# Traces in the Desert

# PRAISE FOR CHRISTOPH BAUMER

'This book is a revelation. Christoph Baumer unravels complex mysteries and shares with the reader his deep knowledge and understanding of living and lost cultures. It is also a tale of high adventure. Neither the seeker of true knowledge nor the merely inquisitive will experience disappointment. Their only regret will be when the last step is taken on Baumer's quest and the final page is turned.'

*John Hare*

## Tibet's Ancient Religion

'A real treasure. Written with the head as well as the heart, its great visual power conveys more than any words can do. Anyone seriously interested in the religious and cultural heritage of Tibet will be greatly rewarded by reading this excellent book.'

*Professor Ursula King, University of Bristol*

'Baumer describes in a thrilling way the history and myths of Bön and demonstrates how alive this religion still is today.'

*Frankfurter Allgemeine Zeitung*

## The Church of the East

'Fascinating and enthralling reading, not only for students of religion but also for the interested general reader.'

*Erica Hunter, SOAS*

'Christoph Baumer's book ranges wide, intellectually and geographically.'

*J.F. Coakley, Harvard University*

'Christoph Baumer's fine book should take its place as the best available general history of the Church of the East.'

*Sebastian Brock*

'Baumer is a scholar to his fingertips…an inspired work of synthesis, containing much original research.'

*Sir Harold Walker, President of the British Society for Middle Eastern Studies*

# Traces in the Desert

JOURNEYS OF DISCOVERY
ACROSS CENTRAL ASIA

*Christoph Baumer*

I.B. TAURIS

LONDON · NEW YORK

Published in 2008 by I.B.Tauris & Co Ltd
6 Salem Road, London W2 4BU
175 Fifth Avenue, New York NY 10010
www.ibtauris.com

In the United States of America and Canada
distributed by Palgrave Macmillan, a division of St Martin's Press
175 Fifth Avenue, New York NY 10010

Maps 3 and 4 reproduced by kind permission of the Orchid Press

ISBN 978 1 84511 337 7

A full CIP record for this book is available from the British Library
A full CIP record is available from the Library of Congress

Library of Congress Catalog Card Number: available

Typeset by JCS Publishing Services Ltd, www.jcs-publishing.co.uk
Printed and bound in Great Britain by CPI Antony Rowe, Chippenham

# Contents

# *Illustrations*

## SECOND PLATE SECTION

## PICTURE CREDITS

All pictures are by the author with the exception of the following:

aps

MAP 1

Christian archaeological sites in Tur Abdin, Turkey

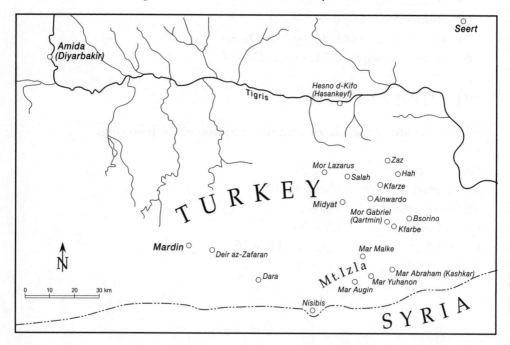

C. Baumer, *The Church of the East* (2006), p. 24.

## MAP 2
### Christian villages in Urmiah, Iran

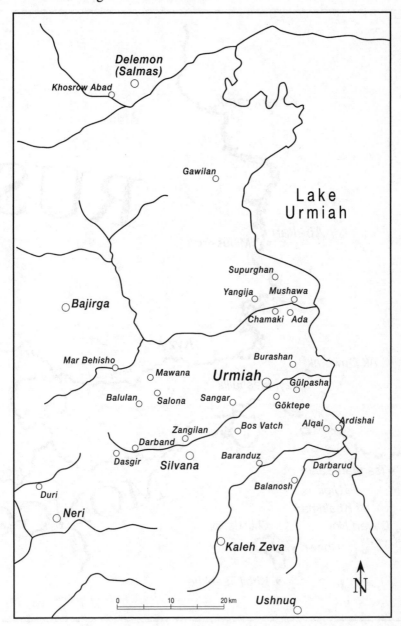

C. Baumer, *The Church of the East* (2006), p. 260

MAP 3
Northern Mongolia and southern Siberia

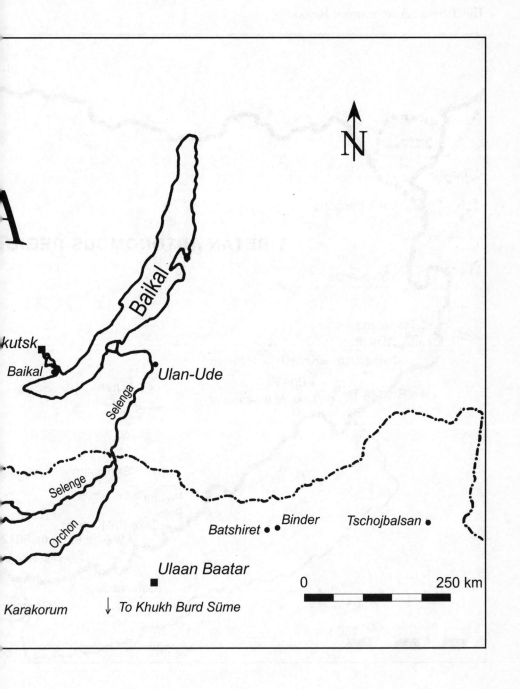

## MAP 4
The Tibetan Autonomous Region

C. Baumer, *Tibet's Ancient Religion, Bön* (2002), pp. 12–13

## MAP 5
Archaeological sites in the Tarim Basin, Xinjiang, China

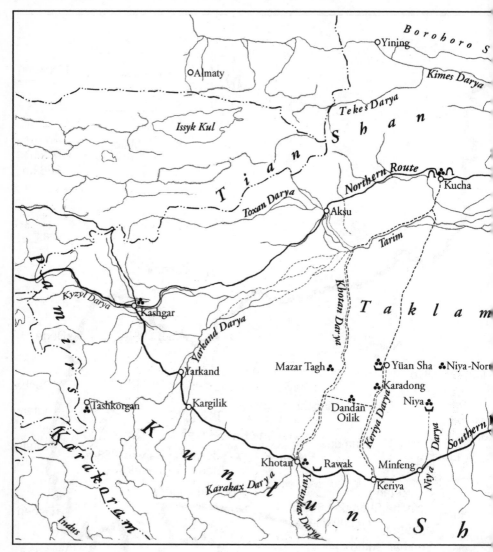

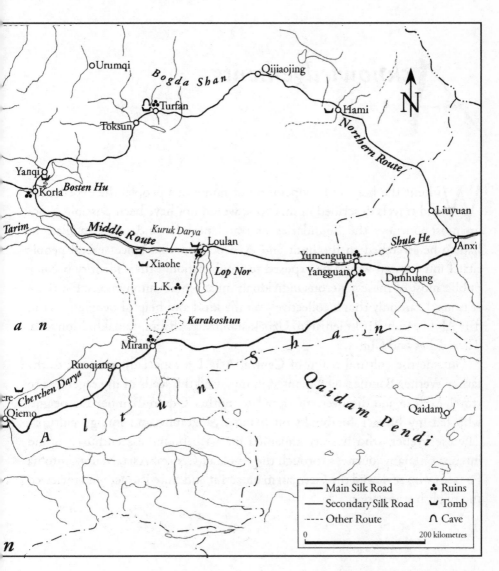

C. Baumer, *Southern Silk Road* (2003), pp. 6–7

# Acknowledgements

Without the help and cooperation of numerous people, the expeditions and travels described in this book would not have been possible. Since on most journeys the boundaries of travel permits and other regulations had to be stretched to the limit and even beyond, and since several people that I interviewed would be exposed to trouble should their identity become public, most of these generous individuals must remain anonymous. For these reasons, I can only thank collectively all the kind and helpful people I met in Tur Abdin, Iran, Turkmenistan, Uzbekistan, Kazakhstan, Ladakh, Mongolia, Tuva, Tibet and China.

Outside the cultural realm of Central Asia I'm especially indebted to my father Werner Baumer, who planted in my mind the seeds of my eagerness to travel, explore and discover, my dear late mother Odette Baumer-Despeigne, who fed my hunger for books on history, geography and foreign cultures, Therese Weber, who has accompanied me with boundless enthusiasm and interest on many journeys through the whole of Central Asia, Maria-Antonia Fonseca who reviewed the German manuscript and Lore Burger who reviewed the English translation.

# Foreword

This book is a revelation. The moment the first page is turned, the reader embarks on a compelling journey through the steppes and high mountain plateaux of the countries surrounding the hostile – and still not wholly explored – deserts of Taklamakan and Lop.

Whether tracking traces of Christian Nestorian worshippers, pre-Buddhist shamans or sifting through the remains of bulldozed and vandalised Tibetan or Mongolian monasteries, Christoph Baumer studiously unravels complex mysteries and shares with the reader his deep knowledge and historical understanding of living and lost cultures. However, there is much more to this book than cultural research. Consistently underpinning Baumer's writing is a deep sympathy for the Mongol, Tibetan, Kazakh, Uigur and other peoples he encounters on his travels. This enables the reader to share his acute anthropological and philosophical insights as well as his archaeological observations. His excavations and well-researched historical flashbacks are enlivened with true humanity.

These personal feelings result in writing that is sometimes tinged with sadness as he reveals how ancient ways of life and religious beliefs are constantly assaulted by the ugly uniformity of what our frenetic world calls 'development'. 'Development to what end?' Baumer ponders, as the tempo of modern life spins on to what he describes in a memorably quoted phrase 'a racing standstill'.

Later in the book he wonders what 'evidence of our civilisation archaeologists a thousand years from now will dig up? Fragments of motorways? Coca-cola bottles? Garbage from the entertainment industry? A rusty tank gun? And what kind of civilisation will they reconstruct from such finds?'

However, his story is not just a description of dying customs or the drawing back of a veil from antiquity. Nor is it merely a lament for cultures on the brink of extinction – it is also a tale of high adventure. In the wastelands of eastern Tibet, the author experiences more than one savage attack by bandits. In the vast reaches of the Taklamakan while on the trail to ancient cities, he encounters mechanical failure and water shortage. His discoveries are gained at the expense of both personal hardship and real danger.

Knowing the deserts of Lop and the Taklamakan, I can readily share the author's feeling of total abandonment when water supplies are nearly exhausted and when a vehicle is comprehensively immobilised in an area of unrelenting hostility. I fully understand Baumer when he writes, 'For all of us who dare to live out our dreams in the vast wilderness of these unyielding deserts, there are still blank spots on the map and they only have to be looked for in the right places.' These sentiments resonate with those of Baumer's hero, the Swedish explorer Sven Hedin. A century earlier Hedin had entered these same 'unyielding deserts', suffered great hardships, lived out his dreams and subsequently written, 'Never before had a white man set foot on this part of the earth's surface. Every step was a new conquest for human knowledge.'

In a memorable paragraph, Baumer states that, 'cultural assets may, however, not just lie hidden in the ground. These remnants of ancient civilisations may stay out of sight and also beyond the compass of our knowledge. Ancient traditions and even valuable religions slip out of our consciousness, threatened by the slow death of forgetfulness.'

It is an urgent priority for Baumer to save from oblivion these assets of the world's spiritual and cultural heritage because, as he asserts, 'Archaeological finds, together with preserved philosophies and religions of the past, represent the memory of mankind.'

With the pace of change taking place at a frightening speed, human memory is constantly tested. The traditional towns and villages of Tibet, Mongolia and China are being relentlessly bulldozed and soulless, uniform concrete blocks are rising in their place. As Baumer notes, 'The unique and diverse cultural heritage of these Central Asian countries is being ruthlessly standardised and ancient religions and customs demoted to the status of folklore' – frequently for the sole benefit of tourists. He unpretentiously explains that by exploring these threatened cultures and recording their past and present riches, he is attempting to make a modest contribution to the preservation of their heritage. Nor does he end on a note of despair. He firmly believes that the strength, for example, of the Tibetan character and their deeply held love and respect for their culture, country and religion will ensure that they survive as a separate and distinct people for centuries to come.

Christoph Baumer's contribution to the preservation of the cultural heritage of threatened peoples is far from modest. Every serious student of Central Asia should travel with him on his single-minded journey of discovery and I would urge the armchair traveller to accompany the student. Neither the seeker of true knowledge nor the merely inquisitive will experience disappointment. Their only regret will be when the last step is taken on Baumer's quest – and the final page is turned.

*John Hare*

*'A settled life is to an explorer what a cage is to a bird.'*

Pyotr Koslov

The author with a lathe-turned wooden column, Endere

# Introduction

All men dream: but not equally. Those who dream by night in the dusty recesses of their minds wake in the day to find that it was vanity; but the dreamers of the day are dangerous men, for they may act their dream with open eyes, to make it possible.

T.E. Lawrence, *Seven Pillars of Wisdom*[1]

I used to live as a dreamer, indulging my yearning for the unknown only by reading the books of great explorers of Central Asia such as Nikolai Przhevalsky, Sven Hedin or Sir Aurel Stein. Their accounts of their travels opened up to me the fascinating cultural landscape of Asia, and allowed my imagination to gain a sense of the excitement of exploring unknown places, discovering new things, and, above all, acquiring new knowledge. I admired not only the courage of these men in embarking for unknown, inhospitable and indeed dangerous regions, but also their single-minded thirst for discovery. Their books exuded a scent of the excitement of discovery, be it the source of a mighty river, unsurveyed mountain ranges or archaeological ruins that brought vanished civilisations and forgotten eras to life.

For years I believed that Central Asia would remain inaccessible to Western explorers for decades to come. I supposed I had simply been born a century too late, but I was wrong. Only a few years after the death of Mao in 1976, China gradually began to open up, and the Soviet colossus – from the ruins of which the Central Asian republics and Mongolia arose to new independence – imploded in 1990. My dreams of exploration were relegated to the night and to the compartment of my mind labelled 'for later', but my passion for and interest in Central Asia lingered in my subconscious.

Chiefly to blame for my addiction to Central Asia was my father Werner. In 1967 he gave me, then aged 15, Sven Hedin's books *The Wandering Lake* and *Across the Gobi Desert*. It was love at first sight or, as the French have it, I was 'struck by lightning'. I devoured these books not once but dozens of times. I was fascinated by Hedin's rafting trip of 1934 along the desert river Tarim, today dried up and swallowed by sand; his discovery in the desert of Lop Nor of mummies thousands of years old; and his fantastic-sounding theory of a lake that migrated with a pendulum-like movement. I felt sympathy for his camels: the drivers had to sew together pieces of leather and affix them to the animals' hooves, cut and made sore by the sharp salt crystals covering the floor of the Lop Nor desert. One thing was clear to me: that was where I wanted to go – no matter when or how. But at that time, the Cultural Revolution was raging in Mao's China; it seemed to me that travelling to the moon would be easier than getting to Lop Nor. I was a victim of the error, widespread among politicians, of projecting the present in a linear manner into the future. In fact, history can change its course and open up new and unexpected perspectives.

For my curiosity and longing for travel, I was indebted to my mother Odette, who was already able to look back on a richly varied life when she married my father. After a period in the diplomatic service in Bucharest, she worked in Finland as a war reporter for the French radio service HAVAS, covering the Finno-Russian winter war of 1939–40, after which her return to Brussels was initially prevented by the German invasion of Belgium and France. She owed this belated return to Sven Hedin. Hedin, whom she visited in Stockholm and asked for help, was acquainted with several leading Nazis; he interceded for her in Berlin and managed to get her a special permit.

Again and again I asked my mother to describe to me Hedin's large apartment, the tall rooms filled to the ceiling with books, and the desks on which more books were piled several feet high; also the signed photos of famous personalities that Hedin had met, among them the Finnish president Mannerheim, whom my mother had interviewed several times concerning the course of the war. I would have loved to have met Hedin personally. He died on 26 November 1952, when I was five months old, but I learned to know him indirectly through my mother.

For my ninth birthday, my mother gave me her 1937 Zeiss bellows camera. On the long holidays through Europe that my parents undertook with me each summer, I photographed every castle, cathedral and locomotive that came before my camera lens. Even then I already felt the pleasurable thrill of lying in wait for a subject – a train steaming towards me, or the sun bursting forth from behind the clouds – together with the corresponding satisfaction on releasing the shutter. I can only agree with the adventurer Wilfred Thesiger that, 'Most men have an inborn desire to hunt and kill.'[2] Thesiger satisfied this desire by big-game hunting, and I did so by taking photographs.

After 15 years of working in marketing, I noticed how the bars of my golden cage – which at least permitted me a four- to five-week journey to Asia every year – increased in thickness; it was turning into a golden prison. And when my boss offered me an important promotion, indeed, a quantum leap career-wise, I was assailed by the fear that not only might the gate to Asia be closed to me for decades, but that I would be definitively walled in within the confines of my career catacomb. For a number of days, I tormented myself with alternative scenarios. After about two weeks of wavering, I made my decision. To the dismay of my boss and colleagues, who thought me crazy, I gave notice, and resolved to sell dreams to others no longer, but to realise my own ones. As a Chinese saying has it, 'With a light hand I grasped the sheep that ran unexpectedly across the road, and led it away.' I became a European nomad in love with Central Asia.

My joy in exploring the unknown was fostered during two journeys I made through Yemen. Like the Silk Road, the Incense Road is surrounded by an aura of mystery. I was fascinated by it and by the southern Arabian kingdoms, their pre-Islamic religions and slender, elegant pre-Arabic script. In 1980, Yemen was still divided into two mutually hostile states: North Yemen, where in 1962 a military revolution had put an end to the ruling theocracy of the Zayidits, and Marxist South Yemen, which had emerged in 1967 from the former British crown colony. My first impression of Sana'a, the capital of North Yemen, was overwhelming. The old town, surrounded by a medieval wall, consisted of hundreds of dwelling-towers or forts, made of grey-brown natural stone and reddish-brown bricks. Inserted into the window openings were panels of finely ground alabaster or panes of glass, ornamented with white plaster grilles with geometric and floral patterns.

A visit to the huge *souk* of Sana'a was like plunging into the fairytale world of the *Arabian Nights*. Tiny shops and workshops were tightly packed together, grouped according to the type of goods. At the southern end of the *souk*, the Bab el-Yemen, meaning 'Yemen Gate', I noticed that the *Arabian Nights* romanticism also had a cruel and shadowy side. From a wooden frame dangled two hands and a foot that had been amputated from three thieves a few days earlier and were hanging there as a warning to others.

Entry to the Grand Mosque of Sana'a was strictly forbidden to infidels, but at the end of my four-week visit, I ventured in at nightfall, after blackening my face with soot in the places still not tanned by the sun. I wore a full-length Yemeni robe with a long dark jacket over it and partly covered my face with a turban. My camouflage worked; no one took any notice of me. I performed the prescribed ablutions, strode with my head lowered through the large courtyard and entered the hall of prayer. Between heavy white pillars the floor was covered by carpets, on which sat men reciting from the Koran in hushed tones. When I cautiously lifted my head, I was amazed to discover Christian crosses on the capitals of some of the pillars. I wondered how this symbol of Christianity had come to be in a mosque that was supposedly founded during the lifetime of the Prophet. I learned much later that in a phase of reconstruction of the mosque, parts of the Christian cathedral of Sana'a, which was destroyed in 770, had been reused as building materials.

This small personal discovery was a key experience to me, for it taught me that even in clearly defined environments one may find totally unexpected things. On a journey it is worth turning over every stone.

Thirteen years later, I had another experience in now reunited Yemen that remained with me. I crossed the southern tip of the Rub' al-Khali desert from the spectacular oasis town of Shibam in the south-east to Marib in the heart of Yemen. Marib is famous, not only for the ruins of its dam, mentioned in the Koran, which collapsed in the late sixth century, but also as the home of wild tribes, who often kidnap foreign explorers and travellers to extort a ransom from them and from the government. While in 1980 I had hired two local armed bodyguards, who accompanied me everywhere, I now thought I could do without them on my planned drive to the capital Sana'a from Marib via the southern mountain route. I was relying on my driver Ali, who possessed a new Kalashnikov. On the way to the capital I wanted to visit the ruins of a pre-Islamic temple dedicated to the moon god, Almaqah, near Sirwah.

When we arrived, Ali warned me of the danger of being kidnapped, and allowed me only ten minutes to photograph the temple. He stayed with the Land Cruiser, to guard the vehicle. Since an unarmed man has no status in Yemen, he gave me a loaded, ten-shot Mauser pistol and kept his rifle for himself. We were both prepared to use the weapons if we had to.

After about six minutes, I heard Ali hooting, and then a shot. This was the signal for me to return at once. I ran to the Land Cruiser and saw two vehicles driving towards us at high speed. One of them tried to cut off my retreat, but I was faster, and just reached Ali. The two cars then blocked our vehicle, and seven armed Bedouins got out. Ali and I stood back to back, and cocked our weapons. The men hesitated but we remained blocked in. When I attempted to defuse the tense atmosphere with the offer of cigarettes, the leader of the glowering men pointed his rifle in my direction, and demanded to be given our Land Cruiser, together with $50,000. Ali lifted his Kalashnikov, pointed it at the leader's chest and desperately attempted to bargain with him. I understood Arabic and was able to follow the threatening interchange. I remembered that one of the heroes of the Yemeni civil war, which raged between republicans and royalists from 1962 to 1970, had hailed from the region between Sana'a and Sirwah. He was the royalist tribal general Qassem Munassar, admired by friend and foe alike for his courage, who brought the republican government to the verge of defeat. I grasped at this straw, and asked the leader in Arabic: 'Did you ever hear of General Qassem Munassar, the late Sheikh of the Bani Husheish?'

The Bedouin was quite taken aback to hear me speak Arabic, and to find that I had heard of the hero of all Yemenis. He flung his head back: 'I am related to the Bani Husheish.'

Hearing this, I at once followed up with: 'I have already been in Yemen, in 1980, and visited several places in the region of the Bani Husheish,' (which was true), 'I met and photographed several blood relatives of General Qassem, and published three newspaper reports on this in Germany,' (which was invented). 'In Marib, I had two Bedouins of Bani Husheish as travelling companions and bodyguards,' (which was almost true).

The Bedouins were thunderstruck. The leader placed his rifle on the ground, and his men followed suit. We put the safety catches of our weapons back on, and I stuck my pistol in my belt. Now it was imperative to keep the initiative and to act fast. I distributed cigarettes, and told two anecdotes about the campaigns of General Munassar I had read about. Then I asked provocatively: 'Do you really mean to kill a friend of the Bani Husheish?!'

'No, by Allah and his prophet Muhammad. Just pay $5 fee to enter, and you are both free.'

What remains to be discovered in the world today, in the age of satellite photography? To me, this is not a rhetorical question; the answer to it is the definition of my goal. What remains to be discovered in the fields of geography, history and civilisation? And what is the difference between discovery and exploration? The discoverer realises the significance of his discovery; he is not just the first to stumble by chance across something without understanding what he sees. As the term indicates, the discoverer removes from some material or ideal object the 'cover' that hides it. The explorer of civilisations, by contrast, can, but does not have to, be the same person as the discoverer. He attempts to understand a find from various perspectives, to expand the limits of existing knowledge and to demonstrate complex interrelationships.

I came to realise the difference between an accidental find that was not immediately understood, and discovery, while studying the 2,000-year-old city of Loulan in the heart of the desert of Lop Nor in north-west China. The inhabitants of Loulan abandoned their city around the year 330 AD for lack of water. Before long, some wooden stakes projecting from the sand were the sole reminders of Loulan. Towards the end of the nineteenth century, a few hunters who had become lost found their way there. They did not see the pieces of 2,000-year-old poplar wood as ruins of a sunken city, only as welcome fuel. The discoverer of the western portion of Loulan, known as L.B., was Sven Hedin's Uigur guide, Ördek, who came across it while lost in a sandstorm in 1900. In contrast to the hunters, Ördek recognised the significance of the dried-up wooden remnants and in 1901 took Sven Hedin to the site. Hedin and, later, Aurel Stein carried out archaeological explorations of L.B. and discovered Buddhist temples, fragments of textiles and antique written documents that gave evidence of trade contacts with both the Eastern Mediterranean and China.

The discoveries of Ördek and Hedin show that for all of us who dare to live our dreams in the vast wilderness of the unyielding desert, there are still blank spots on the map in terms of geography, archaeology and civilisation; they only have to be looked for in the right places.

Cultural assets may, however, not only remain hidden in the ground, The remnants of ancient civilisations may stay out of sight beneath the earth, and also beyond the compass of our knowledge. Ancient traditions and even valuable religions slip out of our consciousness, threatened by the slow death of forgetfulness. It is the second main task of my life to preserve from oblivion such items of the world's spiritual and cultural heritage. Archaeological finds, together with preserved philosophies and religions of the past, represent the memory of mankind.

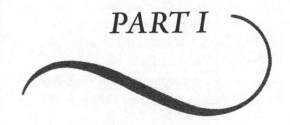

# PART I

## In Search of the Nestorians

# Christian Crosses in the Himalayas

The Nestorian Church is an Eastern Christian Church that is independent of both Rome and Constantinople. It originated in the second century AD east of the river Euphrates, and rapidly expanded eastwards along the Silk Roads, from Mesopotamia – present-day Iraq – via Central Asia to China, into Mongolia and to southern India. It once had over 200 bishoprics and about 8 million adherents; its patriarch was in the city of Seleucia-Ctesiphon, the predecessor of Baghdad. In the year 635, the Emperor of China received the Nestorian missionary and Bishop Alopen. The emperor had the Christian texts brought by Alopen translated into Chinese, recognised their truth and had a monastery built in the capital of China, Chang'an, present-day Xian. The Church was also received with enthusiasm by numerous Turco-Mongolian tribes, one of whose most powerful representatives was Toghril Khan. He ruled over the mighty people of the Kerait from 1175 to 1203 and was the patron of the young Genghis Khan. On his journey to meet Emperor Kublai Khan around 1273–74, Marco Polo encountered several Nestorian communities, also in China.

Nestorianism embodies an Oriental form of Christianity that has retained much of its early Christian heritage, but has also developed its own theology and mysticism. In the second half of the first millennium, at a time when Europe had long forgotten its Greek cultural heritage, Nestorian scholars translated the Greek classics in philosophy, mathematics, astronomy and medicine into Syriac and Arabic. These translations made a decisive contribution to the Muslim tradition of learning, and bridged the gap between Classical antiquity and the European Middle Ages, to the extent that the works translated into Arabic were transmitted to Europe via the Caliphate of Córdoba. However, the Church has had a troubled history, frequently tainted by accusations of heresy from the Catholic Church and plagued by persecution. Today it has around 400,000 members and is fighting for survival in its homeland, Iraq.[1]

The ancient Silk Roads, which ribbon across land and water, are among the most fascinating aspects of the history of Eurasia, for they connected China with the Roman Empire. Not only were goods transported from East to West, including spectacular inventions such as silk, paper and the compass, and in the opposite direction glass, incense or the grapevine; traders also transmitted ideas, concepts and religions. Since I became interested in the Taklamakan Desert in the north-west of China through Sven Hedin's accounts of his travels, I have travelled extensively through this region. Two millennia ago, two routes of the Silk Road ran along the southern and northern fringes of the Taklamakan Desert and several subsidiary routes even crossed it.

Old travel accounts first introduced me to the Nestorians, but at the time I did not pay proper attention. I read in the writings of two Frenchmen, Jules Dutreuil de Rhins and Fernand Grenard, that in 1892 they had acquired an ancient breast cross of bronze, showing a Christian text written in Chinese characters, in Khotan, an oasis town on the southern fringe of the Taklamakan Desert.[2] A cross more than a thousand years old in the western part of China seemed remarkable to me, but I did not then pursue the trail.

I had found other mentions of the Nestorians years earlier, when I was planning an expedition to the lost oasis city of Dandan Oilik, in the heart of the Taklamakan Desert. This city, dating from the fifth to the eighth centuries AD, had last been visited by the German explorer Emil Trinkler and the Swiss photographer Walter Bosshard in 1928, and had since then been regarded as lost. In Trinkler's travel report, *In the Land of High Winds*, I discovered a hint that he had come across very old Nestorian rock inscriptions near the village of Tanktse in Ladakh, close to the Tibetan border. These were first documented by the German Moravian missionary A.H. Francke in 1909. A more detailed account was given by Trinkler's travelling companion Helmut de Terra in his book *Travels through Primeval Worlds along the Indus*, for he had returned there in 1932. He described not only crosses carved in the rock dating from the ninth century, but also Sogdian and Tocharian inscriptions.[3] This excited my curiosity, for the Sogdian script was widespread in Central Asia over a thousand years ago, and had developed from Aramaic, the mother tongue of Jesus. Furthermore, I had also encountered the Tocharian script in 1994 in the Taklamakan Desert, where it was in use during the first few centuries AD.

I wanted to find out what these ancient crosses in the southern Karakorum – which at the time belonged to Tibet – meant: was there a connection with the Silk Roads? Who were the Nestorians? And where did these adherents of the faith still live? Searching in libraries, I soon discovered that there were few books on the subject. None of them provided a general survey; they were out of date, were scarcely illustrated and evidently mostly written by people who had never seen the ancient cultural monuments of the Nestorians themselves. I resolved to go in search of the Nestorians, to document their architectural remains in photographs and to publish a survey of this mysterious community. My objective was to awaken the memory of this Church, forgotten in the West. And so the search began.[4]

In summer 1998 I had been trekking for months in Ladakh and Zanskar. One morning, I set off long before sunrise from Leh to Tanktse in search of mysterious Nestorian crosses carved in the rocks. There were four of us: Sürmed drove an ancient army jeep; beside him sat our Keralan cook Anil, who conjured up wonderfully hot, southern Indian curry dishes. My guide and interpreter was Sherpa Tsering Anchuk, a proud mountaineer who had climbed the 7,616-metre Nanda Devi several times and now specialised in photographing elusive mountain leopards.

The road ran south-east, following the northern bank of the river Indus, the source of which lies north of the holy mountain Kailash in western Tibet, and which I had circumambulated in December 1991. We passed the large Buddhist monasteries of Shey and Tiktse, each perched on a rocky outcrop 30 to 50 metres in height. In the pale moonlight, they resembled ghostly forts. At Hemis, we left the Indus to turn north-east into the fertile Shakti valley. In the village of Shakti we visited the cave monastery of Trakthok, which nestles against a steep rocky wall. Trakthok belongs to the Buddhist school of the Nyingmapas, who follow the Indian teacher, tantric practitioner and magician Padmasambhava. At the close of the eighth century AD, Padmasambhava, called Guru Rinpoche ('precious teacher') by the Tibetans, achieved a limited breakthrough for Buddhism in Tibet and Ladakh by conquering – thanks to his magic powers – the divinities of Bön, the pre-Buddhist religion of Tibet, and transforming them into protective deities of the Buddhist doctrine. At the same time, the Nyingmapas retained much of the heritage of the Bönpos. Trakthok was of great interest to me, all the more so since Padmasambhava is said to have meditated in its innermost cave.

This inner cave, completely blackened by soot, is divided into two parts. In the front, accessible to the faithful, stands a red and gold painted altar cabinet, in the niches of which are small bronze statues of Guru Rinpoche. The ceiling is plastered with coins and paper money that pilgrims have stuck there as offerings. The back of the cave, where monks practise tantric prayers and rituals on special occasions, is behind the altar cabinet. Entry into this part is strictly prohibited to outsiders, but Anchuk made use of a trick, telling the abbot: 'This foreigner is a pupil of the late Drenpa Namkha, one of the most important teachers of Bön. Now Guru Rinpoche appeared to him in a dream and urged him to meditate in this cave.' This had its due effect, and strong monks moved the cabinet aside, one of them illuminating the cave with a burning torch. On the floor were thick woollen rugs on which the monks sit during their rituals. Apart from these, the cave was cold and empty, resembling an ancient rock tomb, across the entrance of which a massive boulder had been rolled.

From the rocky ceiling dripped water, which the monks collect and distribute to the faithful as medicinal nectar. The abbot complained that the cave had been drying out in recent times, so that there was no more 'nectar'. 'This is a bad omen, a punishment for the general decay of morals today.'

A week later, I saw signs of this decay in Trakthok when, on returning from Tanktse, I stopped there to see the two-day Buddhist masked dances. These celebrate Padmasambhava's triumph over Bön. They are a religious festival and should take place at the end of the ninth Tibetan month, approximately in early November, but now are sponsored by a taxi association from Leh, and held additionally in early August as a tourist attraction. Over 80 per cent of the 200 spectators were tourists. The air was pregnant with the fumes of hashish and alcohol from the intensive smoking and drinking, and full of raucous shouts. A large group of young Israelis, who had just finished their military service, were particularly conspicuous. Evidently they were compensating for the frustrations of military discipline to which they had been subjected. Meanwhile, the monastery had sold its soul.

After Shakti, the long climb to the Chang Pass began, at 5,288 metres (17,350 feet) the third-highest pass in the world that can be driven over. Sürmed urged the asthmatic old jeep to its limits, for we wanted to reach the top of the pass before the water from the melting snow flooded the gravel road at noon. The road is a permanent building site, as it has to be repaired each year after the snow has melted. The road workers live in wretched tents barely a metre high and are exposed to constant dampness for weeks on end. Some of them fall ill with tuberculosis and many of them suffer from arthritis in their old age.

At the summit of the pass, I met someone I had last seen 25 years earlier. For half an hour Anchuk had been negotiating in vain with the Indian soldiers on duty to allow us to proceed. On account of the proximity of China, Tanktse is inside a restricted military zone into which foreigners are allowed only with a special permit, which we did not have. A sharp icy wind was causing the numerous Buddhist prayer flags stretched across the track to flap smartly. I was listening to Anchuk's pleading when a Toyota Land Cruiser pulled up and a tall, very well-groomed, silver-haired elderly gentleman stepped out. Images of a small office occupied by a man in his fifties drowning in a sea of books and manuscripts came to mind. Some of his books on Tibetan and Mongolian Buddhism are in my library; I remembered that he had twice been a Member of Parliament. Confident in my recollection, I approached him: 'Are you Professor Lokesh Chandra?'

Hesitating at the sight of this unshaven stranger, he responded: 'Yes, that is correct. But do I know you?'

'I visited you with my mother Odette in Delhi 25 years ago. You discussed Buddhist texts at the time. I remember noticing the hammock in the anteroom to your office. When we left, you gave us a Tibetan longbook that you had published.'

Lokesh Chandra's eyes lit up. He remembered my mother, with whom he had corresponded for many years. And I noticed how I rose considerably in the estimation of the soldiers – a foreigner recognising the well-known parliamentarian. Soon we were on our way with a hastily issued special permit granting me a three-day stay in Tanktse.

Only a few miles on from the pass, a torrential mountain stream that was eating its way through the road brought our descent to a sudden halt. We had to camp where we were – at an altitude of about 4,860 metres. Quite close to the track stood seven tents, widely spaced, made of black yak hair and guarded by loudly barking mastiffs. Four women were milking about 60 Kashmir goats that they had tied by the horns, head to head, in two long rows of 30 animals each. From the goats' fine hair that is combed out, not shorn, the famous pashmina is made. Two more women produced yak milk cheese, which keeps for months and gets hard as stone. After being greeted by Anchuk, the women called their dogs off, chained them up and invited us into the large tent, beside which a solar panel was lying on a stone wall.

The inside of the tent was arranged in the typical manner of the nomads. In the middle was a fireplace and stove fuelled with yak dung. To the right of the entrance was the men's area, where an old man, holding his grandson on his lap, was spinning wool with a hand spindle. To the left was the women's area, and opposite the entrance, between large wooden chests, was an altar, painted red. On this stood two small brass figurines of Padmasambhava and the historical Buddha Shakyamuni, several yellowing photos of the fourteenth Dalai Lama, and a few butter lamps. We were at once plied with *tsampa* (roasted barley) and *gurgur*, the notorious salty butter tea. Whether one takes to this is a question of attitude. If you are expecting tea, it tastes awful, particularly when the butter used is rancid and has been packed in a goatskin with the hairy side inwards. If, on the other hand, you are expecting broth, you will be grateful for the warming drink.

Soon the men returned with their herds, and Tashi, the elected leader of the seven distantly related families, introduced himself, saying: 'Welcome to Chang-Tang, the Tibetan plateau and home of the nomads.' He continued, describing their lives that moved with the seasons: 'We spend the winter in the Tanktse valley, and between May and September we camp on the slopes of the Chang Pass. As the snow melts, we climb higher and higher, up to the present camp; next week we shall commence the gradual descent. Our herds comprise a total of 300 goats and sheep and 500 yaks. All the animals give milk; from the sheep and goats we get pashmina (the fine hair from which cashmere is made); we make the hair of the yaks into felt for the tents and their sinews into ropes. At the beginning of winter the animals are fat, so that we slaughter a few yaks and some sheep and freeze the meat. Unlike the nomads in Tibet, who do not store winter supplies and are dependent on the sparse winter grass, our older family members, who remain in the valley, amass a rich store of hay.'

I asked whether they sometimes crossed the border to Tibet, which is officially closed. Tashi hesitated and looked questioningly at Anchuk, to see if I could be trusted. When reassured by the latter, he fetched a packet of cigarettes from a chest. I realised that they were Chinese cigarettes. Tashi grinned: 'We nomads do not recognise borders. On the other side of the Indian–Chinese border live our Tibetan brothers, nomads like ourselves. So it is quite normal for us to trade with them. On Lake Pangong we buy Chinese cigarettes, tea, leather jackets, shoes, thermos flasks and spirits.'

Tashi invited us to put up our tents next to theirs, saying that the dogs provided an effective deterrent to wolves. As a further protection, also against cattle thieves, an armed man slept in the open every night, next to the animals. Despite the cold and a fall of eight inches of new snow, I slept well enough, at any rate better than the British horse breeder and adventurer William Moorcroft (1787–1825) who, in October 1821, was the first European to cross the Chang Pass. A snowstorm had surprised his caravan while descending and scattered it. He must have spent a most uncomfortable night not far from where my tent stood: the bearers with the food were camping an hour further down, and those with the tents and warm sheepskin coats had collapsed at the top of the pass.

> These three individuals gave themselves up as lost, and, throwing themselves in the snow, declared they would rather die than proceed. Deeply concerned as I necessarily was at their probable fate, it was now impossible to devise a remedy. It was night, the cold was intense. My companion and myself remained without food. Mr. Trebeck doubled himself in a felt carpet, and I endeavoured to sleep in my clothes on the ground: cold and anxiety, however, permitted neither of us to repose.[5]

The following morning, the nomads helped us make the road passable with the aid of a few stone blocks, and after a dizzying descent we reached the town of Tanktse. There were numerous empty barracks, with just a few soldiers sitting around, looking bored – a reminder that more than 30 years earlier a brief war had raged between India and China. After China had occupied Tibet in 1951, it built a military road in secret, connecting western Tibet with the Chinese province of Xinjiang. Two hundred kilometres of this road, however, led through uninhabited territory claimed by India, and was called Aksai Chin by the Chinese. As the border between India and Tibet was poorly guarded until 1959, India did not notice the border infringement until the road had been finished. China, for its part, emphasised the fact that it had never recognised the border between India and Tibet, which had been unilaterally established by British India in November 1914. With this border, known as the 'MacMahon Line', British India had annexed over 90,000 square kilometres of southern Tibetan territory. On 13 October 1962, India began to attack Chinese border posts in the Aksai Chin and the Chinese People's Army embarked on a vigorous counter-offensive a week later, both in Ladakh and in Assam, north-eastern India. The Indian army collapsed in a few days, and on 21 November Mao Zedong declared a unilateral ceasefire, a retreat to the MacMahon Line in Assam, and the final annexation of Aksai Chin. In Mao's words, China had 'taught India a lesson'. The subsequent political détente between the two powers led to an agreement in 1993 that brought about an extensive demilitarisation of the border region.

However, it was not the barracks that interested me, but the Nestorian inscriptions that I found on the fringe of the village. On a six-metre-high rock, and on a few smaller ones, three large and eight smaller Nestorian 'Maltese' crosses were chiselled into the reddish-brown patina, together with a bird – perhaps a dove. Then there were inscriptions in five different languages: Tocharian, Sogdian, Chinese, Arabic and Tibetan. A Sogdian inscription read: 'In the year 210 [according to the Arabic reckoning, that is, 825–26 AD] we sent Caitra the Samarkandian, together with the monk Nofram, as envoys to the King of Tibet.'

A further Sogdian inscription above one of the crosses reads as 'Yisaw' – Jesus. If one assumed that the two Sogdian inscriptions are connected with the three large crosses, we may conclude that a Sogdian trader from Samarkand was accompanying a Christian monk to the King of Tibet in 825–26. Who was this monk, who undertook the hazardous 3,000-kilometre journey from Samarkand to Lhasa, at a time when Buddhism was slowly spreading through the Land of Snows? We do not know. No doubt he hoped to announce his good tidings in Lhasa. I felt a great respect for such people, who took upon themselves unimaginable hardships for an idealistic goal and spent large portions of their lives on this task.

The rock was already thought holy in pre-Christian times, for the upper side, facing the heavens, is covered with Bronze Age motifs such as hunting scenes, yaks, small ibexes, spirals and swastikas, which in this context have peaceful meanings. The fact that this rock had served for millennia as a sacred place, where members of at least four different religions left signs of their belief, impressed me deeply. The four religions were shamanism, Nestorian Christianity, Buddhism and Islam. The geographical situation of the rock was, no doubt, favourable, being at the junction of three trade routes: one led east to Lhasa, the capital of Tibet; the second north to Yarkand and Khotan, two oasis cities on the Southern Silk Road of the Taklamakan Desert; and the third, finally, west to Kashmir and on to Bactria in today's Afghanistan.

I noticed another scene on a neighbouring rock, showing a hunter shooting an arrow at a deer, which is also being attacked by a dog. In Ladakh, which is devoid of forests, there are no deer. Presumably forests still existed in the Middle Ages, so that deer were able to live there. I could imagine that the building of Ladakh's countless monasteries probably contributed to this deforestation.

I was also impressed by the fact that none of the various religious symbols had been destroyed, as is often the case. Was the fact that the rock was large enough the reason why religious testimonies of adherents of other faiths were respected, and not chiselled over? This acceptance of other faiths was echoed by the Mongolian Great Khan and grandson of Genghis Khan, Möngke (ruled 1251–59), when the Franciscan William of Rubruk (c. 1215–95), envoy of King Louis IX of France, endeavoured to convert him to the Catholic faith. Möngke replied: 'We Mongols believe that there is but one god [Tengri, the god of heaven], in whom we live and die, and our whole heart is devoted to him. But, just as god gave each hand several fingers, so he also gave men several different ways for achieving beatitude.'[6] The rock of Tanktse resembles an ecumenical altar to religious tolerance.

When I explained Khan Möngke's statement to Anchuk, he sighed and explained that Indian Ladhakis are, with the exception of the region of Kargil, peace-loving Buddhists, but that they are coming under increasing pressure from extreme Muslims. For the last few years preachers funded by Saudi Arabia have apparently been distributing much money in the south-west of Ladakh, in order to entice the people into newly built mosques, and the children into Koran schools.

Anchuk was referring to two different conflicts. The first involves Kashmir, which was divided between India and Pakistan at partition in 1947, which subsequently led to three bloody wars between India and Pakistan, in 1948, 1965 and 1971. The relationship between the two countries remains tense and until recently artillery duels were an everyday matter. One day in 1998 I narrowly escaped the explosiveness of the situation in Kargil, which has a large Muslim population: at noon, a bomb exploded at a taxi stand, killing nine people. Three hours earlier, I had been at that very spot on my way to Leh.

The second conflict has been smouldering since 1842, when the Indian ruler of Jammu conquered Buddhist Zanskar in the west of Ladakh, and promoted the settling of Muslims, a practice which continues today. After the partition of Kashmir, Zanskar was assigned to the almost-exclusively Muslim district of Kargil. This was hard to bear for the Buddhist inhabitants of Zanskar, since only Muslims were appointed to posts in the administration and in public schools. In 1976, this led to fierce conflicts between the Zanskar Buddhists and Kargil Muslims. Recently, the Islamisation of Zanskar and west Ladakh has been intensified by the building of mosques and the introduction of Muslim institutions, financed by the Gulf States, including Saudi Arabia.

Helmut de Terra, the geologist who had first put me on the trail of the Nestorians, paid his second visit to Tanktse 66 years before me. I thought that it might be possible that there was someone still living there who remembered him. Visiting Tanktse's monastery, which belongs to the Tibetan school of the Drigung-Kagyupa, I asked whether there were any people in the village who were at least 80 years old. The abbot laughed, understanding the reason for my enquiry. He promised to invite all the elders of the village for Ladakh cakes and butter tea in the monastery courtyard, provided I would finance the catering. The following evening half a dozen elderly people had assembled, chattering loudly and gaily. After a while, an old man called Puntsok Namgyal, addressed Anchuk and me: 'Sixty-five to seventy years ago, some foreigners came to Tanktse, two men and also one or two women. One of them ran around with machines that he held to his eyes, and made many notes and sketches on his pad. The other spent hours photographing the rock with the inscriptions, and collected plants. After a few days, they moved on to Lake Pangong.'

I was fairly certain that the first man referred to was Helmut de Terra, and the second his travelling companion, the famous biologist and zoologist George Evelyn Hutchinson, and that one of the women was Rhoda Hoff de Terra. Even if Puntsok was unable to remember further details, his reminiscences created an emotional bridge to de Terra and to the Nestorians.

# *T*he Churches and Monasteries of Tur Abdin

My search continued in the region of Tur Abdin, located in southeast Turkey. I arrived in Diyarbakir, the unofficial capital of Turkish Kurdistan, which forms the western gateway to Tur Abdin. The city lies on the river Tigris – a traveller continuing downstream would eventually reach Baghdad and the Persian Gulf. The black basalt town walls, dating from Roman and Byzantine times lend Diyarbakir a threatening and claustrophobic atmosphere.

In the 1970s a civil war raged between Kurdish rebels, the Turkish army and private Turkish militias who carried out the army's dirty work. In the late 1980s, Hizbollah also became involved. Only the arrest of Öçalan, the leader of the Kurdish Workers' Party (PKK) in February 1999, and a unilateral ceasefire brought about a slight détente. With its mix of these hostile groups and its turbulent past, Diyarbakir is a tense and unwelcoming place, resembling a bowl of scorpions.

I experienced this simmering violence on a small scale when I climbed the city wall to photograph Diyarbakir from one of the wall's 72 towers. A dozen young men followed me up, and attempted to push me from the parapet of the outer wall, which offered protection, to the unprotected inner side of the wall, a fall from which onto the dusty market-place below would have had dire consequences. I know no Turkish, but the demand 'hundred dollars' was not to be misunderstood. I had no choice. At that moment, a shot rang out. Below me stood a man in civilian clothing, with a pistol in his hand, loudly calling 'polisi', which confused my attackers. I took the opportunity to knock the nearest youth to the ground and ran like the wind down a nearby flight of steps. When I went to thank my rescuer he had vanished as if the earth had swallowed him up.

The name of the city of Diyarbakir goes back far into the past. It is most commonly associated with the tribe of Bani Bakr, who live in the surrounding area, but I prefer another interpretation that links the Turkish word 'Diyarbakir' with the Arabic 'Deir Bakira', meaning 'Monastery of the Virgin'. And indeed the city of Diyarbakir, earlier known as Amida, was a purely Christian community up to the late Middle Ages. Today only a few Christian families live there, whose dilapidated houses nestle against the basalt walls protecting the Syriac Orthodox Church of the Virgin Mary, which I visited while I was there. Only after I had knocked several times on the closed iron gate with a stone did a surly man open it, and I found myself looking into a pair of distrustful eyes – a look that I was frequently to encounter when first making contact with members of small Christian minorities. Before long, however, the distrust gave way to traditional Oriental hospitality.

He asked me what I wanted. 'I am working on a book about early Christianity in Asia,' I explained, 'and I would like to visit the church, and look at the Gospel with the silver cover.' I was allowed to enter. Once inside the church, I was struck by the splendidly ornamented wooden altar with a central icon of the Mother of God, and the Gospel on a lectern before it. As I went to photograph it, George, the church warden stopped me: 'Please do not publish any pictures of the Gospel. The more people know about it, the greater is the danger that it will be stolen.'

Two years later, I understood how justified his fears were: one night in January 2003, robbers climbed the high protective wall, sawed through an iron grille, broke a church window, and stole numerous valuable objects, including the famous Gospel with the ancient silver cover.

Tur Abdin is also the site of an infamous period in Turkish history: the Armenian genocide. I had read of a court case against Diyarbakir's local parson, Jusuf Akbulut, shortly before my visit, and enquired after him. George became talkative and told me the story. In the autumn of 2000, the US Congress was debating whether or not to recognise as genocide the 1915–18 massacre of approximately 2 million Armenians, Syriac Orthodox and Nestorian Christians. The Turkish government countered with a media propaganda campaign, into which Jusuf Akbulut became unwittingly embroiled when the conservative newspaper *Hürriyet* interviewed him on the subject. When Akbulut confirmed that the genocide was a 'historical fact', *Hürriyet* published the article under the headline 'The Traitor in our Midst'. Two days later,

Akbulut was arrested and interrogated by the police, who accused him of incitement.

I was shocked. Here was a man being accused of incitement by the state for having confirmed that a historical fact was true. This is as if a German parson had confirmed to a German popular newspaper that the Holocaust had in fact taken place, and the German authorities had thereupon charged him.

The massacres not only of 1915 and 1918 but also of 1894–96, which were first ordered by Sultan Abdülhamid II and then by the Young Turks, cost over 2 million Christians their lives. The subsequent expulsion of 1.3 million Greek Orthodox Christians from the Turkish republic completed the 'ethnic cleansing'. In 1850, the population of today's Turkey was about 30 per cent Christian; today the figure is only 0.2 per cent, the great majority of whom live in Istanbul. In Tur Abdin, the Christian community shrank from 80,000 before 1915 to barely 2,000 today.

I was unable to find any traces of the Nestorians in Diyarbakir – the alleged Nestorian church, turned into a mosque in the fourteenth century, is situated within the barracks area – but I gained a thought-provoking and ultimately disturbing insight into contemporary politics.

The next day, I travelled by shared taxi to Mardin in Tur Abdin. Such a taxi only sets off when twice as many people are seated in and perched on it as the vehicle was built to hold. The name Tur Abdin means 'Mountain of the Slaves (of God)'. Near Mardin, the traveller's eye is caught by a new landmark: the gigantic NATO radar dishes on the crest of the mountain that towers over the town of Mardin. The sight suggests the image of an enormous elephant, its body consists of the mountain mass, with its ears the radar dishes and its trunk the runways of the nearby military airport. It was from here that the American bombers took off to drop their deadly loads on Iraq in the first Gulf War in 1991.

Apart from the Syriac Orthodox Church of the Forty Martyrs, where I took part in the Palm Sunday service, the numerous churches in Mardin are closed for lack of worshippers and priests. During the service, which was held in the ancient Syriac language, I noted that God was praised in many prayers as *al-rachman wa al-rachim*. Was that not the formula with which every sura in the Koran begins? The priest, Gabriel Aküz, enlightened me: 'Certainly, you heard correctly. The ancient Syriac language and Arabic are related, both deriving from Aramaic, Jesus' mother tongue. This formula, which praises God as gracious and merciful, can be found in our liturgy from the fourth century onwards. Islam has simply adopted it.' Father Gabriel added with a smirk: 'You know, we few Christians left in Tur Abdin still speak Turoyo, a dialect derived from Aramaic. If Jesus returned, we would be the only people He could talk to.'

The Syriac Orthodox Church, with its present patriarch in Damascus, is, like the Church of the East, an oriental Christian Church independent of Rome. It was founded following a furious dogmatic battle within the Byzantine imperial Church. These quarrels concerned the definition of the relationship between the divine and the human nature of Christ: whereas the Church of the East stresses the human dimension of Christ, the Syriac Orthodox Church places the emphasis on his divine nature. The respective liturgical languages and writings are related. Both churches use the same version of the Bible, the Peshitta, the counterpart of the Latin Vulgate. Today the Church numbers around 1.5 million faithful, the majority of whom live in southern India and in Syria.

Three kilometres east of Mardin is the monastery of St Ananias which, with interruptions, was the residence of the Syriac Orthodox patriarch from 1166 to 1923. It is situated at the foot of a mountain that, like a Swiss Emmental cheese, is full of niches and caves, dug out by hermits who withdrew to live in them. Especially rigorous ascetics had themselves walled into their caves for years, or even their whole lifetime; novices from the nearby monastery would pass them water and a little food through a small hatch. If a hermit left his bowl untouched for 40 days, his death was assumed, and the stone wall was broken down. This was like an early, voluntary choice of one's own grave, a custom that was also widespread in Buddhist Tibet up to the Chinese invasion of 1950. It was hermits like these that gave Tur Abdin its name.

I was intrigued to hear of Christians practising something that I had only ever associated with Buddhist monks. I asked Ibrahim Türker, the frail-looking abbot of the monastery, what he felt about the hermits. 'It is an extreme path to take,' he said. 'These hermits took Jesus' command to leave everybody and everything and follow him literally. Just as Jesus died voluntarily and was buried, to rise again three days later, they wished to hasten their own deaths, and so had themselves walled in.'

I then visited the subterranean tomb of the monastery and found, in the seven room-size vaults, three Syriac Orthodox patriarchs and four archbishops buried seated on thrones in full regalia. This custom also has a parallel in Tibetan Buddhism, where high-ranking dignitaries were embalmed and buried seated in a chapel, and even in some cases 'exhibited' behind a pane of glass. In 1928 J.F. Rock, an American of Austrian origin, visited the monk king of Muli in south-eastern Tibet:

I was invited to have lunch with the king daily. In the extreme end of the oblong room on a dais sat a life-sized, gilded statue representing Buddha. There was, however, something phoney about that figure. The king noticed that I often looked curiously at the gilded figure, and said: 'This is my uncle. He died sixty years ago. I was given the formula for the preparation of such a body.'[7]

In the burial vault of the monastery I was overcome by the same feeling as in the catacombs of Rome, of being on the threshold of two worlds: behind me the world of the living, and before me that of the dead. The hermits walled in their caves must have experienced similar feelings.

In Midyat, 50 kilometres farther east, a tense calm hung uneasily over the town since the PKK had threatened to resume its guerrilla operations. Military jeeps and armoured vehicles were passing through the narrow streets of the Kurdish quarter and at night enforced the curfew from 10 p.m. I saw that I was not welcome: the few hotels that Midyat possessed refused to admit me, although they were clearly empty. I was wondering what to do, when a young man approached me and asked if he could help. Salim was a Turk who had been studying in Berlin and had returned to Midyat. 'The hotels are wary of accepting foreign tourists, because of pressure from the authorities,' he explained. 'Recently, employees of the German embassy checking on applications for asylum or human rights activists disguised as tourists have been staying in Midyat and have made the authorities nervous. But one of the hotel owners is a relative of mine, and I will help you.' A moment later I was the only guest in a three-storey boarding-house.

My meeting with Salim was fortunate, for in the coming weeks he took me to dozens of Syriac Orthodox churches and monasteries scattered throughout the barren landscape around Midyat. In some of the monasteries, a single monk would keep watch, most of them having only returned from exile to their home region following the PKK's ceasefire. Many not only care for the tiny Christian congregations in their areas, but also work as masons, repairing the worst damage to the buildings themselves. Other monasteries, like many village churches, are closed, if not misused as cattle sheds; they possess the stoic beauty of weathered ruins.

Near the village of Bsorino, where 22 Christian families still live, Salim and I had an unfriendly reception. The footpath led over a low hill to the settlement, where a company of soldiers was guarding the village. Suddenly, three dogs with bared teeth and bloodshot eyes rushed out of a military barracks. Salim told me to stand still. The vicious dogs circled us until, after a few minutes that seemed like an eternity, two soldiers arrived, taking time to light their cigarettes at leisure before calling off the dogs. An officer explained: 'Before the ceasefire, some supposed tourists came to the village and took many video shots. The following night, PKK fighters attacked us. This is why we are suspicious of all strangers.'

So far, I had seen only Syriac Orthodox churches, but close to the border with Syria is the Nestorian monastery of Mar Malke, which dates from the fifth century and was rebuilt in 1955. The track approaching it led through a military post, at which I had to give up my passport and my watch. A young monk guided me round the monastery. His restless and unsteady gaze gave him a sinister look, and I was, perhaps unfairly, reminded of a story that told how the founders of the monastery imprisoned a devil that had been driven out of a princess in the monastery's well.

We continued our journey, delayed by several military checkpoints, to the town of Nusaybin, the Nisibis of antiquity. Nisibis looks back on a turbulent past. The town was once wealthy, for it lay on one of the most important branches of the Silk Road, linking Seleucia-Ctesiphon with Antioch. The Silk Road also served as a military road, and so Nisibis was conquered by a succession of foreign rulers. After the Assyrians came Medes, Persians, Greek Seleucids, Iranian Parthians, Armenians, Romans and Byzantines, Iranian Sassanians, Arabs, Turkish emirs, Mongols, Kurds and Turks. Today, the Silk Road of the past is unrecognisable. Instead of merchant caravans, pilgrims and travellers from the four corners of the Orient, the road is crowded by hundreds of petrol tankers. Salim explained: 'This is petrol smuggling in a big way. The trucks buy up petrol in Iraq as cheap as dirt, and sell it here, making a huge profit. This petrol road leads from Kirkuk in northern Iraq over Syrian territory, where the customs officials are bribed, directly to Nusaybin, and then either to Diyarbakir or to Urfa.'

Three metres below the present ground level of Nusaybin is one of the oldest churches in the world. St Jacob's was founded in 313 AD and until 1616 was the see of a Nestorian archbishop. In the baptistery, dating from 359, time has stood still. The massiveness of the walls, built of huge stone blocks, is made less severe by richly decorated arches. The altar and the lecterns are also of stone. Closing my eyes, I could hear the singing of the mixed choir, smell the incense, and see the pilgrims kneeling in the crypt before the tomb of the church's founder, Bishop Jacob. I was soon jerked back to reality: the old man who had opened the church for me wanted to go home; the last Christians of Nusaybin had been murdered in 1915.

The next day, I drove with Salim eastwards to the Izla Mountains, where there were the ruins of the monastery of Mar Augen. Founded in the fourth century AD, Mar Augen was, for a millennium and a half, a centre of Nestorian spirituality. The last Nestorian monk left Mar Augen between 1838 and 1842, and Syriac Orthodox monks took up residence until 1974. Gertrude Bell, the famous traveller, orientalist and comrade-in-arms of Lawrence of Arabia, gave a vivid account of her visit here in 1909:

> Ten monks are lodged in the rock cells. The cell of St. Eugenius stands apart from the others, hollowed out of the cliff to the west of the church. The prior had spent a lonely winter there, seeing no one but the brother who brought him his daily meal of bread and lentils.

When Gertrude Bell wished to pay her respects to the bishop, the prior

> pointed to a cave some fifty feet above us in the cliff. Three-quarters of the opening had been filled with masonry. The prior explained: 'You cannot see him, he has left the world. He is the father of eighty years. It is now a year he took a vow of silence and renounced the world. Once a day, at sunset, he lets down a basket on a rope and we place therein a small portion of bread.'

'And when he dies?' asked Gertrude Bell.
'When he is sick to death he will send down a written word telling us to come up and fetch the body.'
'And you will take his place?'
'If God wills,' the prior, who was about 30 years old, answered.[8]

What I had heard in the monastery of St Ananias happened less than a century ago. What a contrast to our hectic everyday lives! In these monasteries people achieved a radical departure from material life, which they reduced to an absolute minimum, in hope of spiritual growth. In the twenty-first century, by contrast, we are constantly in motion, mentally and emotionally, often driven by an insatiable inner unrest. And if, at the end of yet another year, we venture an honest look back and ask ourselves how far we have come, we are often at a loss for an answer. We live in a state of 'a racing standstill', to borrow the memorable phrase of the essayist Paul Virilio.

Soon after turning off towards the Izla Mountains, our way was blocked by a barrier and two military checkpoints consisting of sandbags placed at an angle. Salim and I stopped and were taken into a large tent. The officer forbade us to proceed: 'The monastery ruins are sometimes used as a hiding-place by the PKK, and recently Hizbollah too. We only go into the valley armed with machine-guns – Clear out!' And to make sure that we did not make a detour in the forbidden direction, we were accompanied by a military jeep as far as Nusaybin. I was still not willing to give up, and the next day persuaded Salim to drive back to the monastery of Mar Malke, north of Mar Augen.

But the checkpoint had informed the army post at Mar Malke, and we were roughly commanded to turn back immediately. With a meaningful expression, the officer advised me to leave the Tur Abdin area at once; 'someone' might get the idea that I was a PKK agent. A few days later, as I was about to board the plane from Diyarbakir to Istanbul, I was held by the police at the security check. The *corpus delicti* was a mini-screwdriver an inch in length. An embarrassing search of my person and a long interrogation followed; evidently, someone had informed the police. It took more than three hours to convince them that I had no connection to the PKK, and wanted to visit the monastery of Mar Augen for reasons of research. I had presumably been shadowed since Nusaybin.

# Christians in Iran

A quest for the Nestorians is not complete without exploring Iran. Not only does a small community of Nestorians live there, but in the west of the country many of their antique churches have been preserved. These churches, some of which date from the fifth century, have never been systematically documented. It was for this reason that, together with my wife Therese, I met the Cor-Bishop of the Church of the East, Domara Benjamin, and the priest Yussuf Rashidi in St George's Cathedral, Tehran.[9] The cathedral precincts were protected from the noisy street by high walls. Our 'letter of introduction' was a photograph on which Therese and I were standing beside Patriarch Mar Dinkha IV, whom we had visited on 2 June 2001 in his residence in exile in Chicago. Mar Dinkha himself was bishop from 1962 to 1968, and from 1968 to 1976 was Archbishop of Tehran. His successor Benjamin told me that their community numbered around 30,000 members; before the Islamic revolution of 1979 there had been twice as many. Although Islam is the state religion, the constitution recognises Christians as a minority, and grants them representation in parliament, for they belong to the 'religions of the book', which are Judaism, Christianity, Islam and – only in Iran – also Zoroastrianism. Assyrians and Chaldeans have one seat between them, Jews and Zoroastrians one each, and the Armenian Christians two. Although they are not subject to any official discrimination, the Islamisation of their society was so rapid and radical that many young Christians have left Iran. Since it is mostly men who emigrate, there is a dramatic surplus of young women, who either remain single as Christians or, on marrying a Muslim, are obliged to become Muslims themselves.

'In Iran,' Yussuf added, 'you will find neither paradise nor hell. Attempting to convert Muslims is strictly prohibited, but we have no problem in restoring our churches or, if required, building new ones, which Christians are forbidden to do in Egypt, for example.'

'And what about the catechism and textbooks?' Therese enquired.

'All children must attend religious instruction in accordance with their family's faith,' replied the Cor-Bishop. 'The four Assyrian communities – that is, my Orthodox Assyrian Church of the East, the Assyrian Evangelical Church, the Assyrian Pentecostal Mission and the Chaldean Catholic Church – still have separate catechisms. At present we are working on a common schoolbook.' Later, I learned that the state is imposing this new catechism, in which Islam is glorified.

A few days later we acquired a clearer picture of the situation. It was evening and we were wending our way through the narrow alleys of one of Tehran's poorer districts. We finally found the rather dilapidated house we were looking for, and rang the bell of David Leoni. We were able to communicate with him without an interpreter so we sent our Iranian guide home. David had been the Catholic catechist for adults in Tehran since 1969. In his poorly lit living-room, the floor of which was covered with books, and the shutters of which did not appear to have been opened for years, he told us: 'When the Islamic government expelled all foreign priests, I was lucky, since I had received Iranian citizenship three days earlier. And I have my Iranian passport to thank for my work during the bloody unrest of 1978–79, when I headed the ambulance service of a hospital. One of my Muslim neighbours, who knew of my work, was elected to the new parliament, and interceded for me.'

'What are you able to do, in view of the current restrictive laws?' we asked.

'The scope for action is strictly limited, and I have to stretch it as far as possible without breaking it,' replied David with a laugh.

He went on to explain that caring for the Christians was simple; the problem was with young Muslims wanting to convert to Christianity (many of whom did, despite the obvious risks inherent in doing so, but not always for the right reasons). Christianity is appealing to many, perhaps because the Iranian Shiism tends towards a certain mysticism in much the same way that a Catholic or Orthodox Christianity does. Christianity is also a part of the condemned Western world and therefore a tempting forbidden fruit. In addition, there are opportunists who believe that they would be granted asylum in the West more readily with a certificate of baptism. For this reason, converts have to wait three years before being baptised, in secret. Conversion to Christianity involves great personal sacrifice. A convert can lose his civil rights, such as the right to inherit or to marry, as well as the possibility of a career in state employment. Still worse, converts are subject to arbitrary arrest or abuse, are involved in suspicious traffic accidents, or simply 'disappear'. Furthermore, they often suffer rejection by the Christian communities, for fear they may be spies.

We left David full of respect and admiration for his tenacity in the face of such obstacles.

The following day, we visited one of Iran's 21 official geniuses, an Assyrian professor called Samuel Pirah. He began by showing us his private Assyrian museum, which was full of copies of antique works of art from the third millennium BC onwards. Pirah's house was indistinguishable from the museum and both were unimaginably surreal. Covering three storeys, it consisted of over 20 rooms that have seen no sunlight for years. Each room is devoted to a particular topic, and full to bursting with exhibits covering everything from Jesus to Christian crosses, Islam and Assyrian peasant life. There was also an Assyrian chapel, a cinema room full of chairs and an exhibition of kitschy travel souvenirs, arranged according to their continents of origin.

Other rooms were disconcerting – the kitchen, the dentist's surgery and the hospital sickroom being the most extreme. The small kitchen contained a table permanently laid with plastic ware and foodstuffs: a plate of pea soup, two fried eggs, a sausage, turnips, custard, a glass of wine – all garishly painted (Professor Pirah was thus obliged to eat out). The professionally equipped dentist's surgery reminded me of the dentist I was sent to as a child. The equipment was out of date, but everything was perfectly hygienic, without a speck of dust. The sickroom, too, looked ready to use, containing a genuine hospital bed, together with surgical instruments and metal bowls. Having seen no other bed in the house, Therese and I suspected that Professor Pirah slept in this one. At the end of our visit, Pirah showed us the book about the official geniuses of Iran, among whom he was numbered, together with a letter from the University of Tehran dating from the 1990s nominating him as a candidate for the Nobel Prize for Literature. The professor is the author of 565 books, which were exhibited in glass cases in a special room. I paled with envy at his ability to write a book a month and tried to console myself with the thought that empty pages might be hidden between their printed covers.

Pirah's eccentricity amazed me. All human beings dream and live in imaginary worlds at times. Children do this in their role-playing with dolls, so-called madmen do it in fits of abnormality, and 'normal' adults in the fantasies of their minds. But fantasy was not enough for Pirah; he had escaped madness by turning his house into a gigantic doll's house. He reminded me of King Ludwig II of Bavaria, who staged his romantic notions of medieval life with the extravagant construction of a series of castles, and finally paid for this by being forcibly committed to a psychiatric institution.

Our visit to the Assyrian Member of Parliament Yonathan Bet Kolia also took a surprising course. During the interview, he reported on his work: 'The Christians are obliged for their seats in parliament to the socialist Prime Minister Mosaddeq, who was toppled by the CIA in 1953 after nationalising the oilfields controlled by the USA and Great Britain. To begin with, the interests of the Assyrians were represented by the Armenian delegate; the first Assyrian member of parliament took up his seat in 1960. When the mullahs came to power in 1979, we feared for our presence in parliament; but the new constitution confirms the seats of the religious minorities.'

'What are you working for in parliament at present?' we asked Bet Kolia.

'We Christians are heavily discriminated against with regard to blood money,' he replied. 'In the case of a crime such as murder, Islamic law has three possible consequences: the application of the punishment laid down for it, the payment of blood money, or forgiveness. Currently, however, a Christian is worth 13 times less than a Muslim, and a female Christian 26 times, because the blood money payable on killing a Christian is lower than when a Muslim is killed. I am working on the draft for a bill to change this deplorable state of affairs. To bridge the gap, a minister of justice who is well disposed towards us has opened a fund to compensate Christian victims. My initiative is also supported by Imam Khamenei.'

After our meeting had ended, Bet Kolia invited us to a 'simple' meal the next evening.

We spent the following day taking photographs in Tehran, and arrived at Bet Kolia's house in the evening dusty and perspiring. He took us from there to the headquarters of the Assyrian Society. The table was set for a dozen people in all, and we were looking far from respectable. Bet Kolia explained, worryingly, that the table was for the guests' chauffeurs. He then led us into a large hall, where the tables were laid for around a hundred people. Bet Kolia had invited us to a regular meeting of the Assyrians of Tehran. All the men were wearing suits, and the women wore ankle-length dark robes and headscarves. In our bedraggled state we were introduced as guests of honour, after which there were two further surprises. Although the consumption of alcoholic drinks is strictly forbidden in Iran, wine and spirits were served. 'This law applies only to Muslims,' my neighbour explained. 'Christians are allowed to prepare alcoholic drinks for their own use and to consume them in private.'

After greeting each guest personally, Bet Kolia proclaimed: 'We are among ourselves; there are no Muslims in the room.' Thereupon all the women removed their long coats and headscarves, and the shapeless scarecrows turned into tastefully made-up, elegantly dressed ladies. For days, I had been seeing Iranian women only as shadowy figures muffled by the *chador*, their ages to be guessed at best from their gait. And now I saw well-proportioned women with plunging necklines and high-cut evening dresses. Quite a revelation!

Bishop Benjamin and Bet Kolia had both confirmed that there were still many ancient churches near Urmiah in the western Iranian province of Azerbaijan. So, the next day, together with our interpreter Gafaari, we set off. Bishop Benjamin had also spoken of the rumour that the oldest Bible in Iran was kept in a library in the provincial capital of Tabriz. At this I had pricked up my ears and asked Gafaari to find out more. He searched like a bloodhound during the following few days, and in the end found what he sought: the Bible in question was in the safe of the newly constructed state library of Tabriz. Armed with several special permits, we were received by the director of the library and entered our names in its guest-book, below the signatures of State President Khatami and the Mayor of Tabriz. Then the Bible was brought into the conference hall by two men. I could hardly believe my eyes when I saw that the book was a 450-page parchment manuscript written in black ink in the particular Nestorian script known as Estrangela. This Gospel can be dated to between the ninth and thirteenth centuries; it was a real discovery, as it had never been published. Unfortunately, the colophon was missing, so that its origin remained unknown. All the director of the library could tell us was that the Bible had been confiscated from a smuggler on the border to Turkey.

In the nearby bazaar, I was surprised by a fortune-teller who employed the original and distinctly 'un-Islamic' method of 'parrot-forecasting'. He takes his parrot out of its cage, and holds it in front of a small basket filled with prophetic phrases. The bird, which has been trained to do so, picks out a scrap of paper, and the customer learns about his future.

On the journey to Urmiah, we stopped in Delemon, today's Salmas, and visited the church administrator, who showed us the churches and the large Christian cemetery. As in the case of other cemeteries, stone figures of rams stood beside the many gravestones. This custom, which I had also found in Kazakhstan and Mongolia, goes back to the time of Mongol rule in Iran (1256–1335). We drove on to the nearby chapel of Mar Jacob, where the church minister described how, on 16 March 1918, his grandfather was accompanying the Assyrian Patriarch Mar Shimun XIX to Mar Jacob to meet the Kurdish leader Agha Simko, who had invited him to a conference. On their parting, Simko gave the Patriarch the kiss of peace, when suddenly shots rang out. The Patriarch and several of those accompanying him were killed in a hail of bullets. The church warden's grandfather survived because he ran into the chapel and bolted the door.

We left Mar Jacob and followed the western foothills of the Dare Rosh Mountains, into the slopes of which wind and water had gouged innumerable deep channels. The sun was still shining, but a violent thunderstorm was brewing; the snow-covered peaks glittered against the threatening background of grey-black clouds. An oppressive feeling descended on the group and I was reminded of the sufferings of the Assyrians of Urmiah during the First World War, when over 30,000 were killed by Turkish and Kurdish militiamen. We finally reached Urmiah that evening, where we were very hospitably received by the city's Assyrian priest, Eliosh Azizian.

Urmiah is a fascinating town. It claims to be the birthplace of Zoroaster and the site of the oldest church in the world. Legend says that when the three wise men of the Bible, whom many claim were Zoroastrian high priests, returned from the Middle East, they founded a fire temple here. The temple was transformed 35 years later by Thomas the apostle into the Church of the Virgin Mary. While wary of the facts behind this story, I did not doubt the very great age of the church, which rests far below the present ground level.

The entrance leads first into a vault containing the tombs of eminent clerics, and then to the main nave. A side corridor leads to the small baptistery and from there to the apse, access to which is reserved for the clergy. The church feels like a catacomb, offering eternal rest to the dead and temporary rest to the living.

During the following days, Father Azizian took us to dozens of Nestorian churches in small neighbouring villages, in the open countryside and in the nearby mountains. There are over a hundred churches or chapels in the area around the city. Most, however, are closed for fear of vandalism, and are opened only once a year, on the calendar feast day of their patron saint. In two churches, the doors had been broken open and cigarette-ends, empty lemonade bottles, anti-Christian graffiti and human excrement littered the interior. Christian cemeteries, too, had been the targets of vandals. On several occasions I saw gravestones recently overturned or with Islamic slogans scratched on them, and also opened graves. The culprits are never punished. One old Christian from the village of Göktepe commented laconically: 'Those who do not respect the dead do not respect the living either.'

We knew how apt this judgement was. We had visited the former Armenian monastery of St Stephanos, north of Tabriz. Doing so, we had followed the south-west bank of the river Arax, which forms the border between Iran and the exclave Nakhichevan, belonging to Azerbaijan. On the north-east –the Azerbaijani side – of the river we saw a dense collection of rock steles up to 2.5 metres in height, about half of which were still standing. It was the Christian-Armenian cemetery of Julfa. In order to photograph it despite the prohibition to stop along this tense frontier, we hid in a small chapel on the mountain slope and used the telephoto lens. In no time, furious whistles and cries rang out from the Azerbaijani border guards across the river. Through our binoculars, we could see that a number of gravestones were richly decorated with crosses, floral patterns, and Armenian inscriptions. The oldest were a thousand years old, while others were reminders of the Armenian refugees massacred here in 1915–16.

Between the states of Armenia and Azerbaijan, which became independent from Russia in 1990, there has been a fragile ceasefire since 1994, after Armenia had won back the region Nagorno-Karabach, 80 per cent of the inhabitants of which were Armenians. Since that time, there have been repeated offences in Muslim Azerbaijan against the Armenian cultural heritage, in the course of 'cultural cleansing'. By 1998, 8,000 of the originally 10,000 gravestones had been destroyed. Then bulldozers devastated a further 800, the broken pieces being removed by the railway that runs between the river and the necropolis. We saw the 1,200 remaining gravestones. In November 2002, a further wave of destruction followed, and in December 2005 200 Azerbaijani soldiers destroyed the remaining gravestones and threw the pieces into the river.[10]

On a cold morning and under a steely blue sky, Therese and I drove to the Assyrian village of Bos Vatch, five kilometres south-west of Urmiah. We were alone, since Father Azizian had excused himself on the previous day because of a death in the family. On our arrival, however, we ran into Father Azizian and Cor-Bishop Benjamin, who had travelled there from Tehran to officiate at the burial service for Azizian's brother-in-law, who had been killed in a car accident. The two churchmen were glad to see us, and Father Azizian insisted on inviting us to lunch at his parents' house. Once more we were impressed by typical Iranian hospitality. Without wasting many words, we were invited to sit at the long kitchen table, where the bereaved family was already seated, huddled together. Assisted by her three daughters and four sons, Father Azizian's mother served the mourners dried veal, excellent yoghurt made from buffalo milk and freshly baked unleavened bread.

After the meal, we took our leave and climbed the steep hillside to the nearby stone-built double church of St Sergius and St Bacchus. It is supposed to have been constructed early in the fourth century at the place where the two Roman officers after whom it is named died martyrs' deaths for refusing to sacrifice to Jupiter. Bacchus was tortured to death, and Sergius dragged to death by a horse. The exact spot of their graves is kept secret, for fear of desecration, but both Christians and Muslims are convinced that their relics possess strong healing powers. On the north side of the church, which has two naves, a narrow passage leads to a subterranean room where the mentally ill are said to be miraculously cured. The sick individuals are locked in this room and heavy stones are rolled across the trapdoor. They spend at least one night in this room and it is said that 10 to 20 people, both Muslims and Christians, are cured each year. This strange custom was also reported on by the American missionary Justin Perkins, who stayed in Urmiah from 1834 to 1841:

> The church [of St Sergius] is much venerated by both Nestorians and Mohammedans. It has the reputation of possessing the rare power of restoring lunatics. And today, on entering, we found several Mussulmans of both sexes within, who had, this morning, placed a delirious relative in a dark vault. These Mohammedans had brought their sick to the church of these despised Christians and employed a Nestorian deacon to read prayers over him![11]

The practice shows how a living popular belief is able to reconcile adherents of different, indeed antagonistic, religions.

The burial of Father Azizian's brother-in-law took place in the nearby graveyard. Colourful wreaths of flowers in the form of crosses lay on the mound of earth. The relatives, clad in black, formed a semicircle around the newly dug grave and gazed far into the valley. In the distance, the blue strip of Lake

Urmiah fused with the horizon. Father Azizian and Cor-Bishop Benjamin sang and recited prayers in the ancient Syriac language. The Nestorian liturgy for the dead is full of symbolism. The mourning service is not held on the day of the burial, which takes place as soon as possible after death, but on the third day. As Christ rose again on the third day, so the deceased takes part in the mystery of the resurrection through the Eucharist celebrated three days after his/her death. Accordingly, on this occasion the ceremony was to take place two days later, in the Church of St Mary in Urmiah.

At the conclusion of the prayers for the dead, an ancient ritual was celebrated, which has its roots in pre-Christian times. The mourners proceeded to the double church, where a sheep was tethered, awaiting sacrifice. The Presbyterian missionary Asahel Grant, who stayed among the Nestorians of Urmiah and Kurdistan from 1835 to 1844, wrote: 'The Nestorians sometimes offer sacrifices at the death of distinguished persons. The animal is usually slain [by a lay person related to the deceased] before the door of the church, when a little blood is often put upon the door lintels.'[12] On this occasion, I counted well over a hundred crosses painted in blood on the lintel, proof of the fact that the custom is still carried out regularly. Father Azizian explained later: 'The sacrifice is connected with the idea of Christ as the sacrificial lamb, which you call in Latin "agnus dei". This goes back to John the Baptist, who greeted Christ as follows: "Behold the Lamb of God, that taketh away the sins of the world." '[13] The bloody marks on the lintel of the church door are a sign of protection from the wrath of God.[14] As I was able to observe a number of times in eastern Turkestan, present-day Xinjiang, Muslims also observe this custom. On visiting the burial place of a Muslim holy man, a sheep is slaughtered, and its blood daubed at the entrance to the tomb. In the practice of popular belief, the three frequently mutually hostile 'Religions of the Book' are much closer to one another than the fiery speeches of their respective purists suggest.

We found ourselves confronted with death not only in Bos Vatch, but at many homes that we were invited to throughout the country. In the home of each family were photos of young men in prominent positions on the walls of living- and dining-rooms. They had all been killed in the war against Iraq, which caused Iran unspeakable suffering, including well over a million dead. Living victims of this terrible war were the numerous crippled men that we saw throughout Iran. The war began on 22 September 1980, when the Iraqi president Saddam Hussein exploited the chaotic domestic situation in Iran and the weakening of the Iranian army to conquer the oil-rich province of Khuzestan in the south-west of the country. In doing so, Saddam relied on the support of the USA and Europe and was financed by their ally Saudi Arabia. Their common goal was the fall of the Islamic Republic of Imam Khomeini. In order to attempt to stop the Iraqi advance, Iran used poorly trained militias, who with great sacrifices succeeded in driving the Iraqis out of Iran by 1982. Khomeini's attempt to retaliate with futile infantry attacks was met with chemical weapons strikes that killed thousands. The military stalemate ended when the American airforce shot down an Iranian passenger plane with 240 civilians on board on 3 July 1988. Fearing an American invasion, Iran agreed to a ceasefire the following month.

In the western Iranian town of Kermanshah, where we had been invited to dinner, our hostess Nur Bakhtiar told us her experience of the war. For the first two years everyone was living in constant fear of an Iraqi occupation. The Iraqis attacked Kermanshah from the air at night at least once a week, first with bombers and, from 1982, with rockets. Nur's husband and her four sons volunteered for the Revolutionary Guard. Her husband returned from the war badly wounded and two of their sons were killed; all that was left of one son were some bodily remains and of the other nothing but a headband with a sura from the Koran on it. There was a photo of them on the mantelpiece. Her sister lost both a son and her husband. Her second son was missing. They thought that he might still be alive as a prisoner of war.

Although the war had been over for 13 years, the exchange of prisoners was still not concluded in 2001. Many mothers were widows and it was hard to find young men for their daughters to marry.

'My younger daughter was lucky enough to find a husband,' said Nur, 'although he is quite a lot older, but my elder one is still unmarried at 30.' The daughter she referred to, still looking young and attractive, nodded sadly: 'Yes, there are hardly any unmarried men between 30 and 40. Maybe I was too choosy in the past; so now I shall have to be content to be a second or third wife.'

# $M$erv, City of Infidels

I was trudging, heavily laden, through the three-kilometre-wide no man's land that separates Uzbekistan from Turkmenistan. Lorries were lining up on both sides of the blocked roadway; it would take them at least three days to pass the border, but my progress was fast: it only took me four hours to undergo the laborious customs formalities, in the course of which every single item in my luggage was registered in a large book. I was headed for the ruins of the ancient city of Merv, about 300 kilometres from the border, which was the see of a Nestorian bishop as early as the fourth century. I wanted to discover whether the reports of Soviet archaeologists from the 1950s were correct, according to which there was still a church ruin in Merv, something that has been disputed by western experts.

A week before, via a terrible phone connection, I had arranged to meet my driver Hassan at the Turkmenian customs post, but now I was worrying whether he would be there. Thankfully, he was waiting in his 1970s Lada, and celebrated my arrival in Turkmenistan by offering me a fresh cup of coffee. He had installed a coffee machine on the passenger seat of his vehicle, running it from the cigarette lighter, and was fond of working it while driving at top speed, although the countless police checks on the way slowed him down considerably. In the next 40 kilometres, my passport, the entry permit issued by the Foreign Ministry and Hassan's driving licence were inspected thoroughly ten times. Hassan handed over his passport each time with a bank note inside it, which of course 'stuck to' the hand of the policeman or soldier concerned.

Like other Soviet republics in central Asia, Turkmenistan declared its independence in 1991. President Niyazov (who died in December 2006) was previously First Secretary of the Turkmenistan Communist Party; the power structure and those wielding it remained identical, only the label changed. Turkmenistan, 488,000 square kilometres in area and with just 6 million inhabitants, could be prosperous, thanks to its enormous reserves of oil, gas and metal, but remains impoverished, due to huge levels of corruption, which was encouraged by Niyazov, who regarded the country as his private property.

I had read in the weekly *Times of Central Asia* about the megalomaniac cult of personality surrounding President Niyazov. Some of his 'eccentricities' made for amusing reading. The main condition for acquiring a driving licence in Turkmenistan was not a driving test but the study, consisting of 20 lessons, of the *Rukhnama*, a 400-page 'spiritual manual for all Turkmenians' authored by the president. Whilst Niyazov saw his work as a history of the world in which the development of all the cultures of the planet is derived from a Turkmenian 'primeval culture', independent observers saw in the *Rukhnama* a hare-brained collection of pseudo-scientific assertions, mixed with borrowings from the Koran and from Turkmenian epics and sagas. The study of this work was obligatory not only at every educational institution from kindergarten to university, but also in the administration and in every business. Shades of Mao and his Little Red Book . . . Whether this measure – the existence of which Hassan confirmed to me – contributed to increasing road safety is another question.

Imitating the founder of the modern Turkish state, Kemal Atatürk, President Niyazov bestowed upon himself the epithet 'Turkmenbashi', meaning 'Father of all Turkmenians'. Accordingly, the airport of the capital is named Turkmenbashi; the Karakum Canal, which is vital for the country's agriculture, was renamed Turkmenbashi Canal; and you drive along the Turkmenbashi motorway to the Caspian port of Turkmenbashi. Nothing appeared to be exempt from such name changes.

The devaluation of the currency in Turkmenistan since independence has been drastic. At the time of the introduction of the new currency, the manat, in 1993, two manats corresponded to one US dollar; today, for one dollar you officially get 5,000 manats, and on the black market up to 24,000. Meanwhile, petrol is dirt cheap: for $1 you can fill up with 60 litres of 95-octane petrol, or 80 litres of 76-octane. Petrol is 20 to 25 times cheaper than mineral water. However, the cotton harvest ensures that the Turkmenians do not drive too far, despite the virtually free petrol. At harvest time, not only are all students compulsorily recruited for picking, but all the bazaars are closed by order of the police from 9 a.m. to 5 p.m., and the corresponding access roads are blocked with lorries parked across them. Even the petrol stations remain compulsorily closed until 3 or 7 p.m., leading to queues of over 100 cars at a time. This measure is intended to ensure that all those active in agriculture participate in the cotton harvest. It was a wonder that a tourist like me was not roped in to pick cotton too.

In the town of Mary, in the centre of Turkmenbashi Square, stood a shiny golden larger-than-life-size statue of a seated Niyazov. Rumour had it that the figure was made of solid gold. When I stopped to take a photograph of this extravagant memorial, Hassan paled. Both acts were strictly forbidden, he said, and the building opposite the figure belonged to the Internal Secret Service (the successor to the KGB) guarding the statue round the clock. Now I noticed that this huge square in this densely populated city was empty of people. The message was clear, and I decided to go without taking the photo, the consequences of which I was able to guess. In any case, I was not interested in Niyazov, but in the nearby ancient oasis city of Merv, which has a fascinating history.

Merv was founded in the seventh century BC, although its earliest origins date back to prehistoric times. Although it has not been proven that Alexander the Great ever visited Merv, it was for a while named Alexandria. In the fifth century it was the seat of a major archbishopric of the Nestorian Church. For the next hundred years, Merv was alternately occupied by the Seleucids, Parthians and Sassanians until 651 AD, when the last Sassanian ruler, Yazdegard III, was murdered and the city fell to the Arabs, who called it 'Gyaur Kala', meaning 'City of the Infidels', since it was inhabited by 'infidel' Christians, Buddhists and Zoroastrians.

Under the rule of the Abbasid dynasty, Merv developed into the second-largest city in the Islamic world, after Baghdad. Thanks to its location on the main route of the Silk Road, it also became one of the richest and most important trading cities in Central Asia. After several successive Persian dynasties, Merv was peacefully occupied by the Seljuk Turks and grew still further until it was named 'the mother of the world'. Culturally, artistically and intellectually, Merv was arguably the greatest city of its era, comparable to Alexandria itself. The glory of this pearl of the Orient came to a brutal end in 1221, when Genghis Khan had its inhabitants brutally massacred. It is said that between 750,000 and 1,300,000 people fell victim to his armies. The thirteenth-century Iranian historian and governor of Baghdad, 'Ata Malik

Juvaini reports in his *The History of the World-Conqueror* on the successive massacres, and tells how the Mongols lured the remaining survivors from their hiding-places:

> A person who was with them [the Mongols] played the muezzin and gave the call to prayer; and all that came out of the holes in which they were hiding were seized and crammed into the Shihabi college, being finally cast down from the roof. And in the whole town there remained not four persons alive.[15]

Although Merv was rebuilt on a modest scale by Shah Rukh Khan, who ruled from 1407 to 1447, the oasis city decayed in the following centuries and became a no man's land of predatory Turkmenian tribes that lived from trading slaves. In 1884 it was annexed by Russia.

The day after my arrival, I was lucky enough to be accompanied around the ruins of Merv by Ak Mohammed Annaev, who knew its history well. Poring over a map, Ak Mohammed said: 'If we leave out the Bronze Age settlements of Margush, which are 40 kilometres away, the area of Merv is about 55 square kilometres in size. It really consists of ten different towns. Following the destruction of each of them, the ruins were abandoned, and the city rebuilt in a different place nearby. The oldest ruins that are clearly visible date from the sixth century BC, and the most recent from the late eighteenth century.' Our visit would be like taking a stroll through 24 centuries.

At the eastern entrance to the site is the mighty ruin of Kyz Kala, the 'Fortress of the Virgins'. It was here, in 1221, that 40 virgins are said to have chosen suicide rather than enslavement by the Mongols. The windowless brick walls of the fortress, along which still stand 15-metre-high slender columns, date from the later Sassanians period. Instead of windows, there are only narrow embrasures that would have been used by archers; light entered the fort through an atrium and oblique airshafts. From the highest floor, we could see in the centre of the city ruins Sultan Kala, the mausoleum of the Seljuk Sultan Sanjar, who ruled from 1117 to 1153 (d. 1157), controlling a gigantic empire that extended from Samarkand to Baghdad. Above this cubic building rises the oldest double-shelled cupola in Central Asia. Its builders took their inspiration both from the tenth-century tomb of the Samanids in Bukhara and from even older Buddhist temple cupolas in Central Asia. With the finite cube and its eight corners symbolising the earth, and the semicircle of the dome symbolising heaven, the form of this mausoleum expresses the unity of earth and heaven, of the finite and the infinite.

Ak Mohammed sighed and explained that although the mausoleum is recognised as part of the world cultural heritage, this jewel of Seljuk architecture has been not only over-restored, but falsely restored. The walls have been broken through to put in windows, the portal was enormously enlarged, the blue faience tiles are missing in the dome, and the interior painting is garish. I was reminded of the restoration of the Tash Hauli palace in Khiwa in Uzbekistan, also funded by UNESCO, which apparently fails to supervise the execution of its projects carefully.

To the north-east of the mausoleum lay the oldest city in Merv, Erk Kala. I remembered having seen a 2,500-year-old inscription referring to it in Iran three years earlier. The famous inscription of Bishotun states: 'King Darius I [ruled 522–486 BC] speaks: Margiana [then the name of Merv] became a rebellious land. The people elected their own ruler; he was named Frada and came from Margiana. I ordered my Bactrian deputy Dadarshish to annihilate this illegal army. The land now belongs to me.'[16] The 50-acre complex was protected by a clay wall 17 metres high and 20 metres thick at its base. Within its great barrel vaulting were numerous apartments, for the enormously thick walls provided pleasant coolness in the hot summer and retained warmth in winter.

People also utilised the insulating properties of thick clay walls throughout the Iranian cultural sphere, to which Merv also belonged, in 'ice houses'. The largest of the three preserved conical ice houses in Merv is 10 metres in height, with a diameter of 19 metres at its base. At the south side of the ice house was a clay wall that protected it from the direct rays of the sun; although this has since disappeared. The dome, built of clay bricks, has built-in steps on the inside, as does the water storage cistern, which was dug deep into the ground during construction. In winter this was filled with water, which then froze. Thanks to the thickness of the walls and the protective outside wall, the ice was preserved well into the summer. Horizontal wooden beams in the dome suggest that perishable foodstuffs were stored there. In addition, ventilation shafts supplied fresh air along the inside walls.

The citadel of Shahryar Ark also presented a vision of devastation. A group of about 50 dromedaries were grazing where the sultan's palace, the seat of government, the mint, two mosques, barracks and the famous library of the sultan once stood. Only the ruins of the Kitab Khana, one of Merv's nine libraries, are still standing. All the valuable manuscripts went up in flames during the Mongol attack.

I asked Ak Mohammed about the Nestorian presence in Merv and whether or not there were any archaeological remains. Ak Mohammed laughed: 'That is a good question! The Soviet archaeologists Pugachenkova and Dresvyaskaya worked in Merv in the 1950s and 1960s, and identified a well-preserved ruin as a Nestorian church. It is located 17 kilometres north of the mausoleum.' He showed me a photo dating from 1966, in which a long building (41 metres in length) was visible, called Kharoba Koshuk. It was divided into four large and two small rooms, once roofed over with a pointed arch vault, of which one single ogive is still extant. Ak Mohammed countered my anticipation with a bitter damper: 'Unfortunately, the terrain is in agricultural use, and the spring and autumn rains have washed away most of the masonry. Some scholars do not accept the identification of the ruin as a church. You will have to form your own opinion!'

Hassan drove us along sandy tracks, raising a dense cloud of dust. Ak Mohammed had been right: compared with 1966, not even 15 per cent of the former building had been preserved, and the great pointed arch had collapsed. I explored the site, taking careful measurements. The position of the apse, where the altar once stood, can still be traced and the apse faces eastward, corresponding to the traditional orientation of churches. I knew that coins were discovered here, dating from the time of kings Kavad I (ruled 498–531) and Hormizd (ruled 579–90). I felt strongly inclined to agree with Ak Mohammed that the ruin was indeed a Christian church dating from the Sassanid period, and was converted into living spaces in the eleventh century by the Seljuks, which would explain the presence of Seljuk ceramics.

Supposing that, on the site of this extensive heap of clay, more than a millennium ago, a great church once stood, perhaps even the cathedral of Merv, the uneasy question arises about what will remain of our own cities in times to come. The archaeologists of today find ancient works of art of great refinement, such as rich burial objects, well-proportioned figures of stone or metal and fine murals. I wondered what evidence of our civilisation archaeologists a thousand years from now will dig up. Fragments of motorways? Coca-cola bottles? Garbage from the entertainment industry? A rusty tank gun? And what kind of civilisation will they reconstruct from such finds?

Our final visit was to the mausoleum of Mohammed Ibn Said, who ruled Merv from 1112 to 1114 and according to legend was a direct descendant of the Prophet Muhammad. As we drew up to the mausoleum, I was struck by the sight of a gnarled tree beside it, which had countless fragments of textiles hanging from its branches. Pilgrims had tied them up there, hoping for the fulfilment of a wish. Some of the pieces had a verse from the Koran written on them, others a personal message such as the desire for a child or the hope for good health. This is a custom that is also found everywhere in Tibet and Mongolia. There too, solid-colour or printed pieces of cloth are tied to trees thought of as sacred. Years before, I found a most unusual form of this pre-Islamic practice in Uzbekistan, near the town of Urgut, south of Samarkand. Close to the tenth-century tomb of the Islamic missionary and holy man Khoja Abu Talib Sarmast stands a plane tree about a thousand years old. A small Muslim school operated within its mighty trunk up to 1920. The tree-trunk and its tiny schoolhouse still exist today.

At the mausoleum of Mohammed Ibn Said, pilgrims were walking reverently seven times around the structure, after which they entered, and stood by the tomb of the holy man, arms slightly raised, their palms upwards towards heaven. The imam recited a sura from the Koran and finally blessed the unleavened bread brought by the pilgrims, which they then would take home again to distribute among their relatives.

Circumambulating the tomb of a holy man several times is a form of reverence that I had already encountered repeatedly in Islamic Central Asia, for instance at the great mausoleum of the Sufi master Ahmed Yassawi, who died in 1166, in the city of Turkistan in Kazakhstan. There, pilgrims circle the mausoleum counter-clockwise, even late at night, touching the outer wall with their left hands and reciting from the Koran. Women can be seen carrying sick babies in their arms and pressing them against the wall at certain points. Such pilgrims demonstrate the peaceful side of Islam, built of reverence, humility and hope. I saw the same custom near the tomb of the Islamic holy man Jafar Sadik in the south of the Chinese province of Xinjiang, the population of which is predominantly Muslim. At the entrance to the tomb hang horses' tails and the fleeces of sacrificed sheep, bearing witness to the persistence of pre-Islamic, shamanic customs. The two tombs are regarded as a 'second Mecca' by the local population.

I asked the imam of Ibn Said's mausoleum what this circumambulation signified. He hesitated and then replied: 'You are an infidel, which explains your ignorant question. The pilgrims circle the tombs of holy men seven times in reference to the circling of the Kaaba in Mecca seven times on the occasion of the pilgrimage prescribed by the Prophet.' The same ritual is also found in the

Buddhist Himalayas and in Mongolia, where stupas, shrines, monasteries and even mountains are respectfully circumambulated. The best-known example of the latter is Mount Kailash in western Tibet, which is circumambulated by members of four different religions, namely Buddhism, Bön, Shivaism and Jainism. Mount Kailash symbolises the axis of the world, the tree of the world and the ladder to heaven at the same time, the magic omnipresence of which is indicated in Mongolia and Tibet by poles driven vertically into the ground.

I also discovered this shamanic symbol – the shaman using the heavenly ladder to embark on his flight of the soul – in two subterranean mosques with necropolises on the Mangyshlak peninsula in Kazakhstan.[17] In the underground mosques Shopan Ata and Beket Ata of Mangyshlak, a slender wooden tree trunk rises from the floor of the largest prayer room and up through the skylight to the sky; pilgrims circle it three times. The world tree penetrates the various levels of the world: the roots are based in the underworld, the trunk gives our world orientation, and the top provides the connection to heaven. In another skylight of the mosque of Beket Ata are placed over two dozen sheep skulls with huge horns – a further custom from the Mongolian shamanic cultural sphere. I have observed repeatedly in Central Asia the heads of sheep, deer and antelope or even bear hanging in trees, facing west. This kind of ceremony pays respect to the spirit of the species of the animal concerned, urging it to reincarnate itself again in the area.

In Central Asia, the mausoleums of Islamic holy men and Sufi mystics form a fascinating overlap between Islam and shamanism. I imagine that the closeness of the Sufi to the shamans greatly facilitated their missionary work with the originally shamanic Turkic peoples of Central Asia. Their main connection was in the conviction that they could, in ecstatic states of consciousness, and thanks to assistant spirits, make contact with the world of gods or spirits in the here and now, not only after death.

At the end of my three-day visit to Merv, Ak Mohammed showed me a book from his library containing numerous old photographs dating from 1891. At that time, many structures that today have become unrecognisable through decay were still mighty and impressive ruins. Although Russian scientists had asked the tsar to intervene with the local sultan to stop the destruction of these ancient buildings, it continued. The sultan justified himself by saying: 'The buildings will not be damaged; only the old bricks will be removed to use them to build new houses.' If one compares old photographs of Merv and Samarkand, one is forced to conclude that Merv could have been restored as

Samarkand was, if the exploitation of the ruins had been stopped at the close of the nineteenth century. Now the tourists flock to Samarkand, whereas in Merv the dromedaries graze.

Since I had heard rumours that the mysterious subterranean dwellings at the Kazakh peninsula of Mangyshlak were possibly linked to Nestorianism, I decided to explore them myself. These caves, which today serve as mosques, are either hewn deep into the mountainside or can be reached via a narrow staircase.[18] Near their entrances there are huge necropolises studded with medieval and more modern tombstones. Next to some stand large stone figures of a ram, called *koshkar-tas*. I had already found the motif of the stone sheep, which comes from the Turkish-Mongolian cultural area, in Nestorian cemeteries in Iran, in Maragha, Delemon and Göktepe. Among Turks and Mongols, the ram was regarded as a tribal totem and protector. Inscriptions in Arabic are chiselled on the backs of the stone figures, and on their sides are swords and axes or bags. At the cave of Shakpak Ata, the cemetery is immediately adjacent to the mosque. To the left and right of the entrance, two and five niches respectively have been hewn from the rock, and inside these are tombs at ground-level. The dead are covered with loosely laid stone slabs; in one of the graves, a centuries-old skull can be seen.

Such cemeteries are more 'lively' than their European counterparts. Next to the necropolis of Hanga Baba, we saw an extended family camping, remembering a relative who had fallen victim to the Stalinist 'cleansing' of 1937. The people had spread out colourful carpets immediately beside the grave of their relative and had slaughtered a sheep, which they at once gutted, cooked and ate, offering a portion to the dead man. It was a ritual, in which the dead man was drawn into the lives of the living and vice versa.

The Kazakh archaeologist Andrei Astafiev believes that these caves were never connected with Nestorianism but that they served the Sufi as monasteries in the Middle Ages. In fact, the local people believe that all these monasteries were founded by pupils of the twelfth-century Sufi master Ahmed Yassawi. A connection with the Sufi is also suggested by the extremely low passages, which permit only a creeping gait, obliging people to adopt a posture of humility. Indeed, Sufis used to meditate in tiny dark cells, the entrances to which were closed for a certain time with huge rocks.

In all these mosques there are also clear signs of pre-Islamic rituals. There are sacrificial stones rubbed and blackened with sheep fat, reminiscent of a cult of fire. In Shopan Ata, the elderly guardian of the shrine performed a fire ceremony at midnight. She is both revered and feared as a magician. She crouched at the entrance to the subterranean mosque, in front of a hollowed-out stone on which she poured some oil. Then she ignited the oil and took out of a bag a number of scraps of paper with verses from the Koran written on them, which she threw into the fire while reciting these. About 20 people stood reverently around her. Finally, all those present rubbed their hands in the fire and applied them to painful or sick parts of their bodies.

This ritual is reminiscent of the fire cult of old Turkic and Mongol peoples. Thus the Byzantine envoy Zemarkos, who in 568 travelled to the Talas valley in southern Kazakhstan to visit the khan of the Western Turks, Istämi, reported that the Turks 'purify themselves with fire'. The fire ritual observed at Shopan Ata also creates a bridge to the Sufis of Kazakhstan. In the Sufi monasteries of the followers of Ahmed Yassawi, a holy fire glowed night and day. Every time a Sufi left the monastery, he placed his hands in the fire, and then passed them over his face. This purification ritual shows that Islam also adopted pre-Islamic religious concepts.

After the exploration of all-important subterranean mosques I reached the same conclusion as Astafiev. There are no signs of a former Christian presence, neither inside the mosques nor in the graveyards.

# The Mystery of Khukh Burd Süme

The Nestorian missionaries did not stop in Merv, but penetrated much farther east. As early as 635 AD, they reached Chang'an (Xian), the capital of China at that time, and, in around 1000 AD, Mongolia. The first Mongolian tribe to accept conversion were the Kerait, whose home territory extended from today's central Mongolia far to the south into the Gobi Desert. Tradition has it that in 1007 the khan of the Kerait was caught in a snowstorm while hunting and lost his way, when St Sergius is said to have appeared to him in a vision and promised to save him if he had himself baptised. After being saved, the khan sent messengers to the Metropolitan Bishop of Merv, who sent out two priests to baptise him and his people, numbering 200,000 souls, on the spot. The khan, who from then on officiated as priest himself, laid the foundations for the medieval legend of Prester John.

The transformation of the historical khan of the Kerait into a mythical powerful Christian priest-king in Asia took place against the background of the Crusades. Following initial successes, the crusaders had suffered their first defeat in 1144, when they lost the earldom of Edessa, in the south-east of Turkey, to the Muslims. It became apparent that the crusaders were hopelessly outnumbered and isolated, so allies were urgently sought. It is thus no accident that the historian Bishop Otto of Freising reported, only a year after the fall of Edessa, on a Christian king who had beaten a Muslim army in Asia and wanted to liberate Palestine.[19] To encourage the European rulers to send more troops to Palestine, the chancellor of the German Emperor Frederick Barbarossa forged the so-called 'Letter of Prester John' to Emperor Manuel I of Byzantium in 1160.

Prester John was, of course, a myth, and the first-baptised khan of the Kerait remained anonymous; but there were indeed several Nestorian Christian rulers and tribes in Mongolia, such as the majority of the warlike Naiman in the west, smaller minorities of the Oirat and the Merkit in the north, the Öngüt in the south, Tungusic tribes in the east and the Kerait in the heart of Mongolia. In the twelfth century, two khans of the Kerait, who evidently bore Christian names – Marghuz and Cyriacus – succeeded in uniting a number of Mongolian tribes, thus anticipating the life's work of Genghis Khan. But the most powerful Nestorian Mongolian ruler was Toghril Khan, who ruled from 1175 to 1203, a nephew of Cyriacus Khan, who held power over large areas of present-day Mongolia. It is a little-known fact that Genghis Khan was a vassal of the Nestorian Toghril for over a decade. Knowing this, the myth of a priest-king hastening to the aid of the hard-pressed crusaders seems to take on the shape of reality. But, as reported by Marco Polo, Genghis Khan rebelled when Toghril refused him the hand of his daughter and killed him in battle.

Is there still architectural evidence of these Christian Mongolians in Mongolia? My hopes were low, because the Mongols built few solid dwelling houses and no religious buildings for four centuries, up to 1235. Their Nestorian churches were tents and the clergy followed the migrations of the nomads.

As far as the Nestorian churches are concerned, I was aware of two exceptions. One I explored in present-day Inner Mongolia – the ruins and necropolises of Olon Süme-in Tor, the northern capital of the Öngüt during the thirteenth and fourteenth centuries. The second church is known from the travel account of the Franciscan friar William of Rubruk, who stayed in Karakorum, the capital of the Mongolian Empire, on commission from Louis IX of France in the year 1254. Rubruk described not only individual tent churches, but also mentions a solidly built church in Karakorum. Although a German–Mongol archaeological team has been excavating Karakorum for several years, the church ruins have not been found yet.

However, 250 kilometres south-east of Karakorum I came across a trace of the elusive, long-since-vanished Church of the East. It is the mysterious stone ruins of Khukh Burd Süme, which lie on a small island in the lake of Sangiin Dalai Nuur. The lake was partly overgrown with reeds; a narrow dam coated with mud gave access to the ruins. Around them loud twittering and croaking could be heard, but the birds remained invisible in the morning mist. The mood was reminiscent of Arnold Böcklin's painting *The Isle of the Dead*, in which a dead man in a white shroud is being rowed by moonlight to an island in the shape of an amphitheatre, in the middle of which black cypresses grow towards the sky.

Here stood the ruins of three buildings; all made of superimposed layers of flat stones. Inside the thick walls the masonry is reinforced with clay. To the east of the site stands a five-metre-high tower with embrasures and a square ground plan. To the west, there is a long one-storey building with a central entrance hall flanked by groups of four rooms. The third building, having at least two storeys, and being up to seven metres in height, surprisingly has the ground plan of a cross, its shape corresponds to the Greek cross, with arms of equal length. In the east–west axis there are two windows, the entrance being in the middle of the south-east side, while the north-west façade is windowless.

What was the function of this ruin? Mongolian archaeologists believe that a palace was built in the seventeenth century on the ruins of a considerably older temple or monastery dating from the eleventh or twelfth centuries. This raises the question as to what kind of monastery that may have been. At that time, Buddhism had not yet gained a foothold in Mongolia, and in any case a ground plan in the form of a cross is rather alien to Buddhist architecture. In those days, the majority of Mongolian tribes worshipped the god of heaven, Tengri and countless lesser deities in whose honour, however, no permanent shrines were built. If the supposed later palace corresponds to the original ground plan, the cross shape raises the question of a possible Nestorian origin. I found this hypothesis plausible, since Khukh Burd Süme was in the heartland of the Nestorian people of the Kerait. But this will only be solved by excavations far in the future.

On leaving the island, I was painfully aware that I may never learn the solution to the mystery of Khukh Burd Süme. There are no definitive conclusions to explorations, only provisional partial goals, following each other in endless succession.

# PART II

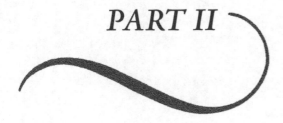

# The Nomadic Land

# Searching for Genghis Khan's Tomb

Approaching the Mongolian capital Ulaan Baatar by air reveals a conflict that seems to describe the country itself. After an hour flying over the rich green meadows and blue lakes of nomadic north-west Mongolia, the oppressive haze of the capital comes into sight. On the ground, Therese and I were greeted by power stations and concrete factories belching smoke and soot. The sky was dominated by a confusion of electrical wires and the sides of the asphalt road leading from the airport to the city centre were covered with garbage. However, in the midst of the monotonous grey Soviet architecture, there were signs of Mongolia's nomadic culture tenaciously clinging on. Amongst the 1950s and 1960s housing blocks clustered on the outskirts of the city, there are areas where hundreds of *gers* (yurts), surrounded by wooden fences, stand in rows. Many inhabitants of the city prefer to spend the summer, or even the whole year, living in these traditional *gers* as opposed to purpose-built concrete blocks. In other parts of Ulaan Bataar there are areas of single-storey wooden houses, between which horse-drawn carts laden with food wend their way: mobile mini-shops offering dairy products, meat and vegetables for sale. A number of cranes rising above the suburbs and the city centre are signs, however, that this peculiar architectural mix will soon be a thing of the past.

Ulaan Bataar's traditional name Urgöö (Urga) means 'City of Felt Tents'. It was founded in 1639 as a nomadic settlement near a Buddhist monastery, over 400 kilometres west of what is Ulaan Baatar now. For the first 140 years of its history, the town changed its location 20 times, as the surroundings became unable to support large herds of animals. It was not until 1778 that the city of Urgöö was established on the current site, which offers protection from the howling winds of the Mongolian winter. Although it became a permanent place of residence, Urgöö remained a city of *gers* until Mongolia's independence from China in 1911. The only solid buildings were 12 temple complexes and the depots of several trading firms. In 1924 it acquired its present name Ulaan Baatar, meaning 'Red Hero', in memory of Sukh Baatar, one of the revolutionaries who led Mongolia to independence and who died in 1923.

Apart from a few monasteries that have been converted into museums, the city centre is at first dominated by the expected and depressing view of Soviet-style uniform building units. There are, however, exceptions: street cafés are sprouting up, and as a change from the monotonous and ubiquitous McDonald's, one snack-bar intices customers with the name Genghis Khan Beer Saloon. The omnipresence of Genghis Khan is a remarkable feature of the city; he is without doubt one of the most controversial and enduringly fascinating historical personalities. Seen from the Mongolian perspective, it was he who in 1206 unified the Mongolian and Turkic peoples into a nation, which then embarked on a mission to conquer the world. To the Chinese, he is the worst of a long series of Mongol invaders who regularly plagued the Middle Kingdom like a natural catastrophe. To the Muslim countries of Central Asia, he brought about the destruction of their architectural splendours, and to Russia and eastern Europe he was evil personified, appearing as if out of nowhere from the wild steppes, reaping death and destruction wherever he went. The people he conquered saw him and his successors as flaming comets that set the whole of Eurasia on fire and which, after decades of destruction, burned out and finally disappeared.

In contrast, the Mongols venerate Genghis Khan as the creator of the Mongolian nation, who gave it direction and meaning. Between the sixteenth and the nineteenth centuries he was deified as a reincarnation of Bodhisattva Vajrapani, the protector of Buddha Shakyamuni.[1] During the Soviet era, he was regarded as a reactionary nationalist. Today, he serves as a figure of national identification, the symbol of a better future. The cult of Genghis Khan, as promoted by the government, almost amounts to a new state religion. He is also useful as a general instrument of advertising. In the capital, I found Genghis Khan beer, mineral water, wine and countless kinds of spirits; Genghis Khan soap, cigarettes, chocolate and chewing-gum. One could continue the list indefinitely.

The monastery of Ganden Dechen Ling, in Ulaan Bataar, was and still is the most important monastery in Mongolia. Building commenced in 1838; a century later, it was closed by the Bolsheviks, who converted it into a museum.

Since independence and the democratisation of Mongolia in 1991, it has become active again, and houses around 500 monks and novices. I was struck by the large number of young people visiting the temple, in contrast to places like Tibet, where the majority of temple visitors are often the elderly. In the main temple of Ganden Dechen Ling stands a 25-metre-high statue of the Bodhisattva of Compassion, Avalokiteshvara, surrounded by life-size figures, much in the same way that the Lilliputians surrounded the sleeping giant Gulliver.

Inside the monastery, a young monk who came to talk to me complained that American missionaries – Mormons or Jehovah's Witnesses – often aggressively try to recruit new members by presenting nomads with a bag of flour, a sheep or some tobacco. A true purchase of the soul. The missionaries also apparently invite urban Mongols to the disco, or offer them English courses; a select few are even tempted with a grant to attend a 'Biblical college' in the USA. In nineteenth-century China, hundreds of thousands of 'rice Christians' had themselves baptised in order to receive rice regularly; in Mongolia today, one could talk about 'green-card Christians'.

Islamic missionaries, who enjoy the massive support of financially powerful states, proceed in a similar manner. A gigantic mosque is being built in Ulaan Baatar, although hardly any Muslims live there and in some cities in Mongolia and southern Siberia there are Turkish educational institutions open only to boys. There they not only receive a good education, including English and Turkish, but are encouraged to convert to Islam. As a reward the best pupils are sent to Istanbul, where they are trained as imams.

After a few days of exploring the capital, we set off in a Russian jeep eastwards on a journey that would take us in search of the tomb of Genghis Khan. We were glad to be leaving the world of sterile hotel enclaves for that of tents and *gers* and wide open spaces. We were accompanied by Professor Damba Bazargur of the Mongolian Academy of Sciences. After several years of field research, he believed he had come closer to discovering the solution to the riddle surrounding the tomb of Genghis Khan, and to have found the site in the north-eastern *aimag* (province) of Khentii, south of the town of Batshiret. A team of 30 research workers, financed by a wealthy American, were being led by John Woods of the University of Chicago and Damba Bazargur to investigate.

Genghis Khan was born in 1162 as Temüjin in eastern Mongolia, near the river Onon. At a young age, following the murder of his father, Temüjin had learned to survive alone and to kill anyone who did not conform to his will, including one of his brothers who refused to recognise his legitimacy as successor to his father. For several years, he began to assemble comrades-in-arms around him, consolidating his power and influence. Around 1189 Temüjin had himself proclaimed Genghis Khan, 'the ruler like the ocean', by several Mongol tribes, and in 1206, an Imperial Diet confirmed his absolute power over the Mongolian tribes; the Mongolian nation was born. As a state-forming measure, he smashed the traditional tribal bonds, and organised the people and the army according to the decimal system formerly used by the Xiongnu, thus creating a new military aristocracy. He also had the Mongolian alphabet developed from the Uigur script, and established a code of laws. He was now able to turn his attention to the world outside Mongolia.

Letting his armies loose to all points of the compass, Genghis Khan systematically conquered western and northern China, central Asia, Afghanistan, Iran, Georgia and the Russian principalities and even pressed on as far as Poland and Hungary. Flourishing cities such as Bamyan, Balkh, Herat, Merv, Nishapur and Bukhara were razed to the ground and their inhabitants butchered. Some places never recovered from this apocalypse; regions of Afghanistan became permanent deserts as a consequence of the wilful destruction of the irrigation canals and the extermination of the population. At its peak, the Mongol Empire exceeded that of Alexander the Great several times over. Mystery and hearsay surround the death of Genghis Khan: some say that he fell off his horse, others that he was killed by an arrow while besieging a hostile city. It is generally assumed that his body was returned to Mongolia and transported to his birthplace near the river Onon in north-eastern Mongolia. In this way, the spirit of Genghis Khan would continue to protect the Mongols from there, and this would also follow the custom of burying the dead next to the graves of their ancestors. Genghis Khan's father Yesügei had already found his last resting place by the river.

The precise site of Genghis Khan's tomb has, however, remained a mystery as the burial ceremony itself was kept secret. Legend tells that the accompanying troops systematically murdered eye-witnesses. Marco Polo reported:

> When the corpse of a Mongol ruler is borne to the imperial necropolis in his home area, the escort of the funeral procession slay all those they encounter on the way, with the words: 'Go and serve thy lord in the other world,' in the belief that the spirits of the slain would serve their dead ruler in the life beyond. When

Khan Möngke [ruled 1251–59] was borne to the site of his tomb, 20,000 people whom the mourning procession encountered were slain.[2]

Genghis Khan was buried by 50 soldiers, who were then killed by another 50, and these in turn suffered the same fate. At the burial site, no monuments above ground, for instance a burial mound or a stele, were erected, in order not to attract grave-looters.

Like that of Alexander, Genghis Khan's final resting place is one of the great mysteries of archaeology. The Mongols of the Ordos region believe that he was buried in the Ordos desert in Inner Mongolia, but others are convinced that he was buried near his birthplace and near the tomb of his father, which is said to be in the vicinity of the mountain Burkhan Khaldun, a site of worship in the thirteenth century. It was here that Professor Bazargur and his team were carrying out their dig.

During the 386-kilometre journey to Batshiret, Professor Bazargur explained that the traditional descriptions of Genghis Khan's tomb are contradictory. One source states that his last resting place was on the peak or in a cave on the mountain of Burkhan Khaldun, another that it was at the foot of this mountain. Another tradition says that a herd of a thousand horses was driven over the grave-site to obliterate all traces of it, or else that a river was diverted over the grave. In addition to Genghis Khan, his sons Ögödei and Tului, and his grandsons Möngke and Arik Böge, as well as several princesses, were supposed to have been buried in the same place.[3] In effect, Professor Bazargur and his team were searching not only for the grave of Genghis Khan but for the royal necropolis, comparable perhaps to the Valley of the Kings in Egypt.

To find Genghis Khan's burial place would reveal much about the religious ideas of the time, including whether human sacrifices were really made, and about the social hierarchies of the Mongols. To date, nothing has been found of the countless riches plundered by the Mongols in the countries they conquered and it may be that they were placed in the graves of their dead rulers, in which case the discovery of Genghis Khan's grave could lead to finds as spectacular as that of Tutankhamun.

Bazargur quoted the Persian chronicler Mohammed al Jurjani in 1260:

> There is among the Mongols the custom of excavating an underground chamber for the dead ruler. The floor is covered with carpets, on which they place a throne, numerous vessels, weapons and personal belongings of the deceased. After the body has been seated on the throne, the tomb is filled in, by night.

A number of archaeologists have sought the tomb of Genghis Khan in vain. Most have looked for it in the province of Khentii, near a mountain situated 60 kilometres south of the Russian border, which is officially described as the real Burkhan Khaldun. Bazargur, however, disagrees, as it does not correspond to clues contained in the *The Secret History of the Mongols*, written for the Mongol royal family in 1240, and considered to be the single most important contemporary account of Genghis Khan. Bazargur thinks he has found Burkhan Khaldun on the unspectacular hill Öglögchiin Kherem, 90 kilometres south-east of the official site. But why there? It is located very close to the upper reaches of the river Onon, where Temüjin first saw the light of day, near the present-day town of Binder, and where there used to be a summer pasture for cattle. Second, the great Imperial Diet of 1206, at which Genghis Khan united the Mongol tribes to form the Mongolian nation, took place on the nearby plain, at the confluence of the Khurkhin and the Onon. And third, a nearby place bears the name 'Graveyard of the Hundred Soldiers'; there is presumably a connection here with the 100 soldiers who were killed after the burial of the khan.

The morning after our arrival at the site, Professor Bazargur showed us around the area being excavated. It covered the southern flank of the mountain, the lowest point of which is 1194 metres and the highest 1416 metres above sea level. A stone wall three to four metres high and 3.2 kilometres long dating from the twelfth to fourteenth century surrounded the site. Inside this wall ran a second, older stone wall about a kilometre in length. If this really was a necropolis, the function of the inner wall would be to protect the older graves.

The archaeologists working on the site had identified over 60 untouched graves, 40 of them on the mountainside and about 20 around the peak. They had now started digging at two points in the lower sector: at the first, they had uncovered dozens of flat carefully joined stone slabs, measuring between 60 x 40 cm and 100 x 70 cm. Were they a path? Or foundations of buildings? Or gravestones? Finding out what they were would show whether the stone wall of Öglögchiin surrounded an ancient city, or indeed a necropolis.

After intensive excavations in Öglögchiin, it became clear that the site was indeed that of a cemetery, although not the hoped-for necropolis of Genghis Khan and the royal family. In two graves three skeletons were uncovered. In the first, the roof of which consisted of five-metre-long stones decorated with wolf motifs, lay a young, socially important woman – perhaps a ruler's wife – as identified by the possessions she was buried with. Beside her lay a wooden coffin containing a male skeleton, together with the bit of a bridle and iron objects shaped like flatirons. In the neighbouring grave was the skeleton of another woman, with jewellery and precious stones. All three skeletons dated from the Iron Age (600–400 BC) or the Xiongnu Empire (fourth century BC–first century AD); there was also the iron tip of a standard dating from the Middle Ages. Bazargur was very pleased, even though the dead were at least a thousand years older than the generation of Genghis Khan. Even if the Öglögchiin site was not the grave of Genghis Khan, it was still a sensational find.

Three weeks after we left Öglögchiin, we contacted Bazargur over satellite phone, to gauge whether we could return. However, things did not turn out as expected. On our return to Ulaan Baatar, the front page of the leading weekly caught the eye of our interpreter, Ningjie; the finds near Öglögchiin had aroused much attention. In the leading article, the former prime minister, Byambasuren, was quoted as saying: 'I am deeply perturbed that the grave of our ancestors has been disturbed, and the purity of the necropolis besmirched, for the sake of a few dollars. This place must be kept forever undefiled for the souls of the dead.' He went on to demand an immediate end to the excavations, the expulsion of the American archaeologists, and the declaration of the site as a protected natural area. Shortly after this, we learned that the expedition had been banned completely.

Bazargur was indignant: 'If the scientists are prevented from exploring, the treasure-seekers and grave-looters will swarm there like flies. The find site is known, and interest in it has been aroused.' I was also disappointed that the project had been broken off. At the same time, I understood the government's decision. Would we permit Mongolian archaeologists to dig in Europe for the bones of our historical heroes such as Charlemagne, Martin Luther, or the popes of Rome?

While we stayed at Öglögchiin a nomad took us to a rock wall named Arschaan Khod, near which the Imperial Diet took place. The wall and the surrounding rocks are covered with Mesolithic engraved symbols called *tamgha*, which resemble hoof prints, as well as with medieval inscriptions in Old Mongolian, Chinese and Arabic script. Beside these are hunting scenes and representations of animals dating from the Bronze Age (1600–600 BC). Like countless other sites that feature prehistoric petroglyphs, Arschaan Khod is a holy place, a shrine with the sky as its roof. The fact that the nomads still show their veneration for such places can be seen from the numerous blue ribbons that hang from crevices in the rock.

These ribbons, called *katha*, are a sign of respect borrowed from Tibetan Buddhism. They are presented as a greeting, laid around statues, or tied to long poles that symbolise the mythical tree of life. From such trees of life, connecting heaven and earth, hundreds of ribbons frequently hang, with banknotes between them bearing the portrait of Genghis Khan. They cascade to the ground like a waterfall, symbolically bringing the blessings of heaven down to men. The colour blue is very popular among Mongols because of its relationship to the sky, which they venerated before their conversion to Buddhism as the representation of eternal truth and supreme divinity. The colour blue is one of the bridges between shamanism and Buddhism. Meaning is also attached to other colours: red symbolises bliss and the courage to overcome all obstacles; yellow symbolises life and eternity; white represents human kindness and success, green growth and fertility.

Wandering around the wall, I came upon a cross with arms of equal length chiselled in high relief in the rock, and surrounded by a circle. Since some Mongolian tribes of the thirteenth century were Nestorians, it is quite possible that the cross represented a first small trace of medieval Christianity in Mongolia. However, the cross is also an age-old, pre-Christian symbol. Being a double connection between opposite points, and a point of intersection between the basic figure of the circle – symbolising heaven – and the square – representing the earth – it is the symbol of the unity of extremes, in other words perfect reconciliation and orientation. The pre-Christian cross can be found both in Stone Age and Bronze Age petroglyphs in Central Asia, Scandinavia or California, as well as on 6,000-year-old ceramic vessels from Elam in south-west Iran. The omnipresence of the symbol of the cross in widely varying cultures can be explained by the fact that it is immediately derived from man himself. When a human being stretches out his arms, he becomes a cross; he orders the world into above and below, right and left, north and south, east and west, and the horizon becomes the circle that encloses him. In the form of the cross, the human being becomes the shaper of the universe.

# Among the Eagle Hunters

The Russian minibus, a four-wheel-drive Tatra high off the road, was an ideal vehicle for cross-country driving. There were six of us crammed inside: Therese and I, Ningjie, a cook, the driver and a local guide, for we would not see a single signpost for the next three weeks. In addition to all the food and supplies we would need for the trip we had 550 litres of diesel oil. In the province of Bayan Ulgii, situated in the far west of Mongolia, diesel depots are very few and far between, and even more rarely do they actually have any fuel. The filling stations are in some cases 300 kilometres apart, reflecting the low population density and the fact that in many places the car has not yet replaced the horse, camel and yak as a means of transportation. In Mongolia, there are just 1.5 people per square kilometre (compared with 365 in the Netherlands) and for 2.8 million people there are 33 million farmed and working animals – the only real economy that can be adapted to the extreme Mongolian climate. Agriculture is possible only in a few places, and the soil requires a great deal of fertiliser. The animals, however, feed themselves, and provide people with food.

After a few days of driving we stopped at the foot of Mount Khairkhan, 3943 metres high and topped with permanent snow. In the magnificent desert landscape of black rock dotted with a few green pastures stood a few lone white felt *gers*. In two of these lived eagle hunters. Cautiously, we approached a *ger* guarded by snarling and barking watchdogs as large as wolves; fortunately, they were chained up. Beside the *ger* huddled a huge golden eagle, also chained, on a tower of stone blocks. Its body was almost a metre in length, and its beak resembled a curved dagger. It was blindfolded by a leather hood. A man of about 40 with a sun-tanned face stepped out of the *ger* and motioned to us to approach. After a brief conversation with our interpreter, Iktamer Baymanday welcomed us into his *ger*. Hospitality is warm everywhere in Mongolia, something of particular importance in a land with no guesthouses.

The red-painted, south-facing wooden door was open, and on entering we took care to avoid touching the threshold. Treading on it brings bad luck, its function being to prevent evil spirits from entering. In the Middle Ages, anyone who crossed the threshold of a nobleman's *ger* paid for this transgression with his life. The inside of a *ger* is divided according to sex and the points of the compass. The west half, to the left of the entrance, belongs to the men, who are under the protection of the god of heaven, Tengri, while the right, eastern half is apportioned to the women, who are protected by the sun. At the rear, in the north, is the place of honour and the Buddhist altar. The walls are lined with beds and chests containing the owners' possessions. In winter, new-born animals sleep to the right of the door, and to the left of it sits the hunting eagle. 'Taking a new-born animal into the *ger* saves it from dying of the cold, but raises other problems,' explained Iktamer's wife, Bajar. 'The young animal then acquires the smell of humans, so that its mother no longer recognises it as her own and refuses to suckle it. In such a case, there is only one thing to do: the small animal is rubbed with salty water, or with its mother's milk, and led to her. While the mother licks the baby clean, I sing a special plaintive song, sometimes for hours. This melancholy song softens the mother's heart, and she takes her baby back.'

In the middle of the *ger* is a wooden pole that symbolises the tree of life and the axis of the world, for the *ger* is thought of as a microcosm of its own. From the apex of the pole dangles a blue bag. This represents the connection between the generations: it contains some ashes taken by the young master of the house from the hearth of his parents. Also in the middle of the tent is the stove, the chimney of which passes through the centre of the roof, without touching the felt or the wood.

The heart and centre of the *ger* is the stove and the fire, which is protected by several taboos. It is forbidden to spit into the fire, to pour water on it, to burn garbage in it, or to sit with the soles of the feet stretched out before it. These taboos are relics of the ancient Mongol cult of fire, which is said to go back to Genghis Khan, but in fact is much older. Bajar explained their belief that a fire queen lives in the fire of the hearth, which was lit by the ancestors of Genghis Khan and must never go out. If the hearth fire is extinguished, it is a bad omen for the family. Every evening they perform a particular ritual to apologise to the fire, should it go out while they sleep. When the *ger* is moved, they take smouldering embers from the fire to light the hearth at the new camping site. And when their sons marry and found a new household, they will light their hearth fire from the original. This practice contains evident traits of ancestor worship, for the fire, which is female, provides a connection with the protecting ancestors, and thus ensures the continued existence of the family.

To protect the family from the dampness of the ground, the structure of the *ger* – consisting of five wooden concertina barriers tied together with leather straps – is placed on a wooden floor. The inside is hung with warming and colourful felt tapestries, richly decorated with appliqués. Some patterns are reminiscent of the embroidered burial fabrics from the Xiongnu period, showing mythical animals, elks and deer antlers. Other forms are derived from deer stones, on which highly stylised stags with long, birdlike beaks are engraved.

Iktamer offered us fermented mare's milk, *airak*; cheese as hard as iron and dried lamb's meat. In accordance with ancient custom, he first drank a small mouthful of *airak* before passing the bowl on to me. This was not a sign of rudeness: the custom is meant to protect the guest from possible poisoning. Like most nomads in the province of Bayan Ulgii, the family was Kazakh. Mongolian Kazakhs are assumed to be descended from the Nestorian tribes of the Kerait and Naiman. Iktamer was proud of his Kazakh heritage.

'The name Kazakh means "free man",' he said, 'and this is how we feel; especially now that communism is gone. Since 1991 we have been able to live as independent nomads again, to own our own herds, and to move where and when we want. Before that we were tied to a collective farm; private property was mainly forbidden, our work was paid for with coupons for goods and we were not allowed to leave the area to which we were assigned. We were serfs of the Communist Party.'

'Did the political change also have some disadvantages?' I asked.

Iktamer and Bajar nodded. Bajar was the first to reply: 'Since the collective was closed, there is neither a doctor nor a school for 100 kilometres. In summer, our children help in looking after the animals; in winter, they go to school in the town of Ulgii, which is very expensive. And then there is no longer an old-age pension. We can only hope that one of our children will stay with us when grown up.'

Iktamer added: 'What has been more serious is the end of the state feed stores, so that if we have catastrophic weather – a *zud* – there is little for us to survive on. In a white *zud*, a large amount of snow falls, and in an iron *zud* the melting snow in spring freezes into a thick layer of ice; a black *zud* means drought. In all these kinds of *zud*, the animals cannot find food, and since we traditionally do not store hay, we are dependent on aid. Fortunately, the people around here have organised themselves in a voluntary cooperative, so that we set up a common feed store in summer.'

In a white *zud* several years before, Iktamer lost hundreds of his animals, but he would have lost more if there had been no common store. I remembered the numerous carcasses of horses, donkeys, camels and sheep I had often seen in the steppe while driving through the province – life and death are inextricably linked in Mongolia

Iktamer proudly told us a legend of Genghis Khan that gave them strength during such hard periods: 'Our wise ancestor once called his four sons, and gave each of them an arrow, telling him to break it. Each son broke his arrow without difficulty. Then the Khan tied four arrows together, and commanded each of his sons to break the bundle. Each of them failed, for the bundle of arrows was stronger than the strongest of his sons.[4] The same applies to us: each of us alone is too weak, but together we can withstand the worst *zud*.'

Another major concern for these families was the government's approach to the nomad way of life. In fertile areas, the government supports agriculture and animal breeding in order to supply towns with meat. The animals are kept on a minimum of land, with exclusive rights granted to one owner. Sometimes these pastures, and even water supplies, are fenced in with barbed wire. It is also rumoured that the government intends to privatise the land in such places. Land laws like this completely contradict the traditional nomad way of life and Mongolia's very identity.

After we had finished our meal, Iktamer's neighbour, Arslan, came to sit with us, leaving his hunting eagle tethered outside the *ger*. In contrast to Iktamer, with his round Mongol features, Arslan was of the Turkic race. A hooked nose projected from his narrow face and he had a dense pointed beard. He resembled his own eagle. As a greeting ceremony, the two men exchanged their snuffboxes briefly, taking a pinch each. Then Arslan began to describe their work with the eagles: 'Training an eagle for hunting takes six months, and is very intensive. We catch young birds with a net and adults by using a lamb as bait. We use only females, which are stronger and more aggressive than the males. Immediately after catching one, we put on a special feast, at which we recite poems in praise of hunting eagles. Then older women place owls' feathers on the captured bird, for owls have excellent sight and are clever hunters. After this, the training begins. First, the bird must become accustomed to me and people in general, and accordingly spends the night in the ger. Recently caught eagles also like the gers, since they are afraid of the large screech owls when chained up. The eagle learns to sit, first on a piece of wood, then on my padded glove, without losing its balance or trying to fly away. I then teach it to return to me on command by giving the bird meat only on its return from a flight. The third step is to teach the bird to hunt, by pulling a stuffed dead fox behind my horse, which it must catch in order to be given meat. Fourth, the eagle must become accustomed to the movements of a galloping horse. And finally we begin the real hunting, first for hares and marmots, later foxes, and even wolves. Since we use or sell the skins of the animals caught, the eagle must be taught only to kill its prey, but not eat it. Every catch is at once rewarded with meat.'

We left the ger to have a closer look at Arslan's eagle. Although golden eagles can reach an age of 30 to 40, they are usually released at the age of 12, 15 at the latest, so that they can mate. Iktamer would give his eagle its freedom back next year in September, in an area with plenty of prey. On these occasions, they will hold a feast and kill a sheep for the eagle. After not having fed it for some days, they release it high on a lonely mountain. Being hungry, it seeks food for itself at once. At the same time, they move their winter camp, to prevent its return. The parting is painful.

'When I give an eagle its freedom, it is like losing a child,' said Iktamer.

'In this province,' Arslan continued, 'there are about 400 families that have hunting eagles. We meet each year for the opening of the hunting season, which runs from 10 October to 10 March, celebrating this with a special feast. We take part in various competitions, which we hold in honour of Genghis Khan, who was a passionate eagle hunter.' And indeed the eagle plays an important part in the lives of Mongols and Kazakhs. It is not only a hunter, but also a symbol of male power, which can be seen in the eagle dance performed by wrestlers after each victory. They dance slowly in a circle and move their outstretched arms up and down, imitating the flight of the eagle. Female and male shamans wear a wreath of eagle feathers as a headdress, believing they make the flight of the soul to invisible worlds possible. In the art of early western Mongolian and southern Siberian nomads, the eagle was given great esteem. On many ancient bronze buckles or plaques, eagles or griffons are shown attacking a deer, a yak or a horse – a bird of prey attacking an herbivore, as hordes of Mongolian horsemen attacked Chinese farmers for millennia.

Unfortunately, we were not able to accompany Arslan and Iktamer on a hunt, because the season had not yet begun. To hunt earlier than custom permitted would mean breaking the taboo that states that no one can hunt more than is necessary for survival. However, they were ready and willing to demonstrate a flight. They mounted their horses and fastened the T-shaped wooden arm-supports in a holder on the saddle. Then they approached the stone towers where the birds were sitting. Iktamer's eldest son grabbed the birds and placed one on the thick glove of each hunter, whose forearm rested on the carrying frame. They galloped off over the crest of the nearest hill and in a short time returned, man, horse and eagle forming a compact whole – resembling a winged centaur, the birds keeping their balance with slight movements of their wings. The riders stopped, removed their eagles' leather hoods, and raised their arms. The two eagles opened their pinions, with a wingspan of over two metres, and soared into the air. They circled slowly over our heads in search of possible prey, their dramatic silhouettes dominating the blue sky. With piercing cries the two hunters called their birds, which folded their wings and dropped like stones, falling at a speed of more than 100 kilometres per hour. A few metres above the ground, they opened their wings again, stabilised their fall, and landed with a noisy rustling of feathers on the outstretched arms of the horsemen: a perfect example of cooperation between man and bird.

As we prepared to leave the ger, Bajar filled a ladle with milk and with her middle finger spread a few drops on the ground, enjoining the gods to protect us on our journey.

Since the Kazakh Mongols live almost 1,000 kilometres from the capital or any other large industrial town, they largely avoid the problems of over-grazing. Apart from copper and gold mining, the entire Mongolian industry had been geared to the Soviet Union and its satellite states, which provided a measure of security. Before 1990, there was practically no trade contact with industrial countries of the West, but with the collapse of the Soviet Union these secure markets for the relatively low-quality products of Mongolian industry disappeared. At the same time, cheap Chinese products flooded the market, so that one factory after another was forced to close down and dismiss its workers. This was made worse by the fact that the Soviet subsidies that had constituted over half of the Mongolian gross domestic product ceased. It was as though the body of the Mongolian economy had suddenly had half of its blood supply cut off. As a Mongol proverb says, 'Mongolia is a raw egg squeezed between the two rocks called Russia and China.'

Huge debts led to three-figure inflation rates in the early 1990s, and to a dramatic loss of purchasing power among the urban population. Only the nomads, as self-sufficient, escaped this vicious circle. In view of the lack of new jobs and inadequate social security, for many unemployed in the provinces the only way out was either to migrate to the capital or to return to a nomadic existence. Many chose the latter, but the rapid growth of the herds of animals led to overuse of the pasture land, and increased the danger of turning the essentially rich land into a desert.

The collapse of Mongolia's industry in the 1990s led to the rapid depopulation of many of the new towns that had been built to provide an industrial workforce. Some years ago, Therese and I travelled on the trans-Siberian railway from Ulaan Baatar to Irkutsk and on to Krasnojarsk. On the 1700-kilometre train journey the sights on entering and leaving each town were the same: miles of decayed industrial complexes with dilapidated factory buildings that resembled giant elks that had been attacked by packs of hungry wolves. Beside the factories stood rusty warehouses, cranes and railway trucks, smothered in overgrown bushes, among which goats foraged. The industrial decline had led to the decay of whole districts and huge levels of unemployment. The only trades that boomed were prostitution and the sale of vodka.

North of Kyzyl-Mushallik, in the autonomous Republic of Tuva, we lingered briefly in one of these ghost towns, which had previously been the site of an asbestos factory. All that remained were the people who used to work there. In some parts of the town, dozens of housing blocks were abandoned, like captainless ships. Windows, doors and staircases had been removed; in one a sheep was decomposing in a pool of water from a broken pipe. The sole restaurant in town was closed for a wedding party – a sought-after opportunity for getting drunk free of charge – so we bought some bread and sausage and sat down in a barren square. Well over half the people who passed by – both adults and children – were limping, without doubt a consequence of long-term, though now hereditary, asbestos poisoning. Many people had noticeably scarred faces, arousing associations with Chernobyl. By early afternoon, with nothing else to do and little hope, half of the people in the streets were drunk. Therese and I left as soon as we could, though the memory of the town lingered long after. A Russian friend told us, 'With the disappearance of the Soviet Union, many former workers became lost people, abandoned in the nowhere.'

# Art in Stone and Men of Stone

Within a single hour, we had experienced driving rain, sometimes mixed with hail, and blazing sunshine. Living up to Mongolia's epithet 'land of raging winds', the only constant feature was indeed a violent wind that blew from every direction. We were on our way to explore the ancient rock carvings of Tsagaan Salaa – the visual record of the dawn of Mongolia's nomadic society.

Along the way, we passed several shaman shrines, or *obos*, at the tops of passes. These piles of stones, up to two metres high, are venerated as the homes of local protective spirits and decorated accordingly with blue ribbons. The traveller, on passing an *obo*, must dismount from his horse, circle the *obo* three times clockwise and add three new stones to the pile. In addition to the blue ribbons, banknotes, coins, fat, items of clothing, empty bottles and even wooden crutches or medicinal plasters are left behind as votive offerings. In remote areas, the skulls of horses or yaks, or deer antlers, may also be found. Like the burial mounds that are found throughout Eurasia, *obos* are sacred sites, where the dead were commemorated in earlier times. Up to the sixteenth century, every family or tribe had an *obo* of its own. As part of the cult of the ancestors, the community would sacrifice a horse at the beginning of spring and place its head on the *obo*, accompanied by a spread of food. Then the spirits of the dead would be invited to take part in the meal and they were informed about the events of the past year. In this way, the world of the living became connected with that of the dead.

Towards evening we reached the river Baga-Oygur and set up camp on its banks. We had come across neither *gers* nor people all day and so were sure the area around our campsite was unpopulated. This was a mistake: the steppe is never empty. In the twilight, two armed horsemen suddenly appeared from nowhere, illuminated like wolves in the pale moonlight. An exchange of snuffboxes took place between the horsemen and our guide and after some discussion we learned that one of the men was the self-appointed guardian of the rock carvings of Tsagaan Salaa. Ningjie showed us the man's dubious credentials: a membership card of the Communist Party. A bottle of spirits later and the horses carried their alarmingly swaying riders back to their camp.

We set off for the rock carvings early the next morning as the sun was already high in the sky by 6 a.m. Tsagaan Salaa, which dates back to late Paleolithic times, is an enormous open-air art gallery that runs alongside the mountain rivers Tsagaan Salaa and Baga Oygur. There are over 10,000 carvings covering the rocks and all are, without exception, angled to the south, south-west or south-east: the sides of the mountain that face the setting sun.

When the glaciers melted in the last Ice Age, thick forests and swampy plains took over, inhabited by aurochs, elks and red deer. About 4,600 years ago a desiccation started which led to the extinction of the aurochs. At the same time, the camel spread. Throughout western Mongolia the forests shrank and with them the habitat of large forest animals. From the later Bronze Age, 3,000 years ago, there was a decline in the number of wild hoofed animals such as the yak and an increase in herds of tame cattle with only smaller red deer, bears and boars still being hunted. The carvings of Tsagaan Salaa are an extraordinary document of this evolution and also show the beginnings of Mongolia's nomadic way of life. Representations of laden oxen and herds of cattle on the move, led by herdsmen and guarded by dogs, show that the people of the time frequently changed their pastures, although carvings of huts and stables show that they also had fixed winter residences.

We explored Tsagaan Salaa for several days, finding hundreds of representations of mammoths, aurochs, giant elks and deer, birds of prey, horses, boars, camels, yaks and cattle, masks, hunting scenes, battles with bows and arrows or lances, as well as depictions of two- or four-wheeled vehicles, and even a man on skis.[5] The latter appeared to be pursuing a deer or an elk bearing a round disk between its antlers. Although we found only one skier, we found several deer with disks or balls on their heads. They reminded me of Egyptian representations of the god of fertility and the underworld named Apis, who was worshipped in the form of a bull with the disc of the sun between its horns.

A few weeks later, in Ulan Ude, the capital of the Buryat, we met an ethnologist who was able to interpret these remarkable scenes:

The Evenki people, who live in this region, have a myth according to which the giant elk Kheglen impaled the sun on his antlers and carried it away to the north, threatening humanity with eternal night and cold. To save them, the divine hero Ma'en pursued the elk and wrested the sun from him, bringing it back to men at dawn. The Evenki believe that this cosmic drama unfolds each night. The carved skier of Tsagaan Salaa certainly represents Ma'en chasing Khegel.

The carvings of Tsagaan Salaa mark the progress of life in the course of climatic changes from a hunting-gathering society to mobile pastoralism. The valley floor of Tsagaan Salaa is also covered with burial mounds, called *kurgans*, dating from the first millennium BC. These *kurgans* are more recent than the majority of the carvings, which suggests that the necropolis was intentionally built in the vicinity of the petroglyphs.

We also saw several depictions of empty or laden horse-drawn carts. In the flat grasslands of Mongolia, heavy wagons would have been used to transport goods and *gers* during the movements of the nomadic groups. Such carts, with thick wooden wheels without iron rims, are still in use today in central Mongolia.

Whilst many motifs were frequently repeated, we also came across rarer carvings, such as a dancing man with the head of a deer, the antlers clearly visible. For centuries, hunters have used a trick, still widespread today, of donning a fur and a cap crowned with horns or long ears to track their prey. Alternatively, the image could depict part of a ritual in which a hunter would show his respect for the spirit of the animal prior to setting off on the hunt. This latter interpretation is supported by an ancient hunting ritual of the southern Siberian Evenki in which, dressed in deerskins and wearing deer antlers on their heads, they dance at a holy place to put the spirit of the deer species in a favourable mood. Similarly, the image could also be that of a dancing shaman. The belief that shamans were able to turn themselves into animals shows that for the nomads of Mongolia the borderline between the world of men and that of the animals is fluid.

Two types of deer carving at Tsagaan Salaa were particularly striking. One from the Scythian period (c. ninth/eighth to third century BC), has highly stylised antlers tending towards the form of a bird's beak. In another, the antlers take on the form of a tree. In this context, the deer with the tree-like antlers also has a female symbolism, for the annually discarded and renewed antlers symbolise the cycle of life and death, the ability of humans and animals to reproduce, and the general fertility of nature. Other, more direct, pictures of female fertility are birth scenes, copulating cattle, or representations of pregnant does with their young clearly visible in their bellies.

A further spectacular motif is the 'Lord of Animals'. A man is standing between two ibexes rearing on their hind legs and arranged in a mirror-like pattern opposite one another. The man is touching their heads with his outstretched arms. A year before, we had discovered this image in the Gobi Desert in southern Mongolia, in the Sirven Mountains, where the Lord of Animals stands between two huge wild yaks. This motif celebrates the domination of the fauna by the shaman or by humans in general. In the world picture of the Mongolian peoples, humans, fauna and flora represent differing but equally valuable elements of a common world. Man is part of nature, not above it.

Great respect is accorded to animals by Mongolian nomads; they may be killed only for food or clothing. The purposeless killing or tormenting of animals is forbidden, as is the pointless felling of trees. A nomad living by the Baga Oygur River told us that breaking such taboos could lead to sickness or to the disappearance of the animal species. Then the souls of killed animals would refuse to reincarnate in the area concerned. The incensed animals' souls could also persuade other animals to abandon the region. This system of beliefs, which is still widespread among the nomads of Central Asia, is nothing other than an ecological philosophy of life.

The image of the 'Mistress of Animals', however, is not limited to Mongolia or Central Asia, but can be found in many parts of both Asia and Europe, the middle figure frequently being a winged woman. For example, we find it in ancient Iran and on a gold plaque from Ugarit in today's Syria. Here she is standing on a lion and holding two ibexes firmly in her hands, while two snakes appear behind her hips. The most famous representation is on a sixth-century BC bronze jug from Lower Italy. Here the Mistress of Animals is taming four lions, two hares, two snakes and an eagle. The animals symbolise the three spheres: the bird of prey the air, and the lion and hare the earth, while snakes represent the connection with the underworld. Thus the Mistress of Animals becomes the great goddess, the mistress of all life. This pan-Eurasian image springs from a common mythological heritage. It originated in Iran, and was taken over by Indo-European peoples when they came into intensive contact with the Middle East. As they migrated in several waves to the west and the east, they spread this archetypical idea there as well.

Surprisingly, the carvings of Tsagaan Salaa were not created by Mongols but Indo-Europeans, who had migrated from their Caucasian and eastern

Ukranian territories of origin. Early in the seconnd millennium BC, Mongols advanced westwards and mingled with the Indo-Europeans, creating the Karasuk culture. In around 1600 BC, a second wave of Indo-European immigrants followed, founding the culture of Andronovo in southern Siberia, which perfected the art of making bronze and spread the use of the cart and the war chariot, as well as equestrianism. In the second millennium BC Indo-European nomadic horsemen populated the Eurasian region from the Black Sea to western Mongolia.

It was not, however, these eastern Indo-Europeans that achieved the transition from loose associations of tribes to organised states, but the Xiongnu, predecessors of the notorious Huns. The Xiongnu society was based on a mixed economy of cattle raising and agriculture, from which the first hierarchically structured steppe state in eastern Eurasia emerged around the year 209 BC in present-day Mongolia. At the same time, Mongolian and Turkic peoples began their trek westwards, which was to last almost two millennia, coming to a standstill only in 1683 before the gates of Vienna.

On the evening of the final day of our stay in Tsagaan Salaa, a traditional Kazakh meal was served. Our local guide had had a sheep slaughtered by nomads, which they prepared in our camp. A stew of lamb, potatoes, turnips and freshly made noodles was served on the grass before our tents. As throughout Central Asia, the sheep's head, which is placed at the top of the pot, is considered a delicacy. The head was turned towards me as the oldest member of the group and a dozen pairs of eye turned expectantly in my direction. As guest of honour I had to begin the feast. I cut an ear off the sheep's head and took a small spoonful of brain. Now the others were allowed to help themselves. Fortunately, I was saved from another delicacy that is the prerogative of the guest of honour in Central Asia: the eyes. I was also lucky enough to have two children next to me, their gaze greedily fixed on the sheep's head. Within a quarter of an hour the skull was polished clean.

As I gazed at the starlit sky that evening, I wondered about the significance that the petoglyphs of Tsagaan Salaa had for the people of their time. In view of the work involved in carving and painting the stone, they could not have been just the whimsical self-expression of an artistically gifted few. Perhaps they served to commune with the forces of living nature and the ancestors of spirits and divinities. Maybe they were a record of the peoples' history, just as a history book is for us today.

Perhaps remembered dreams suggested to early man both the existence of independent dream worlds and of entities existing independently of the body. Dreams opened up the gate to the spiritual for mankind. It is therefore surely no accident that the earliest objects of art are cave paintings; being in a dark cave that barely provides any impressions for the senses comes closest to the state of dreaming while asleep.

Regardless of their symbolism and purpose, many petroglyphs in Central Asia radiate such elegance and expressiveness that they can be called true works of art. Even in the eternal darkness of the deep caves of Khoit Tsenkher in south-west Mongolia, there are 15,000-year-old paintings depicting mammoths, antelopes, snakes and birds that are still visible.

Leaving Tsagaan Salaa, we headed south, and after a few hours of travelling stopped by a lonely *ger* in the rocky steppe of Ulaan Hus. Suddenly a couple of cross-country vehicles roared up and the inhabitants of the *ger* ran out and as a greeting threw sweets on the vehicle and the emerging passengers. It transpired that the visitor thus honoured – a man in his mid-50s – had grown up here. He had been the Mongolian ambassador to Cairo for several years, and had run a private business in Dubai for the past two years and now he had come home on holiday to his old home, travelling via Iran, Turkmenistan, Uzbekistan, Kazakhstan and Russia. A week later, this eminent man was celebrated in the provincial capital of Bayan Ulgii with a public festival. An army parade, official speeches and triumphal music filled the main square of Ulgii, the people basking in the renown of this former nomad child.

We followed the valley carved out by the river Khovd, on the way to Lake Dayan Nor, close to the Chinese border. The narrow roadway was cluttered with a busy jam of lorries exporting scrap metal to China, which has an insatiable hunger for steel as a result of its economic boom. We were moving through what looked like a lunar landscape: dotted all around were mounds of earth and large piles of rocks. It was a Bronze Age cemetery. We stopped the car to explore and were taken aback by the way the ground was humming and moving. As we moved closer, we realised that the cemetery was covered with locusts – a plague was infesting the region. As we moved around we couldn't help crushing them under our feet.

From the burial mounds, known as *khereksur*, stone paths radiate out like the spokes of a wheel, 10 to 25 metres in length and oriented exactly to the points of the compass. The outside edge of the complex is marked by a circle of rocks. There are other burial sites, where the margin is in the form of a square. The archaeologist Ehdel-Khan from Bayan Ulgii believes that the stone circle symbolised the sun or the heavens, and the stone square represented the earth. This kind of symbolism, a circle for the sky and a square for the earth, is also widespread in China.

We reached Lake Dayan, and the purpose of our journey, two days later. On the banks of the river is an extraordinary stone figure that was discovered by the Russian explorer G.N. Potanin on his journey through Mongolia in 1876–77. Potanin was delighted by the figure, and wrote: 'As concerns the quality of the manufacture and the degree of preservation, the stone man of Dayan Batyr is the best of such stone figures that we saw in north-west Mongolia.'[6]

The figure is made of granite and faces east. It has a fine moustache and a chain around its neck from which hangs a stylised eagle, which may be the totem animal of the man's tribe. Other large stone figures found in Mongolia are depicted holding a drinking vessel in front of their bellies, with a dagger hanging at their belts. Beside the figure at Lake Dayan stands a slender, uncarved stele. On one side of it Chinese characters are chiselled, reminding us that the Chinese border is less than 10 kilometres away. Behind the two steles, a rectangular arrangement of rocks indicates the location of three graves.

Most stone figures of this kind, which Mongols call *balbal*, originated during the time of the Turkish empires (AD 552–745) and the rule of the Turkic Uigurs (AD 744–840). The *balbal* of Dayan Batyr probably dates from this time. Whilst the stone figures dating from the time of the Turkic people have Mongol facial features, and show a person down to the waist or the knees, in Mongolia there are considerably older and rarer stone figures up to 80 centimetres high, showing only a head with clearly European features.[7] The latter are reminiscent of the famed stone figures of Easter Island.

The figures represent the dead who are buried in the vicinity, and serve as sites of ancestor worship. As we were able to observe several times, Mongols and Tuvans still show respect to the stone people, who tend to have a blue *katha* tied round their necks; their hands, folded on their bellies, are blackened with rubbed-in fat. Not only do people ask the ancestors for their blessing, but shamans also carry out rituals in which they magically transfer the illnesses of the sick into the stone figures.

In Mongolia and southern Siberia, the stone figures almost always represent men, but among the Cumans, the confederation of whom extended from

1 The author's bodyguards (first and fourth from left) in Marib, Yemen, 1980

2 Ladakhi woman with a *perak* (headdress) decorated with turquoises

3 Rock with Nestorian crosses and inscriptions in Sogdian, Tocharian, Chinese, Arabic and Tibetan, Tanktse, Ladakh

4 The fortified church of Ainwardo, Tur Abdin, Turkey

5   Women near Susa, Iran

6   The citadel of Bam, Iran, destroyed by an earthquake in 2003

7  Nestorian cemetery at Göktepe, Iran

8  Woman picking cotton, Uzbekistan

**9** Dromedaries grazing near the ruins of the palace library Kitab Khana in Merv, Turkmenistan

**10** Mosque in the former subterranean Sufi monastery of Shakpak Ata, Mangyshlak, Kazakhstan

11   The cross-shaped ruin of Khukh Burd Süme, twelfth–seventeenth century AD, central Mongolia

12   The three *madrasa*s on Registan Square, Samarkand, Uzbekistan

**13**  A Mongolian horseman captures a young horse

**14**  The motorbike competes with the horse among Mongolian nomads

15 The omnipresent Genghis Khan on a Mongolian banknote

16 Damba Bazargur and the author on the search for Genghis Khan's tomb, Öglöchiin Kherem, eastern Mongolia

17    Iktamer the eagle hunter at the foot of Mount Khairkhan, western Mongolia

18    Stone figure in front of a Turkic grave, sixth–ninth century AD, central Mongolia

**19** Bronze Age petroglyphs at Tsagaan Salaa, Mongolia

**20** Stone balbal, sixth–ninth century AD, near Kyzyl-Mushallik, Tuva, Russia

**21** Deer stone with a woman's face, eleventh–tenth century BC, Ushkin Uver, central Mongolia

**22** Stags with birds' beaks on a deer stone, Ushkin Uver, central Mongolia

23  Female shaman, Seren Ojun, summons spirits, Tuva, Russia

24  Young Tibetan nomads

25   Herd of yaks crossing a river, central Tibet

26   Riders in the desert north-west of Mount Kailash, Tibet

28    Buddhist shrines, palace ruins and the citadel of Tsaparang, western Tibet

27    The western flank of Mount Kailash and the monastery
of Chuku Gonpa, western Tibet (facing page)

**29** Tathagata Ratnasambhava in the Marpa chapel of Sekhar Guthog monastery, Lhodrak, southern Tibet

**30** The monastery of Taranatha at Phuntsoling, destroyed during the Cultural Revolution, central Tibet

Kazakhstan to the Ukraine in the eleventh to twelfth centuries AD, there are numerous female stone figures. These *balbal* also caught the attention of European travellers of the thirteenth century, such as the famous missionary and explorer William of Rubruk: 'The Cumans raise a large mound over the deceased and erect a statue to him facing east and holding a bowl in its hands in front of the navel.'[8] When Rubruk was travelling through Mongolia, the steppe would have been populated by a far greater number of figures than the 370 known today, for Buddhist missionaries in the sixteenth century beheaded them or knocked them down. They now lie in the grass like fallen warriors on the field of battle, instead of gazing towards the rising sun.

A few days after leaving Lake Dayan, we set up camp near the small town of Mörön, in the province of Hövsgöl, at the foot of the Ushkin Uver Mountains. Nearby was an impressive arrangement of 14 deer stones. Mongolia is not only the land of petroglyphs and *balbals*, but also of 'deer stones'. These are sandstone, marble or granite steles up to four metres in height that stood from the middle Bronze Age (c. 1300 BC) near groups of graves or cemeteries, and also in some cases at magic sites such as the confluence of two rivers or the foot of a holy mountain. They owe their name to the unique engravings characterised by deer motifs. They show deer or reindeer stylised in a very lively manner, and in rare cases horses or antelopes. The deer have slender bodies, excessively long necks, and unusually large and richly branching antlers lying along the total length of their backs. Often the deer's muzzle is replaced by a bird's beak, which emphasises the dynamics of the upward orientation of the deer. In the upper part of the stele, the sun and sometimes also the moon is engraved, and in the lower part bows and arrows, battle-axes, curved daggers and knives.

This large necropolis of Ushkin Uver, with several huge *khereksurs*, smaller stone graves and also stone altars, extends over about 25 square kilometres in total, and contains over 200 stone structures above ground. All of the deer stones are at the eastern side of the site, and face east towards the rising sun. Engraved on all four sides, the deer stones can be dated back to the eleventh to tenth century BC.

The southernmost, 2.6-metre-high deer stone is unique: at its upper end a three-dimensional human head is engraved, with ears and earrings clearly recognisable. In the central and lower parts at least 26 deer, an axe, a curved dagger and a pentagonic shield are engraved. Only six such deer stones exist in

Mongolia and the one at Ushkin Uver is arguably the most beautiful. Stones like this one, featuring human-like qualities, suggest that they represent human beings, presumably tribal leaders and glorified warriors. The deer stones are distant precursors of the Turkic period stone figures. The anthropomorphic stele of Ushkin Uver has fine, feminine features, with no moustache or beard and so could have been erected in honour of a female ruler or a female divinity.

This stele of Ushkin Uver, with its mysterious face gazing into infinity, lent a surreal, Dali-esque, character to the landscape. Above it, in the blue sky, intricate cloud formations appeared, then dissolved again into nothing, creating fantastic images of fire-spitting dragons, marine monsters or giant locusts. Every now and then the idyll was interrupted as aeroplanes dimly droned far overhead, leaving nothing but a fading rumbling and a pale vapour trail.

Therese made a rubbing of the stele, placing a thin sheet of Japanese paper around it. As she was wrapping the 'body' in paper, leaving the head free, a herdswoman passed by with her daughter, and gazed at the suddenly mummified stele in astonishment. She watched with great interest as one deer after another appeared on the paper, conjured up by Therese's chalk. Two hours later, she confessed: 'To me, there was just a stone standing here before; now it is an image, and the place has come to life.'

The deer stones served in the past to mark sites near graves, where the ancestor cult was celebrated, and where people made sacrifices to venerated leaders of their tribes. They sacrificed milk and animals and perhaps also human beings – around several deer stones horse skulls were excavated with their snouts oriented towards the east.

The representation of deer and reindeers flying towards the symbolic sun is mysterious. It is possible that the deer stones not only evoke the presence of a deceased person, but also signify a three-levelled cosmos. Below, in the earthly world, human attributes figure, such as weapons, tools or mirrors, and at the top, the sun and moon mark the heavenly sphere. Between these are the deer, which are breaking free from the earth and striving for the sun. On a few steles I noticed many smaller deer below the belt, reaching down to the ground. They perhaps suggest a connection to the underworld.

On other journeys I found indications that antlered animals and mountain goats were regarded as companions of the dead on the journey into the Beyond. Among them are archaeological finds, nearly 2,500 years old, from the Scythian graves of Pazyryk and Tuekta in the Russian Altai, and Berel in the Kazakh Altai. Here, in the eternal ice, sacrificed horses were discovered wearing deer masks and antlers, as well as masks of ibexes with huge horns made of felt, leather or wood. Other horses were buried with wooden deer heads that had leather antlers. In other graves of the same period, small wooden figures depicting horned horses were found. It is clear that the horse, symbolically transformed into a deer, or occasionally into an ibex, served the dead as a mount on which to ride to the Beyond.

After long searches I also found this ancient symbolism among the petroglyphs of Tamgaly in Kazakhstan and Saimaly-Tash in Kyrgyzstan, dating from the second half of the second millennium BC. At Saimaly, pairs of such hybrid beings between horse and deer are pulling a single-axle wagon guided by a human. At Tamgaly there are dozens of representations of large horses with great forward-pointing horns, most with a small rider. Based on these finds, it is likely that the deer striving for the sun and moon on the deer stones symbolise the successful transition of the dead to the Beyond.

That night, just before full moon, I gazed at the tall stele with the female face rising above the other, darker deer stones. The tallest of all of them, it resembled the female leader of an army of deer stones. I would not have been surprised if the deer stones had begun to move off in response to her command. At first sight, it was surprising to find this prominent female stele at the centre of the warlike world of the Mongols, but we must not forget that the highest divinity of the Scythians and of their Indo-European forefathers, who also settled in western Mongolia, was female. Herodotus reported that the three chief gods of the Scythians were Tabiti, the goddess of the hearth, Papaios, the god of heaven, and Api, the goddess of the earth and of fertility.[9] Tabiti's status as leader can also be seen on the felt carpet from the Scythian grave V of Pazyryk, dating from the fifth century BC: the crowned goddess is seated on a throne, holding in her right hand the tree of life; a horseman is approaching her respectfully. She appears to be the mistress of life itself.

# A Shaman from Tuva

When Buddhism began to spread in Mongolia from 1578, it integrated numerous local spirits and deities into its own pantheon by assigning them the function of protective deities. At the same time, it forbade rituals such as animal sacrifice, which directly contradicted its principles, and persecuted shamans as sorcerers. But shamanism in Mongolia did manage to survive. Many shamans became Buddhists and continued, as travelling monks who were not tied to monasteries, to carry out traditional rituals under the cloak of the doctrines of Buddha. In the twentieth century, however, Stalin plunged both Buddhism and shamanism into an existential crisis. In 1930, the extermination both of shamans and of monks and nuns began in Tuva and Buryatia and was extended to Mongolia in 1935–36. Only with the collapse of the Soviet Union did freedom of religion return.

For most Mongols today, Buddhism complements shamanism, which is not so much a religion as a system of rituals to promote the wellbeing of people. Put simply, shamanism relates to life this side of the grave, and Buddhism to death and the life beyond. Shamans are neither lamas nor priests but mediators between the world of humans and that of the spirits.

Among the most important tasks of the shamans is the healing of the sick. According to shamanic belief, a person becomes ill when the shadow soul has left him and become lost, or has been attacked by a hostile spirit. The shaman heals by having his own soul seek out the lost soul of the patient and bringing it back to him. Or an evil spirit may have occupied the body of the sick person, and has to be driven out by the shaman. Other responsibilities are the averting of misfortune, the blessing of animals and pastures, predictions, the restoring of a disturbed cosmic order and accompanying the soul of a dead person to the Beyond. This last function is also very important for the living, because the shaman ensures that the soul of the dead stays in the Beyond and does not return as a dangerous ghost to the world of men.

In the shamanist world perception of the Mongols and Tuvans, the god of heaven and creation, Tengri, does not concern himself with the everyday lives of living creatures. This is the sphere of the countless nature deities and local spirits. Here, an important part is played not only by female deities such as the mother of the hearth and fire, but also by female auxiliary spirits. In contrast to Buddhism or the monotheistic religions, in which women play at best a subordinate role among the clergy, female shamans enjoy the same degree of respect as male ones.

At the end of August, we met such a female shaman in Kyzyl, the capital of Tuva. The Institute of Tuvinian Shamans is picturesquely situated at the confluence of the rivers B'eg-Xem and Kaa-Xem, which join to form the mighty river Yenisei, which flows northwards to the Arctic Ocean. The site of this confluence is considered to be the centre of Asia, as it is supposedly situated equidistantly from each of the world's oceans. The spot is marked by an obelisk on a triangular base, which rests on a globe. The female shaman, Seren Ojun, was a young woman of about 35. She received us in her office and asked whether we were sick. Seren would begin all her consultations by diagnosing people's illnesses. After diagnosis, she would decide whether or not she could help, or would send the patient to a doctor with Western training. We replied that we would like to take part in a shamanic ritual and she readily agreed to perform one designed to prevent illness.

Before starting the preparations for the ritual, she told us some details of her life. Her forebears had been shamans for generations and belonged to a group of shamans of earth and water spirits. When she was 17, Seren fell seriously ill and was delirious with fever. In a trance she experienced her body being divided into pieces by spirits, who mixed them up and re-composed them. She was then reborn as a shaman. Her training was frightening to begin with: spirits that were summoned appeared like huge hailstones and flew towards her, circling inches from her face. Only after some time did she learn to control them.

In the late afternoon, we called for Seren and drove to a spring outside the town. She was accompanied by a second, older shaman named Darja Kendenova, and her assistant, Sajana Dargan. The three women, clothed in traditional Tuvan silk robes, were heavily laden, not only with ceremonial clothing and headdresses, but also with biscuits, cigarettes, vodka, milk, butter, pine wood and the head of a deer, which had had a fair part of the meat removed and was thickly spread with melted butter.

Seren donned robes of reindeer hide, from which hung bundles of coloured fringes and strings of beads, two tiny bows with arrows affixed to them and some other amulets. Then she put a headband around her forehead, closely set with eagle's feathers. From the wreath of feathers hung little metal bells that served to call up her attendant spirits. The function of the shamanic regalia as a whole was to protect her against attack by hostile spirits or demons. The sight of the shamanic robe and the wreath of eagle feathers reminded me of the stone carvings of deer and reindeer with birds' beaks. Both the deer, stretching towards the sun, and the shamans are supposed to contribute to the smooth transition of the souls of the dead into the world beyond.

Darja was wearing a dress of violet silk, at the back of which hung broad strips of deer hide and coloured fringes. She wore a headband with feathers from a falcon, and from her neck dangled a large mirror made of shining tin. In this mirror resided an auxiliary spirit; the mirror also indicated that Darja belonged to the group of shamans of the heavens. In this way, the two women between them covered the two spheres of existence normally inaccessible to humans, the higher world and the underworld.

The ceremony could now begin. Sajana began beating time on a brass sounding-bowl. To gain the benevolence of the local tutelary spirits, the two shamans cast milk, vodka and millet grains over a neighbouring *obo*. Then Seren piled pieces of pine wood artistically around the deer's head to form a square and an adjacent triangle. With a burning juniper twig, she ignited first the fire and then a cigarette, gazing absently into the slowly smouldering fire, as if her contact to our world was loosening.

All of a sudden she shot up, and took hold of the flat drum covered with reindeer skin that was lying ready, and the wooden drumstick covered with bearskin. With these attributes, the most powerful animals in the world of Mongolian shamans are represented: eagle and falcon, reindeer, deer and bear. These animal spirits, whose language the shaman had learnt during her training and initiation, support her during the ritual. Once more I realised how strongly the Mongols, Burjats and Tuvans are connected with animals.

By now the two shamans were beating their drums ceaselessly. Seren danced in a circle at various speeds, summoning her chief spirit and other auxiliary spirits with song. She conjured them to keep evil spirits from us, and to take care of our health. The flat drum is the shamans' most important tool, for its sound not only helps them to go into a trance and to call their spirits, but also serves as a symbolic mount for the ascent of the soul to the upper world. After an hour or so of this, Seren sank exhausted to the ground, then knelt before the *obo* and touched the floor with her wreath of eagle feathers. She had dismissed the spirits and returned in mind and spirit to the dimensions of ordinary life. The ceremony had ended.

On the way back to Kyzyl, Seren, still in a state of exhaustion, aptly summed up the goal of shamanism: 'We shamans attempt, with the aid of spirits that are favourably inclined towards us, to promote the health of and harmony between men, peoples, animals and nature in general.'

# Genghis Khan's Capital

Karakorum was the centre of the largest empire of all times, yet its capital has vanished. On our travel to this mysterious site, Therese and I stopped in the small city of Tsetserleg after quarantine had been lifted after an outbreak of plague. Before the communist seizure of power in 1921, one of the largest Buddhist monasteries in Mongolia, Zayain Khuree, had stood here. The main temple was converted by the new rulers into a department store, and most of the minor temples and meeting halls had been pulled down. A museum was opened in a small remaining part of the complex in 1960.

In the inner court of the museum, a surprise awaited us. On top of a stone tortoise stood a two-metre-high stone pillar bearing inscriptions. Such steles were used in China from pre-Christian times onwards for the proclamation of important laws and decrees. On the upper part of the stele, instead of the representation of dragons common in China, I saw a female wolf stooping over a baby. But the legend of a wolf suckling a human child was related to the foundation of Rome! My surprise grew when I found texts on the stele in Sogdian and Brahmi, that is, in Iranian and Indian script. The stele, dating from AD 571, was further proof of the international links of early medieval Mongolia. The upper part of the stele illustrates the primeval myth of the Turkic tribes at a time when they still inhabited Mongolia. According to this myth, a female wolf brought up an orphan child in a cave, and subsequently conceived by him the 10 forefathers of the 10 Turkic tribes.

An old monk from the nearby monastery of Buyan Delgeruulech showed us around the museum. In dusty rooms he showed us ceremonial clothing of nomads, old furniture from a yurt, and musical instruments. We then entered the roughly reconstructed assembly room of a Buddhist monastery. On the walls hung yellowed photographs, newspaper cuttings and paintings illustrating the history of the revolution. In one picture, General Sukh Baatar was shown with a blood-covered sabre, in the act of slaying a monk on the ground whose picture-scroll, depicting a Buddhist tutelary deity, lay in the mud. In another picture, tanks and soldiers with fixed bayonets are advancing on the monks of a monastery.

In a tremulous voice, the monk said: 'This happened 1936 in Tsetserleg. I was still a junior novice when the rumour circulated that the monastery was about to be attacked. We hid the most valuable books and the holiest figures by night in caves in the mountains. When the red bandits appeared they soon noticed that many statues were missing. So they shot several monks on the pretence that they had stolen property belonging to the people.'

Others were cruelly tortured to wrest from them information about the hiding-places. But all of them remained steadfast and died in immense pain. The monk we were speaking to managed to escape because his family had smuggled a soldier's uniform into his cell a few days before the attack on the monastery. More than 40,000 monks were less fortunate: they were shot as alleged spies for Japan, agitators or counter-revolutionaries.

It is impossible today to imagine that Karakorum was once the capital of an empire. Sheep and camels graze on the site of the city, the only remains of which are three monumental granite tortoises that served as bases for stone steles bearing texts. The tortoise symbolises stability and durability. Only such a strong and long-lived animal was suited for bearing imperial inscriptions designed for eternity. The symbol has remained, but the city has completely disappeared, ravaged by time and looting. For many years, even the precise location of Karakorum was disputed, because many explorers equated it with the Uigur city of Ordu-Baliq, which was several centuries older. Its ruins were finally discovered in 1889 during the last expedition of Nikolai Przhevalsky, but only after his death. The last doubts about the identity of the sparse field of rubble near the Buddhist monastery of Erdene Zuu as the city of Karakorum, however, were not dispelled until 1949 by the Soviet archaeologist Sergei Kiselev.

A Chinese-Mongolian stone inscription dating from 1346 tells how Genghis Khan chose the place in 1220 as his imperial residence. This choice was symbolic, representing a demonstration of the legitimacy of his rule, for Karakorum was situated not only close to the former capital of the Uigurs, Ordu-Baliq and the still older Turkic capital, Höschö Tsaidan, but also in the heartland of the Nestorian Kerait, whose last khan, Toghril, was Genghis Khan's patron. As the inscription has it: 'He founded a city, thus creating the precondition for a state.'[10]

However, it was Genghis Khan's son and successor Ögödei, who ruled from 1229 to 1241, who developed the former *ger* settlement into a real city with solid buildings from 1235 onwards. He had a palace, a Buddhist temple and protective walls built, and reorganised the imperial administration. Genghis Khan had founded the Mongolian nation; Ögödei founded the Mongolian state. In doing so, he followed the advice of his chancellor Yelü Chukai: 'You can conquer an empire on horseback, but cannot administer it from there.'[11] Almost 600 years later, Talleyrand said to Napoleon: 'One can do everything with bayonets except sit on them.' However, Karakorum was to remain the imperial capital for only 40 years, after which Genghis Khan's grandson Kublai Khan, who ruled from 1260 to 1294, moved it to Khan-Baliq, today's Beijing. In 1388 a Chinese army destroyed Karakorum and the builders of Erdene Zuu took care of the rest, using the rubble to build their monastery. Thus vanished a city from which a chapter of world history had been written.

The most precise description of Karakorum was left by William of Rubruk, who stayed there for two months in the spring of 1254. Although he travelled as a simple Franciscan friar, he was in fact a spy in the service of King Louis IX of France, tasked with collecting information about the numbers and strength of the Mongols and their intentions towards Europe. As regards the latter, he received a menacing piece of information from Great Khan Möngke (ruled 1251–59), who wrote to Louis: 'As soon as you Christian rulers are willing to obey us, send envoys to tell us so. Then we will be sure whether you wish war or peace with us.'[12]

Rubruk, who observed the people and customs of Mongolia with a keen eye and was admitted to several audiences with Möngke, was not particularly impressed by Karakorum:

> As far as the city of Karakorum is concerned, know that, apart from the Khan's palace, it is not even as impressive as the market town of St Denis [now a suburb of Paris]. And the monastery of St Denis is ten times as important as this palace. The city has two quarters: that of the Saracens [Muslims], where the markets are held and many merchants meet. Then there is the Chinese quarter, most of whose inhabitants are artisans. Outside both are the large houses belonging to secretaries at court. For the various groups of inhabitants, there are 12

[Buddhist] temples for the worship of idols, two mosques, and at the extreme end of the city, a Christian church.[13]

He compared Möngke's palace to a church with five naves. Here he saw the magic fountain recently created by the French goldsmith Boucher, in the form of a silver tree:

> Maître Guillaume from Paris erected a large tree of silver, at whose roots lie four silver lions. Inside them is a pipe through which white mares' milk flows. Inside the tree itself, four pipes run up, the upper ends of which are bent downwards again. There is a golden snake curled around the end of each pipe, with its tail wrapped around the trunk of the tree. From one of these pipes flows wine, from another fermented mares' milk, from the third a drink made from honey, and from the last, rice beer. At the top of the tree the artist has placed a statue of an angel holding a trumpet. Whenever the head cup-bearer has to have a drink served, he calls upon the angel; this call is heard by a man concealed in a [subterranean] cavity, who then blows hard into the pipe leading to the angel. The angel then puts the trumpet to its mouth, and it sounds very loudly. When the servants in the pantry hear this, each pours his drink into the pipe destined for it.[14]

No doubt the guests in the palace were duly impressed by a silver angel that could conjure up four kinds of drink out of the earth.

The site of the ruins, a few hundred yards north of the monastery of Erdene Zuu, was a hive of activity when we visited, for archaeologists of the German–Mongolian Karakorum Expedition had been exploring them since 1999. In some places, digging had only been going on for the past few months. A young German archaeologist informed us that digging was taking place above all in two locations: the site of the artisans' quarter, at the junction of the two main streets, and the site of Ögödei's palace in the south-west of the city. On the site at the city centre, the first traces of stones forming the roadway were being unearthed, and at the presumed palace site wall foundations and the square bases of pillars. Since the Nestorian church was located at the northern edge of the city and the archaeologists were working in the centre and the south-west, it had not yet been found. Meanwhile, the archaeologists had discovered four kilns which were the first kilns dating from the thirteenth–fourteenth centuries found in Mongolia. They had been used to manufacture terracotta Buddhist figures, as well as roof tiles and tiles for walls and floors.

The excavations brought a surprising result to light. The archaeologists discovered a large hall of a square ground plan with seven naves having 8 x 8 pillar bases, a total of 64; this tallied more or less with Rubruk's description. However, countless Buddhist finds, such as three-dimensional figures of the Buddha, fragments of eight Bodhisattva figures up to five metres in height, Buddhist murals, and over 100,000 small Buddhist votive figures suggested the conclusion that the excavated hall was not a palace but a Buddhist temple of the thirteenth–fourteenth century. This hypothesis was strengthened by the Sino-Mongolian inscription of 1346, which describes a seven-nave Buddhist temple with a square ground plan. The question remained, where was the palace of Ögödei that Rubruk described? There are two possibilities here: either the excavated hall originally served as a palace and was converted into a Buddhist shrine, or the palace must be sought elsewhere, perhaps beneath the present-day monastery of Erdene Zuu. A preliminary indication of this was provided by a trial excavation on the east side of the monastery, which brought to light a layer of a wall from the Karakorum period.

This monastery was the object of our next visit. It was certainly no accident that Abadai Khan, who ruled from 1554 to 1588 over the mighty federation of the Khalkha Mongols and was a supporter of Buddhism, had the first Buddhist monastery in Mongolia built in 1586. The monastery of Erdene Zuu, named after Buddha (the name means 'precious lord'), symbolised the legitimacy of the Khalkha's claim to leadership. Their power was said to be founded in the teachings of Buddha and the heritage of Genghis Khan. These are the two principles that have defined the national identity of the Mongols for the last four centuries – with the exception of the communist intermezzo.

The monastery complex is surrounded by a square wall and is crowned with 108 white stupas, in some of which the bones of venerated monks are immured. These were first mummified and coated with clay, then whitewashed and finally covered with gold paint. Erdene Zuu was badly ravaged by the Stalinist purges: of the 62 temples and shrines, only a handful remained. Yet, despite this destruction, the fascination of the monastery persists, not least because of its architecture. In its western part is a temple complex purely Chinese in style, consisting of three well-preserved shrines; in the northern part, a purely Tibetan temple, the Dalai Lama Temple; and between them, a gleaming white stupa. The Dalai Lama Temple is watched over by two stone lions, which without doubt originated in the city of Ögödei. The three temples built in the Chinese style contain not only remarkably well-preserved and valuable picture-scrolls and bronze figures, but also life-size Buddhist sculptures made of papier-mâché. The basic construction of the figures – their skeletons, as it were – consists of wood and reeds, over which a mixture of dissolved paper, clay and plaster was moulded and, after drying, was painted over with coloured and gold paint.

Only the Tibetan temple is in active use today. Inside, Buddhist monks recite sutras for hours and every now and again novices hurry up with large jugs and fill the monks' drinking bowls with butter tea. At the same time, pilgrims show their reverence for the statues inside the temple by depositing small banknotes before them. Prosperous believers donate larger amounts, for the monks to address a prayer to a compassionate Bodhisattva as an intercession. In one corner, a monk was selling printed sheets to serve as amulets against ill fortune and sickness. They reminded me not only of the paper amulet, over a thousand years old, that I had found in the Taklamakan Desert at Dandan Oilik,[15] but also of the printed slips of paper that Buddhist itinerant physicians sold to their patients. On such slips one could read, for instance, 'Eat in case of stomach-ache' or 'Swallow in case of flu'. These 'physicians' suggested to the sick that swallowing the amulets would miraculously cure them.

Close to Erdene Zuu stands a figure that is quite surprising to find near a Buddhist monastery prescribing celibacy for its monks: a stone phallus over two metres in length. It points in the direction of a hill that is said to have the shape of a recumbent woman with her legs apart. According to legend, a monk was castrated at this spot for having broken his oath of chastity and so the stone phallus serves as a warning to other lustful monks. Today, it is mostly women who visit the monument in order to pray to be blessed with children.

Karakorum's predecessor, Ordu-Baliq, was also built near the river Orkhon, which was thought holy by the Mongols from the earliest times. This city was the capital of the Turco-Mongolian people of the Uigurs, whose empire lasted from AD 744 to 840, when it was set on fire by rebellious Kyrgyz.

The inner city is surrounded by a clay wall, where watchtowers would have once stood at each corner. In the south-west corner is a large rectangular bastion, and on the north side rises another bastion that used to frame the main gate. The east side is reinforced with two additional fortified towers. To the north is a building made of air-dried bricks, which served the ruler as a palace. The Arab historian Tamim ibn Bahr, who visited Ordu-Baliq in

821 and was impressed by its wealth and its pulsating life, mentioned that the palace was crowned by a golden yurt, visible from several kilometres' distance, and which could accommodate over 100 guests.[16] Within the city walls resided the family of the ruler, the imperial administration and the higher Manichaean clergy; the merchants, soldiers and the remaining inhabitants lived outside the walls in the outer city. The great size of Ordu-Baliq is indicated by broken steles bearing inscriptions, two stone lions, and the ruins of a Manichaean temple outside the city walls. An inscription discovered in the inner city, dating from the early ninth century in three languages – Uigur-Turkish, Chinese and Sogdian –underlined the international character of Mongolia at that time. In those days, there was here a Babel of languages, people speaking Uigur-Turkish, Chinese, Tibetan, Sogdian, Arabic and Persian. Contrary to our prejudices, the Turco-Mongolian peoples of the first millennium were not 'barbaric' nomads, but constructed cities and fortresses, of which dozens of ruins are extant.

About the year AD 762, a curious thing occurred in Ordu-Baliq. The Uigurs, who were one of the most warlike nations in history, made the most pacific world religion of their time, Manichaeism, their state religion. Metaphorically speaking, this was the marriage of fire and water, or of a tiger and a lamb. Manichaeism was founded by the Iranian Mani (AD 216–76), who proceeded from the Zoroastrian dualism of light and darkness, good and evil. To Mani, this dualism develops, as cosmic history, in three ages. Originally, the two opposing principles were separated, whereupon darkness attacked the light and fused with it. From this arose the world and the human being, everything material, including the human body, being the bad work of the powers of evil. The soul alone has a share in the light. In a third, future step, light and darkness will become distinct again and be separated for all time. Mani considered himself the successor of Zoroaster, Buddha and Jesus.

This view gave rise to an ascetic, indeed life-hostile anthropology. Since the cosmic process of salvation aims at liberating the particles of light imprisoned in the evil material, individual salvation presupposes the rejection of the corporeal. The consequence of this was a draconian code of morals, according to which not only marriage and reproduction were forbidden, together with the consumption of meat, vegetables and wine, but physical labour and medical treatment were also banned. Since persons striving to achieve perfection in this way were not viable, and the vast majority of people were unable to meet these excessive demands, Mani divided the faithful into two categories, the 'elect' and the 'hearers'. The elect obey all the commandments and are able to save their souls; the hearers, by contrast, have to serve, clothe and feed the elect. As a reward, they will be reborn as elect in a future life.

Despite continual persecution, Manichaeism had spread rapidly in the Mediterranean region, but gave way to Christianity in the fifth and sixth centuries, spreading eastwards instead, so that by the late seventh century it had reached China. However, in 731 the Tang emperor Xuanzong condemned Mani's doctrine as a misleading and deceptive belief falsely claiming to belong to Buddhism. The tide turned in 755 with the rebellion of General An Lushan, when in desperation the Emperor of China requested military aid from the Khan of the Uigurs, Muyu. The Uigur allies not only put down the revolt in a great bloodbath, but also mercilessly plundered Chinese cities, and blackmailed the emperor into handing over vast treasures. The Middle Kingdom had to all intents and purposes become a vassal state of the Mongolian Uigurs.

On this Chinese campaign, Khan Muyu encountered Manichaean missionaries, following which – although a warlord who was the equal of Genghis Khan as to cruelty – he elevated the peace-loving religion of Manichaeism to his state religion. We can only guess as to his motives in doing this. It might be assumed that he wished his multinational state to have a religion of its own that had nothing in common with Chinese Buddhism. Or else the ascetic spirit of Manichaeism appealed to his soldierly nature. Good soldiers are not attached to life and do not fear death. But just as water can wear down the hardest stone, Manichaeism and China's enormous tribute payments led to a softening of the Uigur society, leading in 840 to a devastating defeat in battle against the Kyrgyz. Thus the spirit of Manichaeism and Chinese luxury goods together formed the Trojan horse that put an end to the Uigur Empire.

That evening, we invited a folklore group to our *ger*, whose members were students at the academy of music in Ulaan Baatar. Their instruments were the traditional deer-head fiddles, instruments resembling the balalaika, and a kind of harp. Particularly impressive were the 13-year-old 'snake girl', who performed the most incredible acrobatic feats, and the overtone singer. He stood alone in the middle of the *ger* and treated us to a duet sung by one voice alone. One tune comes from a deeper, 'normal' voice, while the other is a great deal higher, floating through space with crystal clarity, as though coming from another world. This eerie-sounding double tune suits the magic of the infinite Mongolian steppe perfectly.

The horse-head fiddle player was also a master of his art. The melancholy music produced by this two-stringed viola da gamba describes the sad legend of its origin. Once, a beautiful elf fell in love with a married man, and presented him with a magic horse that brought him to her every night. She told her lover to rub the horse dry each time on his return home, so that no one would suspect the effort of the long ride. For three intoxicating years, the man spent his days with his family and his nights with his beloved. One night, however, he forgot the precautionary measure and his wife noticed that the horse was drenched in perspiration. Her suspicions aroused, she killed the animal. Now the man was unable to reach his beloved. To relieve his sadness, he carved a fiddle from the head of a horse, and played and sang of his lost love in melancholic tunes.

# PART III

# Discovering the Treasures of Tibet

# L and of Snows

Tibet has captivated me ever since my childhood. My love affair with the land of eternal snows began with *Tintin in Tibet*, in which the pictures of towering snowy mountains, Buddhist monasteries, monks and the yeti held me spellbound. When I was young, Tibet was relatively familiar to the Swiss. The failed Tibetan revolt of spring 1959 and the ensuing flight of the Dalai Lama frequently filled the evening news on the radio, and I listened to it attentively, even though I understood little of its complexities. In 1961 the Swiss government had decided to grant asylum to a thousand of the approximately 100,000 Tibetans fleeing their country. Two or three years after this, my parents invited a few Tibetans to our home, and I showed them my Tintin book. I can still remember the pleasure on the faces of our guests when they found written Tibetan, Nepalese and Chinese characters in the book. After a brief examination, they confirmed that all three types of script had been correctly reproduced and contained a meaning appropriate to the drawings. Their visit fuelled my dreams of exploring Tibet one day.

I was first able to breathe the heady air of Tibet in the summer of 1988. As a consequence of violent riots in Lhasa the preceding autumn, individual travellers were not allowed into the country, so I had joined a group of tourists and crossed the Nepal–Chinese border with them. Fifty kilometres beyond the Chinese border post of Zhangmu I was met by a Chinese jeep that I had organised from Kathmandu. I was free to move around the country by myself for about three weeks, until meeting up with the group again. I did not have a personal visa, only a bad photocopy of the group visa so in the event of police checks, my girlfriend at the time had to feign serious illness, which explained our separation from the group.

My first impression of Tibet was contradictory. I was enchanted by the landscape and by the nomads moving across the plains with their herds of yaks. I was equally impressed by the honesty of the people and by the few Buddhist monasteries that had escaped the destruction of the Chinese invasion with their fantastic murals and picture scrolls intact. But the sight of the majority of Tibet's monasteries in ruins was depressing. Nor could I communicate with the Tibetan people: my guide was Chinese and either did not know Tibetan or was unwilling to speak it. The driver, also Chinese, was of the 'old school'; he kept strictly to his prescribed eight-hour working day, and took a two-hour midday break every day, so our progress and scope for travel was slow.

Parts of the journey from Zhangmu, close to Tibet's border with Nepal, to Lhasa were eerie; everywhere the crumbling ruins of destroyed monasteries and fortresses pointed heavenwards accusingly. There seemed to have been recent attacks from the air, bringing to my mind images of cities that were destroyed in the Second World War, like Coventry or Dresden. Even in and around Lhasa, the devastation inflicted between 1959 and 1976 was still evident. In the summer palace of Norbulinka I entered a room that was out of bounds and found myself faced with a huge pile of smashed bronze and brass Buddhist figures. The arms, legs, heads and torsos of the statues lay scattered around and I felt as though I were standing beside an opened mass grave looking at a pile of corpses.

Still more shocking was the sight of the monastery of Ganden, 45 kilometres east of Lhasa, founded by Tibet's great reformer Tsongkhapa (1357–1419) in 1409. Until 1959 about 3,000 monks had led a peaceful life in over 100 temples, shrines and houses, now I could see only ruins. Since Ganden is particularly holy to Tibetans, the Chinese wreaked particular havoc here during the Cultural Revolution from 1966 to 1976, cruelly and systematically destroying this significant monument of Tibet's ancient cultural heritage. Following the murder or internment of most of the monks, they used artillery and vast quantities of dynamite to raze the buildings to the ground. However, amidst the rubble of destruction, hope glimmered: the reconstruction of the 6,000 monasteries obliterated during Mao's Cultural Revolution had begun. Tibetan Buddhism triumphed over the communist idea of a uniform socialist human being.

Some years later, the gates of Tibet opened to me again. This time, my goal was located in the west, where I intended to circumambulate the holiest mountain in Asia, Mount Kailash. Individual journeys to this region, near the borders of Nepal and India, were prohibited so I joined a seven-strong Dutch group. The 2,000-kilometre journey from the Nepalese border to the beginning of the pilgrims' trail near Darchen, in a lorry roughly converted into a bus, took 12 long and bitterly cold days. It was the beginning of November, and the seating area, separated from the driver's cabin, was unheated. On the return journey to Lhasa the cold, which in December was becoming unbearable, coupled with the lack of exercise, was to give two of my companions frostbite, with the resulting loss of several toes. It was so cold that the oil sump of the truck had to be heated with a gas burner for several minutes each morning before setting off.

The journey took us from Zhangmu northwards over the 5,100-metre Lalung La ('la' meaning 'pass' in Tibetan). From here a phenomenal view of the 8,012-metre mountain Shishapangma to the west and the 8,153-metre Cho Oyu to the east opened up. We then drove around the Pal Khyung Tso ('tso' meaning 'lake') – where I would make one of my most important discoveries.[1] Our journey was fraught with obstacles. Winter had set in early that year and blocked the southern route to Mount Kailash with snow. Now a thaw was forecast, which would make it into an impassable muddy trail, so we were obliged to make a detour of 1,000 kilometres via the north route, passing the monastery of Mendong near Tsochen, Gerze and Shiquanhe. One of the most agreeable diversions were the geysers north of the 5,080-metre-high pass Bertik La, where fountains of boiling-hot sulphurous water over 10 metres high shoot out of the ground, instantly turning into thick clouds of steam. The thought of a hot shower was tempting, but the water was too scalding to even get close to and the icy wind banished all ideas of removing my clothes.

The Chinese garrison town of Shiquanhe was a cultural shock. The town consisted of ugly prefabricated housing blocks and military barracks; in the main square tipsy Chinese soldiers and Tibetans were thronging around about 20 billiard tables that were set up in the open air. Between the tables, prostitutes from the Chinese province of Sichuan wandered in search of clients. While taking a photo of three of them forcing their attentions on a Chinese subaltern, I was surrounded by soldiers, who grabbed my camera and took me to a barracks building. Luckily, our young interpreter, Lakpa, had observed the scene and hurried after me. After two hours of negotiation in a dark, smoky office, an officer wearing sunglasses announced that they would confiscate my film and impose a 'fine' of US$50 for insulting the Chinese People's Army.

When we protested, the officer threatened to confiscate our group visa and, worse, to arrest Lakpa for inciting a riot. I got the message and paid up. On our way to the lorry, Lakpa calculated that with my $50 the officer could buy either 17 prostitutes or 60 bottles of liquor.

From Shiquanhe, we travelled to the former kingdom of Guge, which borders on Ladakh in India. To get there we drove by night through successive canyons, where small rivers had eaten their way deep into the mountains and the wind had sculpted the rock still further. By the light of the moon, my imagination conjured these features into fantastic fortresses and enchanted castles.

Guge, which was founded in the mid-ninth century AD, was in the eleventh century the origin of a wave of Buddhist missionary activity, which rapidly spread to the whole of Tibet. The citadel of Tholing, the more recent of Guge's two capitals, rose about 200 metres above the valley floor. The slope leading to it was dotted with chapels, shrines and caves that once served as cells for hermits. Here too, Mao's Red Guards caused huge destruction. In the White Temple, dating from the eleventh century and situated on the river Sutlej, all that survives are fifteenth-century Buddhist murals, and two of what were originally four *chörtens* or relic shrines, called stupas in Sanskrit. The large mandala-shaped temple built in honour of the pious King Yeshe Ö, who initiated the revival of Buddhism in Tibet around 980, looked as if it had been bombed from the air. It was now used as a stable.

In a shrine in Upper Tholing I came across fragments of clay figures at least three metres in height. One of the decapitated heads had a gaping mouth and protruding eyes, an expression of horror frozen permanently in stone. In one *chörten* that had been broken into, I made the macabre discovery of a pile of skulls and bones of five or six people, which were very clearly not ancient relics. Other *chörtens* were full of thousands of small votive figures, either representing Buddhist deities or shaped like miniature stupas. These small figures made of unfired clay, called *tsa-tsa*, were made by the tens of thousands with the aid of moulds.

I could not believe my eyes when I shone my torch through a small hole in another, more remotely situated *chörten*: it was full of Tibetan long books. In contrast to the temples in the village, where piles of half-burnt documents lay abandoned in niches, this 'library' had not been plundered. The pages were more or less undamaged; the sheets were covered on both sides with Tibetan characters, applied with golden ink to the dark blue paper. My photos of two pages of text revealed that they belonged to the 108-volume Kanjur, the canonical text of Tibetan Buddhism in which the words of Buddha are recorded. The extremely dry climate of Guge has preserved these centuries-old documents from decaying. When I left, I closed the hole with fragments of brick and clay, to preserve the *chörten* from plunderers.

The following day, we set off for Tsaparang, the older of Guge's capitals, which is situated 26 kilometres west of Tholing. Five members of the expedition were suffering from slight altitude sickness and so they stayed in Tholing for a couple of days.

   The truck got stuck while crossing a small river, so we walked the last few kilometres through the canyon of the Sutlej. The rocky cliffs by the northern bank of the river were riddled like a Swiss cheese with caves that had once been monks' cells. Rounding a spur of a mountain, Tsaparang came into view. Blanketing the northern slope of the mountain were six Buddhist shrines, *chörtens* and countless monks' cells. Above them, at the top of a 200-metre-high rock with a broad peak like a chimney was the citadel. Tsaparang is a marvel of early Tibetan architecture and a jewel of art history. It is all the more valuable due to the fact that it was relatively unscathed during the Cultural Revolution, because it had been abandoned in the late seventeenth century. Several clay figures had been swept up into piles of rubble or otherwise smashed, but in the shrines there were still murals dating from the fifteenth and sixteenth centuries, that are among the most splendid in all Tibet.[2] In these murals, which blaze with various shades of red and gold, deities from the Buddhist pantheon are depicted, as well as more mundane scenes, such as the building of a temple.

   As in the case of Upper Tholing, the citadel of Tsaparang is accessible only through a sequence of subterranean chambers hewn out of the mountain and finally by a secret tunnel. As we were crawling through these chambers, I noticed a pile of rocks, which presumably served to block the tunnel in times of war. From the citadel, the walls drop vertically at least 40 metres. At the very top, situated next to the royal palace, is the Mandala Temple – the spiritual centre of Tsaparang. The temple is named for a three-dimensional mandala which once stood in the centre of the shrine and which was dedicated to the deity of meditation, Demchog (or Cakrasamvara in Sanskrit). Since Buddhists venerate Mount Kailash as the spiritual home of Demchog, there is a direct connection between this temple and the mountain that was my goal. Just as those who meditate penetrate in spirit from the outer rim of the mandala to the central figure of Demchog, so the pilgrims at Kailash who physically circle the mountain can approach the deity. Various other deities connected to Demchog are represented in the excellently preserved murals of the Mandala Temple.

Below these murals runs a macabre frieze representing the eight most important cemeteries in India. The frieze depicts people being impaled, devoured by wild animals, or hacked to pieces by skeletal figures; birds of prey are pecking the intestines from abdominal cavities and in the midst of all the horror, yogis meditate on the transitory nature of human existence. I was to come across two such holy burial grounds while circumambulating Mount Kailash.

In August 1624, two ragged, snowblind and exhausted men entered Tsaparang. They came from India, and had crossed the Himalayas via the 5,600-metre Mana Pass. The snow on the pass was so deep in parts that the men had to crawl forward on their stomachs. The two men were Jesuits: António de Andrade and Manuel Marques and were the first Europeans to reach western Tibet. They were there to investigate stories of Christian communities living north of the Himalayas. Although they did not find any Christians, they were received cordially by the King of Guge, who saw in the Christian faith a possible way to rid himself of the domination of the Buddhist clergy. As the Jesuits were leaving to continue their journey into India, the king invited Andrade to return soon, and gave him a letter to deliver to his superior in Goa, which said:

> We, the King of the Kingdoms of Potente, rejoicing at the arrival in our lands of Padre Antonio to teach us a holy law, take him for our Chief Lama and give him full authority to teach the holy law to our people. We shall issue orders that he [can] build a house of prayers.[3]

Andrade returned the following year to Tsaparang, where he remained until 1629. There he observed a superstitious custom that I also encountered several times among Mongolian nomads. 'Out of fear of demons, they give their children at birth as names the terms for things or animals of little value. Thus a father will give his sons names like "dog", "mouse", or "cold", so that the demon will dismiss them as unworthy of his attention.'[4] In Mongolia, I heard other names given to small children such as 'nothing', 'not there', or even 'shit'!

As far as the church was concerned, the king kept his word. He had some houses pulled down in the best area of Tsaparang, including a palace belonging to his grandmother, and ordered a church to be built, the foundation stone of which he laid in person on 11 April 1626. Then Andrade had the church painted by Tibetan painters. In a letter to his superiors in Rome, he wrote: 'Pictures from the life of the Virgin are being painted, not to mention those of the altar-piece, on which five rows of paintings are beautifully arranged. In the nave, pictures of the life of Jesus will be painted.'[5] Christian pictures painted by Buddhist artists – this must have been a unique synthesis of Catholic content and Tibeto-Buddhist iconography! Unfortunately, despite an intensive search I could not find any trace of Andrade's church, which had already been plundered in 1630 by order of the King of Ladakh. At that time, both the brother of the Christian-friendly king and the Buddhist clergy were rebelling against their ruler, and called the king of the neighbouring kingdom of Ladakh to their aid. The latter did not let the opportunity pass and occupied Guge, abducting the defeated king to his own capital of Leh.

From the citadel, I gazed across the barren landscape surrounding the canyon of the Sutlej, thinking of how these once-great capitals had declined. According to one story, the rulers gave up Tsaparang around 1640 and moved to Tholing. There is another much more dramatic version, however, which tells of how Tsaparang was attacked again by a king of Ladakh in 1685. After besieging its impregnable citadel in vain, the King of Ladakh engaged Muslim soldiers, who threatened the ruler of Guge that they would kill 50 inhabitants of the city daily until he capitulated. If he did so, he would be granted safe conduct for himself, his family and his ministers. The King of Guge took pity on the defenceless citizens of his town and abandoned his fortress. The last defenders had barely left the citadel when they were beheaded by the mercenaries as infidels; the surviving inhabitants of Tsaparang buried the headless corpses in nearby caves. Recently a number of headless skeletons had been found in a cave, lending credibility to the legend.[6]

# Yaks as Snowploughs

The sight of the 6,714-metre Mount Kailash is overwhelming. It rises like a perfect pyramid from the 4,500-metre plateau. Its peak is covered with snow and glitters like a crystal above its black granite base. Tibetans appropriately call it Kang Rinpoche, 'Jewel of the Snows'. It attracts the gaze of every observer and has for millennia been the goal of countless pilgrims, who often subject themselves to unbelievable hardships in order to reach it. Some travel for years and many never return home. As one of Tibet's smaller mountains, though, Kailash's significance lies in the spiritual, rather than the physical. Its religious importance is, however, rooted in the geography of the landscape, which is unique. Mount Kailash is at the centre of the sources of four mighty Asian rivers, which flow in exactly the four directions of the compass: the Indus to the north, the Brahmaputra to the east, the Karnali, one of the principal tributaries of the Ganges, to the south, and the Sutlej to the west. Considered geographically, the region around Mount Kailash forms the centre of a double watershed, and in the religious sense, a huge mandala. The mountain is a gigantic *chörten*, with the four sources representing the four entrance gates of the mandala.

Thanks to its unique location at the point of origin of four life-giving rivers, Mount Kailash is revered as holy by the four most important native religions of the Indo-Tibetan culture area. To Buddhists and Hindus, it symbolises the cosmic world axis, called *meru*. But whereas the Buddhists see in it the palace of the deity of meditation Demchog and his female companion Dorje Phagmo, the Hindus worship it as the seat of the god Shiva and his spouse Parvati. The Jains, adherents of an ascetic doctrine of salvation that also arose in India at about the time of Buddha, believe that the first of their mythical 24 saviours attained enlightenment on Mount Kailash.

To the Bönpos – adherents of the autochthonous pre-Buddhist religion of Tibet known as Bön – Mount Kailash was not some distant mythical mountain, but the concrete spiritual centre of their empire Shang Shung.[7] The political centre of Shang Shung, which was conquered by Central Tibet in 644, was most probably located in the valley of the Sutlej, near the fortress of Kyunglung, halfway between Tsaparang and Mount Kailash. The Bönpos revered Mount Kailash long before the adherents of the other three religions. They call it Tise or Yungdrung Gutse, meaning 'a pile of nine swastikas', and revere it as the residence of the feared nine-headed deity Welchen Gekhö who presides over the 360 Gekhö divinities (the number of whom corresponds to the 360 days of the lunar year). To them, Tise was the 'soul mountain' of their empire, and it is here, too, that the mythical founder of their religion, Tönpa Shenrab, is supposed to have descended from heaven to earth.

Thus Mount Kailash is a truly-ecumenical place, comparable only with Jerusalem. In contrast to Jerusalem, however, Kailash is a place of peace, where pilgrims of all four religions encounter one another without conflict. The swastika, too, is a symbol common to several religions. To the Hindus it represents fire, to Buddhists the wheel of truth and to Bönpos the energy of the primeval whirlwind that keeps the cosmos in place. In the Bön religion, the swastika turns to the left, for which reason Bönpo pilgrims circumambulate Mount Kailash counter-clockwise, whereas the other pilgrims do so clockwise.

It was a chilly November morning and I was in the hamlet of Darchen preparing for the 53-kilometre pilgrimage around the mountain. The only other member of the expedition group wishing to come was Erik Brandt; the others continued to suffer from symptoms of altitude sickness and stayed in Darchen, which was at a relatively low altitude. Several other pilgrims were encamped there waiting for the opportunity to join a larger group, fearing at this late time in the year to be surprised by a sudden snowstorm. Winter has fully arrived in this region by mid-November, as experienced by a Jesuit priest, Ippolito Desideri, who in 1715 was the first European to circumambulate Mount Kailash, during his journey from Ladakh to Lhasa:

> We arrived at the highest point reached during the whole journey in this desert called Ngnari-Giongar [the district including Kailash] on the 9th of November [1715.] Close by is a mountain of excessive height and great circumference,

covered with snow and ice, and most horrible, barren, steep and cold. The Tibetans walk most devoutly round the base of the mountain, which takes several days and they believe will procure great indulgences. Owing to the snow on this mountain my eyes became so inflamed that I well lost my sight. I had no spectacles, and the only remedy, as I learned from our escort, was to rub the eyes with snow.[8]

We engaged Tsering, an elderly Tibetan with a tanned face and lively eyes, as our guide. He insisted on taking his son and four yaks. 'What do we want with four yaks?' I asked, 'We are only going to be away for three days, and will spend the nights in caves. We need neither tents nor water, since we will pass by streams, or can melt snow. One yak would be enough to carry our sleeping-bags and some food.'

'Snow is why we need the yaks,' was his laconic answer.

The evening before our departure, a fight almost broke out among the team that were to accompany us: not only Tsering and his son, but also the driver, Li, wanted to come. Li was Chinese, but a Tibetan at heart, having grown up in Lhasa. Erik and I decided to take the slightly-built Li and a second driver Norbu, a strong, coarse-looking Tibetan, both of whom were greatly pleased.

In the afternoon, I performed a final fitness test, climbing to the most important of the five Buddhist monasteries along the pilgrims' route, called *khora* in Tibetan. The monastery of Gyendrak, stood on a small ridge at the southern foot of Mount Kailash and from the outside resembled a fortress rather than a monastery. The view from the monastery terrace took in the 7,728-metre mountain Gurla Mandatta, with Lake Langnak Tso (called Rakshas Tal in Sanskrit) glittering in the sunlight in front of it. Langnak Tso symbolises, together with the neighbouring lake, Mapham Tso (Manasarowar), to which it was once connected by a canal, the loss of cosmic unity and universal polarity. To the pilgrims, Mapham Tso is the epitome of spiritual purity and the power of light, while Langnak Tso represents the powers of evil. It is thought to be the meeting-place of the worst kinds of demon, despite the fact that it receives two streams that flow into it from Mount Kailash.

One of the six monks of the Buddhist Drigung Kagyüpa school who lived there showed me round the monastery, which was reconstructed in the 1980s.[9] In one dark room I noticed a few rusty old swords, together with fragments of breastplates and some ragged coats of chainmail. In good English the young monk explained that these weapons had been hidden in a cave during the Cultural Revolution. They had originally been taken from soldiers from

Kashmir who were killed in 1841 at Purang, about 100 kilometres south of Kailash. At the time, General Zorowar Singh, in the service of the ruler of Jammu and Kashmir, attacked western Tibet after having conquered and plundered the Buddhist kingdom of Ladakh. On 19 November 1841 a Tibetan army inflicted a crushing defeat on the invaders, saving western Tibet from a dire fate.

At dawn the following morning we set off towards the north-west, passing numerous small *chörtens* and mani-stone walls on the way.[10] After about two hours we reached a place called Darboche, where a huge flagpole stood, adorned with hundreds of colourful prayer flags, which are ceremonially renewed each spring, at the full moon of the fourth lunar month. The flagpole symbolises both the cosmic tree of life and the axis of the world, two interlinked concepts that date from the period of pre-Buddhist Bön.

To the east of the flagpole was one of the two sky burial sites on Mount Kailash – the cemetery of the 84 Mahasiddhas, Tantric masters who had acquired supernatural powers. Up to a few decades ago, sky burials were the most common form of funeral ceremony for the dead in central and western Tibet, since there is hardly any wood available, and the ground remains frozen for a long time in winter. The corpse is cut into pieces, and the flesh thrown to the vultures that circle above the cemetery. The skull and bones are crushed, then mixed with *tsampa* – a mixture of roasted millet flour and butter tea – and also given to the birds of prey. Tsering told us that parents sometimes take their children there to show them the transitory nature of human life. The east wind carried a terrible smell of decaying flesh in our direction and we hurried on, past 13 *chörtens* that had been destroyed during the Cultural Revolution.

Although the path climbed only moderately, Erik's pace grew slower and he began breathing heavily. He confessed that he had been having hallucinations all night and was now hearing voices: clear symptoms of acute altitude sickness. Although Erik had dreamed of the *khora* around Mount Kailash for more than 20 years, a further climb of over 1,000 metres was out of the question for him. He was forced to return to Darchen, where oxygen bottles were available. With a heavy heart, I commissioned the disappointed Li to accompany Erik back and to ensure he received proper medical attention on arrival.

After a further half-hour's hike, I was startled when a man jumped out from behind a large rock and strode straight towards me. In his belt was a long dagger. I had seen him the day before in Darchen and was told that he came from Kham in eastern Tibet. I was aware that bandits still roamed the area around Mount Kailash, robbing lone pilgrims. I remembered reading of an encounter the Japanese pilgrim, Ekai Kawaguchi, had here in 1900:

> My guide informed me that the man [I had just met] was a native of Kham, a place notorious as being a haunt of brigands and highwaymen. He really looked like a typical highwayman, with ferocious features and fierce eyes. Then [I found out] that this fellow was doing penance not for his past offences alone, but also to obtain immunity for crimes he might commit in the future. Yet I was told that this convenient mode of repentance was universal in the robber district of Kham.[11]

Luckily, Norbu quickly explained that the Khampa was not a bandit, but wanted to join our little caravan. I readily agreed. A quarter of an hour later, we were joined by a woman with her eight-year-old daughter and a baby that she carried in a basket on her back. She too had heard of my departure in Darchen and wanted to take this opportunity to carry out the *khora* in company, as the volatile weather could often turn bad without warning. When we stopped to rest, she told us that she was also undertaking the pilgrimage on behalf of a sick elderly woman who was paying her for it. She would share the spiritual merit acquired from the *khora* with the woman.

Soon we were crossing the frozen mountain stream Lha Chu, in order to reach the monastery of Chuku Gonpa or Nyen Ri Gonpa, which could barely be seen from a distance, as it clings to a camouflaging background of rust-coloured rocks. This second monastery of the *khora* was founded in the thirteenth century in a place that was sacred to the Bönpos. The name means 'Mountain (Ri) of the Astral Divinity (Nyen)', which is revered by the Bönpos as powerful and dangerous. The view from the monastery of the western side of Mount Kailash is one of the most impressive of the whole *khora*. Sven Hedin, who made the pilgrimage in 1907, recorded:

> The view one has from the roof is indescribably beautiful. There the icy peak of Kang Rinpoche arises in the midst of fantastic, jagged mountain walls, and in the foreground we have the picturesque superstructures and wimples of the monastery. This valley [that of the Lha Chu] is one of the most splendid in terms of wild natural beauty that I have ever seen.[12]

Unfortunately, the monks refused me access to the inside of the monastery. Their reasons, however, were understandable: only a few weeks before, thieves had broken in and stolen valuable statues. Most likely they had been commissioned by unscrupulous collectors, as so often happens in Nepal.

On our return to the Lha Chu stream an old nun from Lhasa, who had covered the entire journey of over 1,000 kilometres on foot, was waiting for us. More pious believers do not just walk the pilgrimage, but measure it with the length of their bodies. They wear special wooden hand-coverings and thick aprons to protect them from the wear and tear of the road. I saw these pilgrims a number of times later in eastern Tibet. Prostrating themselves on the ground, their arms stretched, they would mark a line in the earth before them with their hands. They then stand up and walk to the line they have drawn, fold their hands above their heads and stretch out on the ground once more, again and again, over incredible distances. The *khora* around Mount Kailash is for these pilgrims a particularly strenuous route as they have to negotiate an extremely steep descent from the pass of Drölma La at over 5,000 metres.

Our group was an eclectic mix: me, two locals from Darchen, two pilgrims, two children and a nun. We were travelling in the same physical space, but mentally we were worlds apart. I viewed the landscape from an aesthetic and religious perspective. For the men from Darchen it was simply a place they saw, mundanely, every day. But for the pilgrims the landscape was full of spiritual places loaded with symbolism and connected with figures such as Buddha, a deity, or a famous monk. To me, Kailash was a photogenic mountain; to them it was the mandala-shaped residence of Demchog. Perhaps the only thing we had in common was an awareness of our insignificance in the infinite chain of pilgrims that struggled, small as ants, around the mountain.

Beyond the monastery of Chuku the valley grew narrower and Mount Kailash disappeared behind walls of threatening dark-grey granite. An opaque veil of high cloud suddenly appeared and rapidly thickened, announcing snow. We hastened our steps and in two hours reached the monastery of Drira Puk which, like Chuku, belongs to the order of the Drukpa Kagyüpa. The most important place at Drira Puk is the cave of the Kagyü master Gotsangpa, who meditated here from 1213 to 1217 and composed the first pilgrims' guide to the *khora*. Shortly before we reached the monastery, the massive north face of Mount Kailash became visible again. I was speechless, and the pilgrims threw themselves down on the ground before the almost vertical 1,800-metre rocky slope. As with the north wall of the Eiger in the Swiss Alps, ice cannot cling to the central part of the steep slope, so that the black rock remains uncovered even in winter. Until late into the night I continued to admire this formidable pyramid of ice and granite; it was only the onset of snowfall that finally drove me into a nearby cave.

The following morning, a few rays of sunshine caressed the north-east side of the peak and we began the ascent, at first gentle, then steep, to the pass of Drölma La at 5,635 metres above sea level. The pass, significantly, bears the name of the most important female Bodhisattva, Drölma (Tara in Sanskrit), meaning 'Liberator'. Pilgrims struggling through the thin mountain air up here must realise that, while Drölma helps them along the path to spiritual liberation from the shackles of human greed, they must also exert themselves and suffer. The snow, which had begun to fall again, and the mist promised appropriate suffering, which the pilgrims uncomplainingly accepted. They believe that the more they suffer on the *khora*, the greater is the merit they will acquire.

We soon reached the second cemetery on Mount Kailash, Shiva Tsal. Here, the dead are carried for sky burial and pilgrims also come to leave an article of clothing, locks of hair, shoes or a drinking-bowl as a sign of discarding their ignoble desires. In the high mountain air, the old, sinful self dies symbolically and the soul is born again, purified.

When we walked by, however, these sacrifices were hardly visible, buried in a deep layer of snow from the night. About a foot of fresh snow was also covering the lower ascent to the pass and 500 metres higher there must have been two feet or more. Drölma La itself was enveloped in thick fog. I began to worry that we wouldn't be able to reach the pass and begin the steep descent on the eastern side before night fell. Tsering, however, was wearing a broad grin. The purpose of the four yaks now became evident. He had known that snow was coming and was prepared. The heavy animals would walk before the group, trampling the fresh snow flat like a steamroller. It would have been tempting to climb on the back of such a sure-footed animal, but to do this would have considerably lowered any moral merit already accumulated and sitting motionless on a yak's back would have increased the risk of frost-bitten feet.

In less than an hour we had reached a huge granite block called Dhikpa Karnak, which essentially means 'White and Black Sin'. Underneath it ran a narrow tunnel. We halted briefly and the nun explained its significance: 'Here, it is necessary to crawl through the tunnel, in order to experience symbolically the time between death and a new rebirth, which takes 49 days.' Sven Hedin provided a different explanation:

Whoever is without sin, or at least has an easy conscience, can crawl through the tunnel; but he who gets stuck in the middle is a rascal. I asked the old man whether it might not happen that a thin rascal might squeeze through, whilst a virtuous fat man would get stuck; but he replied most seriously that fatness or thinness had nothing at all to do with it: success or failure depended solely on spiritual qualities.[13]

Unfortunately for us, the snow had blocked the tunnel and the nun was dismayed that she would not be able to crawl through. Although our bodies were crying out for a rest, Tsering urged us to press on. He drove the yaks forward with whistles and shouts, occasionally throwing small stones at them. We climbed in a steep zigzag; I had to stop every 50 paces and gasp for breath. On many of the surrounding rocks pilgrims had raised pyramid-shaped piles of stones, miniatures of Mount Kailash. Sticking out of the snow, these helped us to find our way despite the mist and swirling snow.

At last the horizon took on a different aspect and walking suddenly became easier: we had reached the saddle of the pass. On a large rock dotted with Bön and Buddhist mantras stood a flagpole held between stones that were piled up in a pyramid. Long ropes, to which colourful prayer flags were tied, connected it with other masts planted in the ground. As at Shiva Tsal, the pilgrims leave something here of their old selves. They spread butter on the rock and press coins, banknotes, or locks of hair into it. Tsering showed me a place where about a hundred teeth were lodged in cracks – a custom that I later saw on the most important pilgrimage route of the Bönpo, at the Kongpo Bön Ri. When the sun briefly dispersed the clouds of fog, the pilgrims broke into cries of joy:'*Lha gyalo, kiki soso lha gyalo*': the gods are victorious! An excellent omen! Full of joy, we presented each other with *kathas* (white ceremonial scarves). The two women and the Khampa extravagantly expressed their gratitude for being allowed to join my small caravan and assured me that Drölma would reward me.

We could not afford to be over-confident, however, for thick clouds were again approaching from the north. We began our descent, which first led to the frozen lake Thukpe Chenpo Dzingbu, the 'Lake of Compassion'. The ice was much too thick, however, for us to break it open and take some of the holy water, as is the custom. By now snow was falling heavily, and with a visibility of less than 10 metres, we made our way cautiously down the step-like slope towards the valley of the Zong Chu. We had to watch our every step but the sure-footed, heavy yaks treading the path in front of us were a reassuring presence. We arrived in the valley in a sombre mood, our earlier elation having vanished. Mount Kailash was once again hidden, the valley floor was covered with sharp, snow-covered scree and shortly before we reached the monastery of Zutrul Puk, a heavy hail shower suddenly came, forcing us to take refuge in nearby hermits' caves.

When we woke, stiff and tired the next morning, we paid a visit to the inconspicuous monastery of Zutrul Puk, which owes its importance to the famous eleventh-century ascetic and mystic Milarepa, who meditated in a cave there for many years. Milarepa was one of the spiritual fathers of the Kagyüpa school of Buddhism and contributed to the final spread of Tibetan Buddhism at the expense of the Bön religion, which became greatly weakened. Buddhism had to lay claim to Mount Kailash, in order to demonstrate its 'victory' over Bön to all Tibetans. This conflict is allegorically portrayed in the epic struggle between Milarepa and the Bönpo master Naro Bon Chung.

The Kagyü tradition tells us that Milarepa, who had been a feared sorcerer in his youth, came to Kailash to challenge the Bönpo master Naro Bon Chung for possession of the holy mountain. After the Bönpo had been defeated several times by Milarepa's magic skills, one final test – a race to the peak of Kailash – was to decide who the winner was once and for all. The contest took place at the site of Zutrul Puk. Naro Bon Chung attempted to reach the top of the mountain through a feat of shamanic magic, by flying on his drum. But Milarepa halted him just short of the goal, transporting himself to the mountaintop on the first ray of the dawn light. Naro Bon Chung, filled with fear, slipped from his magic drum and crashed to the ground. But Milarepa had compassion for his defeated rival and not only allotted him a new place to live, within sight of Kailash – the monastery of Tise Bön Ri – but also allowed him to continue to make the pilgrimage around the sacred mountain. The monastery ceded by Milarepa to Naro Bon Chung stood, until the Cultural Revolution, at the foot of the mountain of Bön Ri, about 30 kilometres east of Mount Kailash. This myth symbolises to Tibetans the victory of the new beliefs over the old ones and also illuminates the tolerance of Buddhism of those times. In time the Bön religion virtually disappeared in its homeland of western Tibet and only continues to be represented there by travelling pilgrims from central and eastern Tibet.

The walk from Zutrul Puk back to Darchen was much easier. Beside the track were countless mani-stone walls, dozens of metres in length, on which millions of mantras are engraved. Not only were the gods victorious, but our small group as well, for we had completed our pilgrimage and the snow and mist that had plagued our journey had disappeared as quickly as it had come.

# Milarepa's Tower

Our march [in August 1922] brought us to a holy temple called Tseguthok – 'Tse of nine storeys'. There is a tower nine storeys high built by the holy man Milarepa, many years ago. He was greatly interfered with by demons, but in the end was successful. It is an act of great merit to walk around the [outer] narrow platform at the top of the [c. 25 metres high] tower, on which chains are tied for safety; but it required a better head for heights than we possessed.

F.M. Bailey, British Political Officer, Sikkim and Tibet, 1921–28[14]

I had long wanted to visit Milarepa's tower, especially as I had heard a rumour that the original murals might still be seen. However, Tseguthok – now called Sekhar Guthog – was in Lhodrak, a militarised zone, near the border with Bhutan and, as such, completely prohibited to visitors. Even Tibetans and Chinese are not allowed to travel there without special permits. The last foreigner to visit Sekhar Guthog was the British ambassador to Lhasa, Hugh Richardson, when he left Tibet via Sekhar in 1950.

Despite the obstacles, an unexpected opportunity opened up when my colleague Michael Henss, who also had an interest in Sekhar, received the news from Lhasa that we had received a special permit. On our arrival in Tibet, however, it became clear that the agent arranging our permits had promised much more than he could deliver – the security police in Lhasa had refused our request. Attempting to travel to Sekhar without a permit would have been pointless as the road was lined with road blocks set up by the police and the military. Unwilling to give up before our journey had even begun, we decided to drive to Zetang, where the road to Lhodrak began, and have one last attempt at persuading the regional security police, whose headquarters were there. After negotiating and pleading through our interpreter, Tashi, the verdict remained unchanged: 'No permit for Lhodrak.'

Despondent, we were about to leave when the police commandant, with the rank of a colonel, walked into the smoky room. Angry that we were taking up the time of his subordinates, he ordered us roughly to leave. At the same time, his gaze fell on the map of southern Tibet that I had acquired in New Delhi. Visibly excited, he grabbed it and hurried into his office. 'Now we are going to be arrested as spies,' whispered Tashi, turning white. The commandant returned in a good mood and explained that my map was more complete than his own. Could we swap? I agreed, of course, and five minutes later we left the post, delighted with the precious permit in our pockets. The commandant had even given me his direct radio telephone number in case of problems. Twice on the way to Lhodrak, military posts prevented us from continuing, despite our permit with its official stamp, for no foreigners had been this far since 1950. But each time, the commandant in Zetang kept his word and confirmed the validity of the permit.

We took our time on the way to Lhodrak. The roads were very bad and we frequently had to ascend high and difficult passes but we also wanted to make several detours. This was a route not travelled by a foreigner for decades and the thought of seeing places along the way that had been forbidden for so long was too tempting to resist. We headed first to Lhünze, where the fourteenth Dalai Lama had spent two nights in March 1959 on his flight into exile in India. It was from here that he announced the formation of Tibet's government in exile. To our pleasant surprise, the beautiful seventeenth- and eighteenth-century paintings at Chilay and Trakor Gonpa were undamaged, because the monasteries had served as granaries during the Cultural Revolution and were therefore not destroyed. We then headed south-west, to visit the monasteries of Mawachok, Benpa Chakdhor, Khoting Lhakang and Kachu. There the elderly abbot confirmed that we were the first foreigners to visit his monastery. These four Gonpas have been under reconstruction since the 1980s, but still contain some old bronze statues that were hidden in caves during the Cultural Revolution. Unforgettable among them is a large statue of a Bodhisattva, dating from the thirteenth century.

In Lhodrak one is struck by the numerous medieval stone towers dotted around the landscape, some of them soaring as high as 30 metres. Many served as watchtowers and are located in lonely positions at the entrance to valleys or at the tops of mountains; others can be found in the centre of small settlements, where they offered protection to the local population in times of war. Although these towers are found throughout Tibet, the two most famous are Yumbu Lhakhang, the royal fortress south of Zetang, and the tower of Milarepa, shrouded in mystery, at Sekhar Guthog.

Milarepa, who was born in the eleventh century, came from a wealthy family, and lost his father at an early age. He and his mother were cheated out of their inheritance by an uncle, and the family sank into poverty. Milarepa's mother encouraged her son to learn black magic in order to wreak vengeance. He obeyed, and in time became a feared sorcerer. At the wedding of the son of his treacherous uncle, he caused the house where the wedding party was taking place to collapse, killing everyone inside. He had hailstorms rage over the fields of his home village, which he then destroyed with flooding. Realising that he had incurred much bad karma and that his rebirth in hell was a certainty, Milarepa repented of his sins and turned to the renowned Buddhist master Marpa to be shown the way to redemption.

In order to remove Milarepa's bad karma, Marpa subjected him to severe mental and physical penances, which brought him to the verge of suicide. Amongst other things, he commanded Milarepa to build a stone tower. But Marpa, who was also a landowner, had made an agreement with his neighbours that forbade the construction of fortified towers. He deceived them by having Milarepa pull down the half-finished tower three times and rebuild it again on another site. The neighbours failed to take the fourth attempt seriously – until it was too late. Marpa now possessed a mighty nine-storey tower that controlled access to the narrow valley. He had cleverly combined Milarepa's spiritual purification with his own political aims. For Milarepa, the fourfold construction of the tower, the ground plan of which was first round, then sickle-shaped, then triangular and finally rectangular, meant the repetitive destruction of his evil self and the gradual rebirth of a new self. Milarepa's penance was finally complete and Marpa began to initiate him into higher doctrines, whereupon Milarepa – whose name means 'Mila clothed in cotton' – devoted himself to many years of asceticism and meditation. He died in his sixties, after drinking poisoned curdled milk given to him by an envious scribe. Milarepa was the spiritual founder of the order of the Kagyüpa, and is regarded as Tibet's greatest poet.

Following the Zhe-Chu River, we reached Sekhar Guthog a week after we had set out from Zetang. Michael and I were keen to see how well-preserved the tower would be and to find out about murals. We weren't disappointed.

Milarepa's tower rose, almost perfectly intact, from the centre of Sekhar Guthog. Nestled at its base were several buildings, dating from later centuries. The 25-metre-high tower itself was made up of nine outer and seven inner storeys; all that was missing was its roof of gilded metal. We climbed into the tower and as we reached the third inner storey, which we named 'Marpa's chapel', our torches revealed wonderful murals of the highest quality, quite unknown outside Tibet. Except for some water damage caused by a leaking roof, they were amazingly well-preserved.

These murals, which have never before been documented or photographed, date from the thirteenth century, shortly after Milarepa's tower was converted to a religious building. They represent the five transcendental Buddhas Amitabha, Amoghasiddhi, Akshobhya, Ratnasambhava and Vairocana as well as the medicine Buddha Bhaisajiyaguru, Buddha Amitayus, the historical Buddha Shayamuni and the one of the future, Maitreya. Even more surprising are the almost life-size depictions of Naropa, Marpa and Milarepa; the latter two being the oldest mural representations of these two Tibetan masters in existence. We were overwhelmed by the find and spent hours gazing at the paintings, which flickered in the light of our torches as if alive.

As we began to climb back down the tower, Tashi stepped out of the highest window and onto a narrow outer ledge. He began slowly to walk round the tower, clockwise, teetering 20 metres above the ground. Michael and I held our breath, praying that the mountings of the thin chain he was holding on to would not come loose from the wall under the strain. Walking round the tower in this way, between heaven and earth, is an exceedingly brave form of *khora*, which I was to witness on a later occasion in eastern Tibet. I refrained from following Tashi, making do with my past *khora* round Mount Kailash.

# The Unknown Bönpos

Tibet is infused, like no other region of the world, with an aura of living spirituality. Buddhism arrived in the land of eternal snows only in the seventh–eighth centuries AD, where it encountered the native religion Bön. Until then, the Bön religion, animistic and marked by belief in a multitude of benevolent and malevolent deities, was widespread. In the Bön world view there was no almighty god governing the cosmos; the universe was regarded as a dynamic balance between creative and destructive forces that exerted their influence on one another. Bönpo priests acted as mediators, ensuring this balance remained constant. Bön culture was marked by warlike values favouring military expansion. A martial culture high on horseback, it was diametrically opposed to peace-loving Buddhism.

From the eighth–ninth centuries, Buddhism from India increasingly rivalled Bön in Tibet but both religions influenced each other in terms of cultic practices and doctrine. Tibetan Buddhism adopted numerous Bön deities into its pantheon, while Bön adopted central Buddhist concepts such as the notion of karma, the entry into nirvana, the structure of the monastic hierarchy and the arrangement of the written canon.

The tradition of Bön lives on in Tibet, both in its own monasteries and within Tibetan folk beliefs, such as prayer flags and spirit traps, the circumambulation of temples and mountains, rituals connected with death and marriage, oracular techniques and countless religious rituals. The historical antagonism between Bön and Buddhism has today been overcome. For the first time a Bönpo representative was, in 1977, admitted to Tibet's exile parliament and the Dalai Lama recognised Bön as the fifth religious school of Tibet.

A few years after I walked around Mount Kailash, I set off for my first circumambulation of the holiest mountain of the Bönpo. Kongpo Bön Ri, meaning 'Mountain of Bön', is situated in the region of Kongpo, about 400 kilometres east of Lhasa. I planned to do the pilgrimage with a group of Bönpo pilgrims and we would travel in the footsteps of the mythical founder of Bön, Tönpa Shenrab. Our journey began in the city of Bayi, the population of which is 95 per cent Han Chinese. Bayi means 'First of August', a name that refers to a day of celebration for the Chinese army. Since Bayi lies about 700 metres lower than Lhasa, the city is very popular with the Chinese, who have difficulty tolerating the altitude of the high Tibetan plateau. In Bayi, the few Tibetans are unmistakably foreigners in their own country. The place swarms with soldiers, who are lodged in barracks located nearby and move apathetically about the city. As in Lhasa, the influx of young Han Chinese increases social tension because they take jobs away from the less well-trained young Tibetans. Unconfirmed rumours say that one day Bayi will replace Lhasa as the capital city of Tibet.

On the morning of our departure for the mountain, dark, ink-coloured clouds hung low over the city. Over the mountain itself it looked as though protective deities and demons were still battling it out in heaven, for sunshine and showers kept alternating. My first stop on the way, the Bön monastery of Sigyal Gönchen, was hidden in threatening clouds. We walked up the densely forested mountainside, past Khasemo, a village notorious for its poison-makers. My interpreter Pasang and I soon became lost, enveloped in a thick and sudden mist. Thankfully, a young monk appeared and offered to guide us to the monastery. He was a Bönpo monk from Sigyal Gonpa and his job was to liaise with the Chinese authorities. He lived for the most part in the village and in this way prevented a Chinese warden from living in the monastery, since the authorities usually place a warden in a monastery once it has as many as 15 monks. Often such 'two-headed dogs', as they are called, are Tibetan monks. They observe activities at the monastery to ensure that no anti-Chinese upheavals occur and that the number of monks does not exceed a certain number. Sigyal, for example, is not allowed to have more than 20 monks. Many of the monks avoid this restriction by alternating with each other in taking the two- or three-day pilgrimage around Bön Ri or by spending time in nearby hermits' caves. Others live with their families, helping to work in the fields and only staying at the monastery on special occasions. Thus the crafty Bönpos succeed in having about 120 monks living in the whole of Kongpo, more than double the number allowed.

After trekking for two hours through the dark conifer forest, a small clearing opened up and the prayer flags of Sigyal monastery fluttered into view. Inside,

Abbot Khedrub Nyima gave us a warm reception and while we drank warming butter tea, he told us of the legend of Tönpa Shenrab: 'About 18,000 years ago, our master Tönpa Shenrab Miwoche, whose name means "outstanding teacher and priest, great man", lived in Shang Shung. One day, a demon prince called Khyapa succeeded in carrying off one of his daughters to hell and marrying her. From this union two demon children were born. Later, Shenrab was able to bring his daughter and his grandchildren back to Shang Shung.'

What I found extraordinary about this introduction was that it initially placed the powers of darkness, personified by the prince of demons, on an equal footing with the powers of light, represented by Shenrab and his daughter. 'But the demon prince wanted his children back,' continued the abbot. 'Since he was unable to find them, by way of retaliation he stole Shenrab's seven miraculous horses and brought them to Kongpo, where he gave them to his ally, Prince Konje Karpo, to keep them for him. Shenrab set off in pursuit from Shang Shung, across central Tibet, to Kongpo. On the way the master had to fight several battles against the armed hordes of the demon prince, which he always won by performing miracles that caused his enemies to convert to Bön. Thus his journey turned into a veritable triumph, as he taught the Tibetans the teachings of Eternal Bön.'

The direct confrontation with Khyapa took place where the southern spurs of the Bön Ri massif join the north bank of the river Yarlung Tsangpo. This gives the mountain its great significance. When Shenrab reached the mountain, the demon horde tried to stop him by causing a colossal black mountain to rise up on the southern bank of the Tsangpo. Shenrab lifted the dark mountain with the little finger of his left hand and made a lofty mountain out of light rays streaming from his heart, which glittered like a jewel. He placed this on the north bank of the Tsangpo.

Next, Khyapa's mother and 99 other female demons transformed themselves into seductive female spirits and tried to poison Shenrab near the village of Khasemo. But Shenrab drank up the poison as though it were nectar. Now Khyapa faced up to the invader and struck a rock with his sword, causing black water to spring forth from it. Shenrab took up the challenge and planted his staff in the earth, which at once began to stream forth turquoise water. The next confrontation took place on the northern bank of the river. The demon set up in a row nine shields made of black iron and vowed to convert to Bön if Shenrab could pierce all nine shields with a single arrow. Shenrab succeeded in this test as well, and a spring came forth at the spot on the rock where his arrow struck. Shenrab captured the father of the demon prince, Gyala Dorje, and Khyapa finally surrendered. Along with the remaining demon hordes, he took refuge in the teaching of Bön. The seven miraculous horses were returned to Shenrab. In reparation, the Kongpo prince Konje Karpo handed his subjects over to the master and gave him his youngest daughter as his wife. Shenrab converted them all to Bön. Before his departure, Shenrab planted a juniper tree, symbolising the tree of life; its offspring still stands today near the monastery of Kushuk, north of Sigyal. The marriage of Shenrab and Karpo's daughter symbolises the reconciliation between the new teaching of 'Eternal Bön' and even older beliefs.

The monastery of Sigyal was destroyed during the Cultural Revolution, like all the Bön monasteries of Kongpo; reconstruction began in 1985. It is the most important monastery on Bön Ri, for it was founded by Ripa Druksa, who instituted the circumambulation pilgrimage of Bön Ri in 1330. The relics of this holy lama are preserved in the main shrine.

When Ripa Druksa was meditating near Mount Kailash, the main goddess of Bön, Sipa'i Gyalmo, commanded him to go to Kongpo and to reconquer the mountain of Bön for the eternal teaching. Having arrived at Kongpo Bön Ri, Ripa vanquished various local spirits and demons and bound them by oath as protective deities. He was the first to walk the route of the *khora* around the mountain, with the goddess in the form of a tiger showing him the way. The nearby monastery of Tagdrosa Darbong, 'Dancing Place of the Tiger', is a reminder of him. Since the goddess Sipa'i Gyalmo is also called Sigyal, this monastery is dedicated to her.

There is another story connected to Ripa Druksa that strongly recalls the famous contest between Milarepa and Naro Bon Chung – but in this case with the results reversed. As a final opponent, a Karmapa lama contested the control of Kongpo Bön Ri with Ripa. Then they agreed that the mountain should go to the one who was able to circle it the fastest. Ripa won and since then Buddhist pilgrims who want to pay homage to the mountain must make their pilgrimage of circumambulation in a counter-clockwise direction.

Two days later I visited the nearby monastery of Gyeri. Although reconstruction had only begun the year before, the temple chapel already contained three large, freshly painted statues. When I visited, all work on the monastery had halted, for the abbot had gone into retreat for three months in a cave near the summit of Bön Ri and five of the seven lamas had gone on a pilgrimage to eastern Tibet. As everywhere in Tibet, at Bön Ri the ancient customs of ascetic meditation are once more being practised. Monks retire to caves to meditate for a certain period, and are brought food by novices at regular intervals. These periods of meditation last for three or nine months, or three years, three months and three days. In some cases, ascetics have themselves walled in for life; they are given food by novices or pious lay persons through a hatch.

In some disturbing cases, a monk does not decide autonomously and of his own free will to spend his entire life thus entombed and is persuaded to take this step. I came across such a case in Aba in eastern Tibet. Near the monastery of Tsanang, I met an 80-year-old monk who had not left his cave in 31 years, although he received visitors once a week. What horrified me was his account of a neighbouring ascetic who had also spent decades in an almost completely walled-up cave and had died three years before. His reincarnation had already been identified: a two-year-old child, who would soon be taken to the monastery and at the conclusion of training there, would spend the rest of his life in the cave of his 'predecessor', to leave it only after his own death.

The provincial government gives financial support for the reconstruction of the monasteries of Kongpo. Most of the medium-sized and large monasteries receive an initial subsidy of about 100,000 renminbi, which was then equivalent to about US$12,000. This sum may seem quite modest, but since the monks, with the help of the local people, do the work themselves, the money is enough to buy the necessary wood and to pay the professional sculptors and painters, who are mostly laymen. The reconstruction of a monastery – regardless of whether it is subsidised by the government – requires a permit. It is also prohibited for monasteries to purchase land or receive it as a donation, if it does not border directly on the monastery – a clever way of the government ensuring that the monasteries do not regain their former pre-eminence.

In the final days of what was an especially mild October, I began the pilgrimage of Bön Ri, following the sluggishly flowing Tsangpo in the direction of the little village of Men Ri, where the ascent to the Bön Ri pass begins. More than once Tashi and I overtook pilgrims measuring the roughly 60-kilometre *khora* with their bodies, throwing themselves on the ground again and again. The 1,600-metre steep ascent from Men Ri to the pass at 4,530 metres, is a tough ordeal for these pilgrims. Especially pious individuals vow to circumambulate the mountain 9, 13 or even 108 times. I estimated that there were about 500 pilgrims doing the *khora* on this occasion. At one stage, the idyllic calm was disturbed by several explosions on the Tsangpo. Chinese fishermen were using dynamite, a sacrilege to both Bönpos and Buddhists.

At the foot of Bön Ri, in a clearing surrounded by fruit trees, was the monastery of Tagtse Yungdrungling. The monastery once housed more than 100 monks, but today there are only 13. Its abbot, Nyan Khyab, from eastern Tibet, received us in his cell. He had spent the previous night with a dying man in the next village, to make his transition from this world to the next easier. In doing so, he had carried out the Po Gyewa ritual, which is similar to the Phowa ritual of the Buddhists. The ritual serves to guarantee that the consciousness – the 'soul' – of the departed leaves his body via the top of the skull, and successfully passes the tests that await him in Bardo, the limbo between death and rebirth. But the Po Gyewa is not merely a ritual performed by an ordained monk with a dying person; it is also a form of meditation anticipating death.

Nyan Khyab explained: 'This type of meditation may only be carried out under the supervision of an experienced master; otherwise, early death or mental sickness threatens. During the meditation, the practitioner repeatedly projects his consciousness with the speed of an arrow to the top of the skull, and then allows it to plunge back into the heart. Once the practice, which lasts several weeks, is concluded, the fontanels of the forehead can be quite easily opened. Then the master tests the roof of the skull, and inserts a blade of *kusha* grass into the opening of the fontanelle. If the grass remains upright in the opening for a whole day, the exercise is considered successful.'

I had observed this final part of the ritual several months previously in the exile monastery of Abbot Lungtok Tenpa'i in northern India. The abbot placed a wheat stalk 30 centimetres in length in the slightly open forehead fontanels of the monk who had conducted the New Year's purification ceremony; this remained upright all day, although the monk moved about normally.

A few kilometres south of Tagtse Yungdrungling is Mijik Tri Durtrö, which means 'Eternal Throne of the Cemetery'. There is a mound of earth five metres in height which is connected with the grave of the semi-legendary eighth king of central Tibet, Grigum. The king failed in his attempt to break the power of the clergy, which at the time was dominant, and succumbed to the cunning of his opponent in a duel. If this interpretation is correct, this burial mound, about 2,000 years old, would be the oldest of its kind in Tibet. The neighbouring land being still in use for sky and earth burials, no archaeological searches can be carried out there. Near the newly dug graves lie broken spirit bottles, ceramic pots, flattened cigarette packets and knives with broken blades. These objects were intentionally destroyed as sacrifices and thus symbolically conveyed to the deceased in the afterlife.

About an hour's journey on foot to the east of Grigum's grave, close to the village of Yungdrung Dzin, stands one of the most important stone steles in Tibet. The Tibetan inscription dating from the early ninth century, which is still legible, but which is known to few, states that the legendary first king of central Tibet, Nyatri Tsenpo, descended from heaven to men on the mountain Bön Ri, which here is known as Lha Ri or 'Mountain of the Gods'. This account contradicts the current view that the origin of the central Tibetan royal dynasty of the Pugyel, which ruled up to AD 923, was in the Yarlung valley, south of Zetang. According to the stone stele of Yungdrung Dzin, which was installed by the Buddhist king Sanalek, the place of origin of the Pugyel kings is supposed to be beside the holy mountain of the Bönpo in Kongpo.[15]

Many pilgrims, some of whom had come from eastern Tibet, several hundred kilometres away, were camped at the foot of Bön Ri. It was new moon. New moon and full moon are considered auspicious dates for the *khora*. By the fire in the centre of the camp, an old monk told me his story. In 1941 he entered a monastery as a five-year-old novice, and at the age of 23 he was ordained as a *gelong*, a fully trained monk, after having taken the 250 necessary vows. He planned after that to enter a monastic university in order to earn the degree of *geshe* by 10 years of further study. An entirely different fate awaited him, though, for in 1959 – after the flight of the Dalai Lama – the Chinese began to force the monks to become laypersons. Thus, shortly after his ordination, Sonam had to leave his beloved monastery and get married. With the beginning of the Cultural Revolution, an orgy of violence and destruction started and Sonam was placed in a work camp near Gyanze.

The living conditions were so terrible that of his group of 140 men only 15 survived. One day Sonam and a group of about 50 former monks were marching on the main road from the camp to the quarry where they worked. They came upon a dead horse on the road in front of them, rotting and swarming with flies. They were so hungry that they all fell upon the cadaver and devoured the putrid flesh raw. After just a few minutes, only the bare skeleton of the horse lay on the ground and they continued marching to work. 'You see, when I die, I will reach straight nirvana, because I have already experienced hell in the Cultural Revolution,' said Sonam.

When he was finally released in 1985, after 18 years of captivity, he returned home to discover that his only son was dead and his wife had married another man. Fortunately, he found a job as a cook in a large school and in 1994 was allowed to return to his monastery, which had been rebuilt.

I set out before dawn with the pilgrims, because I wanted to complete the ascent of Bön Ri in one day and spend the night on the other side of the pass. All along the way, happy singing could be heard, even though the steep climb was hard work not only for me, but also for the pilgrims. In contrast to the pilgrimage route circling Kailash, the rock-strewn path of Bön Ri, which is very steep in places, is impassable for beasts of burden. Physical exertion is in fact part of the pilgrim's ritual of circumambulation. A pilgrimage trek in adverse weather conditions is considered particularly meritorious.

Although the path led through high brush and conifer woods, the route was festooned the whole way with colourful prayer flags or bunches of coloured wool so there was no risk of getting lost. Strips of pressed white wool up to 10 metres long recall the material that sometimes marks the route from the house of a dead person to the burial ground. The eye-catching cloths remind the pilgrim that the *khora* represents inner purification. At five sacred places on Bön Ri the pilgrim is invited to leave his or her bad-karma-ridden past behind.

After pilgrims have passed the monastery of Dzong Khyung Teng, which was destroyed by an earthquake, and Shenrab's Throne, where Tönpa Shenrab is said to have meditated, they reach a sacred tree near Sembon called Thangshing Durtrö. This mighty pine tree, 'the silver pine of Shenrab's consciousness', is a children's cemetery. About 20 little wooden coffins are suspended between earth and sky in its branches, about five metres above the ground. Below them hang the same number of cloth bags containing the clothes and playthings of the dead children. Dead infants are entrusted to the tree so that the spirits inhabiting it may redeem the sins of their previous lives. It is thought that in this way a longer life will be granted to the prematurely deceased children in their next life. Every pilgrim pauses briefly at this moving place and murmurs a prayer. 'Air burial' of little children in the branches of a tree is also still practised by certain tribes in Siberia. The pine tree also serves a more earthly purpose: in the bark of the lower trunk, dozens of human teeth are embedded. The pilgrims leave them behind here, along with the evil deeds that caused the toothaches. For this reason, the tree is also called 'the toothache tree'.

The third sacred place on the pilgrimage route connected with death and purification is called Zhingkham Dzegke, the 'Ladder to Paradise'. Here small sticks of wood with rungs carved into them line the edge of the path. These miniature ladders help the dead souls that always accompany the pilgrims on the *khora* to get to heaven quickly. Beside these ladders to heaven are heaped the skulls of sacrificed animals, as well as sheep scapulae, which are used for divination. The animal sacrifices are supposed to placate malevolent spirits and thus protect households from infection.

Shortly before the Bön Ri pass, pilgrims get their fourth chance to rid themselves of their sins. They sit down on the stone known as Dhikpa Pabsa and rub their backs against the rock wall, which absorbs their sins. After a short but steep climb, the pilgrims arrive at a small clay oven in which they burn juniper branches that they have carried up from the valley in honour of the great Bön teacher Tsewang Rigzin. Finally they come to a big *lhatse*, a stone heap identical to the *obo* of Mongolia, decorated with innumerable prayer flags, at the summit of the pass. Here many pilgrims leave behind a piece of clothing or a tuft of hair as an atonement offering for committed misdeeds.

Hardened sinners, who have managed to carry sins over the sacred pass after all, find the fifth and last opportunity for purification on the north side of the *khora*. Here is Dhikpa Dhotak – the 'Place of the Stones to which you Tie your Sins'. Dhikpa is located in a pine forest. The pilgrims use coloured woollen threads to tie little stones onto the lower branches of a tree or onto a bush. The last remaining sins are transferred to the stone and left behind here. We celebrated finishing the *khora* in a nearby clearing with a sumptuous picnic.

Especially pious pilgrims go on to make a detour of about 15 kilometres to reach the town of Ningchi, in order to go to the monastery of Tagdrosa Darbong, 'Dancing Ground of the Tiger'.

The following summer, I set out on another journey in search of Bön monasteries. Following my exploration of the monasteries surrounding Kongpo Bön Ri, this expedition took me to all the Bön monasteries in central Tibet, frequently difficult to access, as well as those on the Chang Tang plateau, where I undertook the pilgrimage round Lake Dangra, which takes a week. The result of my search for ancient architectural evidence of Bön was unfortunately disappointing, since the Bön monasteries were hit hard by the orgy of destruction during the Cultural Revolution.

Except for the small monastery in Ombu on the northern shore of Lake Dangra, where murals from the 1880s were preserved, all the Bön monasteries had been devastated during the 1960s or razed to the ground. Everything was new. Only small antique bronze figures were ancient, the monks had buried or hidden them in caves. Did this mean that there were no ancient Bön murals left in Tibet at all? My last hope was a remote monastery near Lake Pal Khyung Tso in the region of Kyirong, which I had touched on during a visit in 1991. The spiritual head of all Bönpos, Abbot Lungtok Tenpa'i, living in exile in India, had intimated to me that there was a small Bön monastery to the east or north of the lake which had possibly not been destroyed during the Cultural Revolution. However, he knew neither its name nor its exact location, nor did I find any reference to this in Western publications.

I was camping on the southern shore of Lake Pal Khyung Tso, 4,505 metres above sea level, enjoying the view of the 8,012-metre mountain Shishapangma and the 7,281-metre Kangpenqing. In the surroundings, my attention had been caught by numerous ruins of small temples and fortresses, but I had encountered neither humans nor animals in their vicinity. All that I found, not far from the lake, were the skeletons of two horned antelopes, their sharp antlers still entwined. They were two males that had killed one another in a fight, and soon thereafter had become food for the wolves. The next morning before dawn, my interpreter and I set off on foot to follow the lake shore in a counter-clockwise direction. In order to make rapid progress – the lake is 80 kilometres in circumference – we only took our sleeping bags, water and unleavened bread with us. We made our way for several hours in a northerly direction through the grassy plain, until a marsh forced us to climb higher and find a path through the scree. After having covered 30 kilometres, we found a rock with a Bönpo mantra engraved on it directing us to a nearby monastery, which we soon found on the north-east shore of the lake.

The monastery rose above several simple low houses of clay, the inhabitants of which had never before seen a foreigner. The Bön monastery, called Pa Lha Puk, housed 12 monks, of whom 11 lived with their families. The abbot was much surprised at our visit, since not even Tibetan visitors normally find their way to this monastery. From him, we learned that the monastery was founded towards the end of the eleventh century as a hermitage. It was renewed and expanded in the year 1405. I pricked up my ears when the abbot mentioned that during the Cultural Revolution all the statues had been destroyed, but the main temple had served as a granary up to the 1980s. Perhaps some murals had survived here.

Nor were my hopes disappointed. Very fine murals are preserved on three sides. As in the case of Sekhar Guthog, unfortunately, water damage and cracks in the masonry have affected the paintings. Iconographical details, and the comparison with other Buddhist mural paintings in Tibet, clearly suggested a dating in the first quarter of the fifteenth century. These are by far the oldest Bön murals in all of central and eastern Tibet and have never been recorded. The main figures represent the four highest divinities of reformed Bön. The chief deity is the primeval mother Sati Ersang, in the form of the compassionate goddess Sherab Chamna. Subordinated to her is a group of three male gods: the god of wisdom, Shenlha Wökar; the creator of the world, Sangpo Bumtri; and the deified master Tönpa Shenrab.

On the return journey to the Tibetan–Nepalese border I found that fortune favoured me on this expedition. Shortly after crossing the 5,100-metre-high pass Lalung La, I gave the order – spontaneously and apparently with no good reason – to call a halt at an exceptionally wide point in the steeply descending road with its numerous hairpin bends. The steering of the Land Cruiser failed and, despite the efforts of the driver, the vehicle drifted to the left – which was fortunately the uphill side – and we landed in a pile of snow. A steering rod on the left-hand front wheel had broken, and 50 metres further down, in a right-hand bend, we would have shot over the edge of a precipice.

# Between Heaven and Earth

Close to the city of Rebkong, which is near Xining, the capital of Qinghai Province, an archaic sacrificial ritual takes place annually at the summer solstice. Although it is held within the grounds of a Buddhist temple, the ancient military ideals from the times of Bön carry more weight here than the Buddhist ethics of compassion and harmony. The ritual, called Lu Rol, is conducted by shamans – no Buddhist monks participate – and it is observed solely by farmers in 12 small villages. The word *lu* refers to a mountain song as well as to a category of subterranean deities that can take the shape of snakes, spiders and scorpions. The word *rol* means 'the playing of a traditional musical instrument'. The ritual is thus directed towards both mountain deities, who determine the weather and towards Lu, who can cause illness in people and animals.

The fertile land around Rebkong was the scene of military conflicts between Tibet and China at the time of the later Pugyel kings of Tibet, who ruled from the seventh to the early tenth century. In 710, China officially ceded this region to Tibet and today Tibetans account for 70 per cent of the population. According to tradition, the Lu Rol ritual was introduced to commemorate the peace treaty of 822 between China and Tibet. The ritual dance not only celebrates Tibet's ancient military strength, but is also an archaic fertility rite. On this occasion, the gods are to be appeased through various offerings, including self-mutilations, so that people are protected from illness and epidemics, and a bountiful harvest is ensured. Shamans act as intermediaries between people and gods. They lead the ritual and communicate with deities while in a trance, to ensure that the gods will accept the sacrificial offerings benevolently.

We witnessed this ritual dance in the village of Tewo, where two other villages were also participating in the festivities. The host and head shaman stood before the entrance to the village, waiting for the guests. Suddenly trumpets and shell horns blasted, drummers struck up a wild dynamic rhythm and the guests drew closer. The three leading shamans exchanged lucky scarves and led more than 100 followers to the temple complex, located at the end of a large courtyard. There a large shrine is devoted to Guru Rinpoche, who helped bring Buddhism to victory in central Tibet, and a smaller one dedicated to the pre-Buddhist mountain deity, Nyen Chen Tang Lha.

The two-day celebration involved a series of sacrificial offerings, ritual dances and readings of holy texts. The villagers brought an eclectic mixture of offerings to the temple: bricks of dried tea, fruit, flour, yogurt, beer, spirits and money. On the first day, richly adorned dancers celebrated the ancient military glory of Tibet. Holding swords, spears, bows and arrows, they swung colourful flags and adopted old military formations, kowtowing three times in the four directions of the compass.

The two guest shamans simultaneously performed an act of black magic at the centre of the main shrine. Together they thrust a long knife into a traditional Tibetan book. Inside the book they had placed a curse written on paper condemning a young man to death for refusing to follow the calling to become a shaman.

The second day was dedicated to Nyen Chen Tang Lha and the Lu. Early in the morning, approximately 30 young men climbed a nearby hill, where they made offerings of juniper to the mountain deities. Then they ran down to the Guchu River and each took one white and one black stone from its waters as an offering for the Lu deities. The stones were placed in a sedan chair shouldered by four young men. On the return trip to the temple, the procession stopped in front of the large house of the village headman. When the sedan chair holders staggered into the inner courtyard as if in a trance or drunken, an assistant shaman sprinkled beer, spirits and yak yogurt on the ground. Then, the procession hurried to the temple and placed the sedan on the ground in the middle of the courtyard.

In the centre of the shrine, four men reciting prayers and playing musical instruments speeded up the rhythm of the music to prepare the dancers for a painful test that lay ahead of them. The cheeks of the 30 young men were to be pierced with long steel needles. After the head shaman had blessed the needles with incense, he stepped out of the temple and exhorted the dancers to choose a needle. Immediately, two assistants began to drive the needles through both cheeks of each dancer. Some seemed to take the pain with ease; fear was written all over the faces of others.

Participation in this gruesome ritual is compulsory for young men between 15 and 30. Those who avoid the sacrifice lose respect in society and risk a curse that excludes them from their community. The ritual is a remnant of former blood sacrifices in which men had to offer their blood and pain to Nyen Chen, in order to appease him and to secure a bountiful harvest. Since Nyen Chen also rules over the weather, he can send hail, drought, rain or sun.

The men began to dance again in ancient military formations, striking flat drums and singing old fighting songs, their faces contorted with pain. After two men had completed a dance on stilts on a slippery floor, 12 unmarried women appeared. Each was wearing a special headdress, from which several round silver plates trailed down their backs, each symbolising a star or a planet. The women moved slowly in a circle and held out lucky scarves to Nyen Chen with outstretched arms.

Towards evening the host shaman asked the gods if they were satisfied with the offerings. He fell into a trance and threw three black triangular objects to the floor and read the answer divined from the arrangement of how they fell. The answer was positive and 12 assistants tugged to remove the needle from the cheeks of the first six dancers. They repeated this until all the men were freed from their needles. As a finale, all the participants gathered in the middle of the courtyard round a burning pile of juniper and threw edibles into the fire whilst sprinkling yak yoghurt and alcohol on the ground. While the performance of the dance ritual benefits the community, some participants carry out additional self-mutilation for their own personal benefit. They have long metal spikes stuck into their backs and then try to get rid of them without the aid of their hands, by moving in a wild dance. Others slit open their foreheads and let the blood flow to the ground. At the moment when the leading shaman falls unconscious to the ground, the ceremony ends. The deity who has taken possession of his body has left him to slide lifeless to the floor.

Nomads from Eastern Tibet never steal at the expense of members of their own group. Theft and robbery in this case are considered shameful acts. On the other hand, horse rustling and taking plunder in raids on hostile territory is greatly approved and considered a heroic act by all.

Namkhai Norbu, 1951.[16]

In many respects, eastern Tibet is full of contrasts. In the rugged mountain landscape, high mountains soar towards the sky and raging torrents plunge through dark narrow ravines. Even in summertime, sunshine, rain, hail and snow alternate from one moment to the next. This is the land of a peace-loving Buddhism, where more and more families are sending their sons to monasteries, as in the days before the invasion of 1950, and where pious people buy animals that are destined for slaughter, saving them from death. But despite this and the peacefulness, eastern Tibet is also a region notorious among travellers. The terrain is difficult and there are sudden and violent changes in the weather but the traveller's greatest fear is from bandits and highwaymen.

The custom of mercilessly plundering and frequently killing foreign travellers used to be widespread in the Amdopa and Khampa regions and were regarded as honourable acts. Travellers who ventured into eastern Tibet had to be prepared for attacks. Only heavily armed expeditions could keep the assailants at bay and the most important item of equipment was a good rifle.

The list of Western victims reads like a *Who's Who* of explorers of Tibet. Nikolai Przhevalsky was attacked in 1879 once and in 1884 twice, Annie Taylor in 1892, Karl Futterer in 1898. Jules Dutreuil de Rhins was murdered in 1894, as was Petrus Rijnhart in 1898. Wilhelm Filchner and Albert Tafel were attacked and robbed three times in 1904, and Tafel alone a further four times between 1905 and 1908. The same fate overtook Pjotr Koslov in 1895 and 1909, Major d'Ollone in 1909, Marion Duncan in 1927, Ernst Schäfer in 1930 (three times) and in 1935, and Harrison Forman twice in 1933–35. A worse fate befell Albert Shelton in 1922 and Louis Liotard in 1940, for both were assassinated.

What awaits the individual traveller in the early twenty-first century? Following the brutal suppression of an uprising of Khampas and Amdopas in 1955–59, the Chinese People's Army imposed a kind of graveyard peace in eastern Tibet, which extended to the attacks on foreign travellers. However, since the 1980s the tribes and nomads of Tibet have regained much of their earlier freedoms and, along with it, their custom of robbing travellers.

I first experienced this in Amdo, while travelling from Labrang to Zoige with a Tibetan interpreter called Gyaltsen. He had told me a few days earlier that some Amdopa had once again begun attacking tourists' vehicles and demanding a 'toll charge'. And indeed, about 10 kilometres before Zoige, we saw that two large tree trunks had been placed across the road, just after a bend. As we approached, three young men were dragging a third tree along to close the gap on the left-hand side of the road. Our Chinese driver reacted like lightning. He stepped on the gas and aimed the ancient Land Cruiser straight at the men. At the last moment, they jumped aside and we shot through the gap.

A few months later, I set off westwards with Therese and Gyaltsen to the town of Dartsedo (Kangding in Chinese), the capital of the former Tibetan kingdom of Chakla, one of the numerous principalities of Kham that remained independent into the twentieth century. Our journey took us towards the ravines of Gyarong, where several Bön monasteries and dozens of fortified stone towers are located. One afternoon, a couple of days into our journey we stopped at a place called Lhagang, where a celebration was taking place in its monastery. Stopping here to take photographs was our undoing. We had been noticed, and presumably our driver, waiting in the Land Cruiser, had been questioned as to the next place we intended to drive to.

We were half an hour from Lhagang towards Danba when our progress was suddenly blocked by six large rocks on the road. I remember thinking that it was odd – a bus had been driving not far in front of us and there were no signs of a landslide or any work being done to the road. Gyaltsen, too, was alarmed, but the driver urged him to get out and to remove the rocks. He had just reached them when three Tibetans armed with long sabres jumped out of the high bushes that lined the road. The bandits were not interested in Gyaltsen, but us, so he succeeded in getting away. We hastily closed the doors and windows, but the men threw stones that they had ready at the windows of the car. The driver was unable to turn – he couldn't see out of the filthy back window. Within seconds, the window on the driver's side was smashed and the leader, a wild-looking Khampa, drove his sabre into the inside of the car, as easily as if it were flesh. With a yell, the driver leapt on to the empty front passenger seat and began to wail, while the Khampa opened my door from the inside and confronted me with his sabre, pressing it against my stomach and my throat in turn.

I refused to get out of the car and stayed in my seat. When the Khampa began to tear my shirt open, I gave him my wallet containing Chinese cash, then our watches and, piece by piece, all of our camera equipment. At the same time, I shouted at him incessantly in Tibetan, that I knew the Dalai Lama, and that he was dishonouring his own country. This took him aback; at any rate, he chose not to kill me. Therese, whose door the other bandits had not been able to open, had managed to hide one of her cameras beneath her seat before the Khampa demanded her camera-case. They also luckily missed our passports and plane tickets, which wouldn't have interested them anyway, and the majority of our money. After what seemed like an eternity, they disappeared into the bushes with their booty and the threat was over, as quickly as it had begun.

Not knowing whether or not the bandits would come back, we decided to get moving as quickly as we could. Gyaltsen was nowhere to be seen, but I knew him to be a fast runner and was sure that he had managed to escape. We hastened to move the rocks in the road aside and urged the hysterically weeping driver to drive on. As darkness fell, we came to a place where a landslide had blocked the road, and were obliged to stop again and wait. Suddenly, a motorbike roared up and, to our great relief, Gyaltsen was sitting on the back. He had escaped while the bandits were busy with us and then stopped the motorbike rider on the road and persuaded him to take him to us.

We had hardly opened the door of our hotel room in Danba, when the mayor and some police officers arrived and began questioning us in a most friendly manner. We were told that four other ambushes had taken place at the same place within the previous six months; on one occasion, a Chinese woman from Hong Kong had been murdered. The Danba police were powerless, as the site of the attacks was in an area where the police of the neighbouring district of Tawu were in control. It was cautiously indicated that they were in league with the bandits.

The following morning, Therese and I realised how lucky we were to be unhurt; despite the loss of our money and camera equipment it could have been much worse. In the early afternoon, eight heavily armed policemen from Tawu entered our room. I instantly disliked the commissar in charge, who looked even less trustworthy than the robbers of the previous day. My initial antipathy increased when he proceeded to try turning me from the accuser into the accused. The interrogation lasted for five hours, during which he repeated the same questions and concentrated on absurd details. I was obliged to describe the bandits' clothing exactly, make a precise estimate of the length of the sabre, or answer questions such as: 'When the robber took your camera, was his sabre pointing at your stomach or your throat? And when you handed over the second camera-case? And your watch?' and so on. The same questions were then repeated two hours later.

Each time I went to the toilet, which was located in the corridor outside the room, a policeman followed me with his revolver drawn and stood watching me.

I had gone from victim to presumed-criminal. However, after over four hours the commissar began to yawn and I began to sense that there was light at the end of the tunnel. After a further hour, he wanted to put the same questions to Therese, who replied emphatically that she had nothing to add, whereupon Gyaltsen was questioned, but briefly. Finally, I was required to sign a six-page transcript in Chinese. I refused, on the grounds that I did not understand Chinese. When the commissar threatened me, saying that he would invoke various Chinese laws, I countered that I would instantly telephone the Swiss embassy in Beijing. At that, he gave in – for the moment.

We spent the next two days in Damba, in order to visit the Bön monasteries in the surrounding area. The Tawu police had also ordered us to stay there, because the provincial police in Chengdu wanted to make further investigations. Meanwhile, the Damba authorities did everything to make a pleasant stay possible for us and even placed a police escort at our disposal.

The valley of the Gyarong looks back on a turbulent history, which the Bön monastery Yungdrung Lhateng illustrates. In the second half of the eighteenth century it was caught up in the maelstrom of the war being waged by the Chinese emperor Qianlong against the Bönpo ruler of Gyarong. Initially the monastery withstood two sieges, but then fell in 1763, when Qianlong brought heavy artillery to bear. The emperor had the monastery – which had been burned down – rebuilt, and turned it over to the Buddhist Gelugpas. The monastery was again destroyed in the 1950s, but in 1990 the still-strong Bönpo community demanded the ruins back and commenced rebuilding once again.

Of more art-historical significance is the Bön monastery Yungdrung Darje in Dratheng, dating from the early fifteenth century, where, in the gönkhang, the chapel of the tutelary deities, I discovered wall paintings that to my knowledge have not been written about in any book. These murals, which are nearly 300 years old, survived the destruction of the Cultural Revolution because they were hidden under a layer of whitewash while the monastery was used as a granary. Near the village of Sokpo, a breathtaking view opens up: from here, one can see a 'forest' of 28 slender stone-fortified towers, all of which served for the defence against Emperor Qianlong.

After a couple of days in Damba, we believed we had regained our freedom of movement and so decided to leave and head southwards. We had barely crossed the border of the district of Tawu, when two Tawu police vehicles intercepted us and forced us to drive to their barracks in Pema. There the execrable commissar from Tawu was waiting for us, together with two police officials from the provincial capital Chengdu and a representative of the town of Kandze. One of the officers from Chengdu quickly came to the point: 'Either you sign the statement of the police of Tawu now or we will detain you here indefinitely.' Meaningfully, the officer gazed at a concrete block, two metres in length and one wide, lying on the ground beside my chair. Two thick metal rings were embedded in it. The block, as well as the two handcuffs dangling from the table beside the officer, sent out an unmistakable message. We were prisoners of the police, unless and until we signed a text that we were unable to read, and which Gyaltsen was forbidden to translate. We had no choice. I signed, adding the note 'under duress', and we were released.

Two weeks later, I was in Litang to photograph the annual Horse Festival, which is followed by about 10,000 enthusiastic spectators. On the last day of the week-long festival, a policeman approached Gyaltsen and asked him if I was the foreigner who had been robbed recently. He stated that the police had caught the three bandits and confiscated the property stolen from us, adding that I must drive to Tawu, which was 380 kilometres away, to identify the robbers. I was immediately mistrustful: how could this policeman know that I had returned to Litang ten days after I had left it? I had no trust at all in the police of Tawu and no particular desire to see them again. I also worried that it might have been a trap to have me robbed once again, on the journey to Tawu. Gyaltsen added that, should the bandits indeed be punished, their relatives would attempt to avenge them.

That night, I had an ominous dream. I was back in Switzerland, and entered a medieval castle to see some friends again. Instead of them, however, I encountered relatives on my father's side of the family dining at a long table on the ground floor. I joined them, then soon noticed that a flickering light was coming up from a staircase that led down to the basement. I asked my relatives whether another party was taking place there. No one understood my question, as I was the only one to see the light. I then descended the spiral staircase, and at the bottom found another long table in the middle of a room illuminated by torches. There was one solitary person sitting at the table with his back to me, and between two lighted candelabras, an empty chair on the opposite side. I approached, and saw that the stranger was my grandfather, who had died 32 years earlier. He greeted me and said that he had long been waiting for me. I was to sit down and share the evening meal with him. I woke up bathed in sweat and took the dream as a warning that I might soon find myself joining my grandfather.

I resolved not to go to Tawu, but straight to Chengdu. To trick the by-now impatient policeman, I claimed to have an upset stomach and said we would go to Tawu in three days. We set off quickly for Chengdu. But our plan was in vain; I was being shadowed. After six hours of driving from Litang to Dartsedo, and inside the district of Tawu, an all-too-familiar surprise awaited me. Immediately after a bend in the road, I saw that one side of the road was blocked by a lorry and the other, where the land sloped steeply into a ravine, by large rocks. It was clear that this was another ambush. Instantly, six men armed with sabres sprang from behind the lorry and surrounded our vehicle, shouting loudly. Others blocked the road behind us with rocks. We were trapped. Three of the men were attempting to open the window with their sabres, a fourth was stabbing at the lock of my door with a dagger and a fifth had climbed onto the roof.

Gyaltsen grabbed the initiative. He took out his mobile phone, opened his window a crack and shouted to the leader of the bandits that I was an official guest of the government of Sichuan and that he was about to phone the police in Dartsedo. This bluff had its effect; the leader was unsure what to do and called his men together for a discussion that took several minutes. Their hesitation proved our salvation. A large bus full of passengers suddenly appeared, coming from the other direction, and the driver sounded his horn furiously when he saw the road block. Robbing us in front of so many witnesses was too much even for the bandits and they removed just enough rocks for the bus to be able to pass and rapidly disappear. Gyaltsen shouted to the driver, who was paralysed with fear, to drive off at once through the gap while it was still open, for the bandits had not thrown aside the rocks, but were still holding them in readiness, two men to each rock, to block the road again. We got through by the skin of our teeth and raced off headlong in the direction of Chengdu.

Eastern Tibet is not only a country of bandits, but also of monks and nuns, both Buddhists and Bönpos. There are, however, eight to ten times fewer nuns than monks, and they are accorded much less respect. In contrast to nunneries, communities of monks are shooting up like mushrooms in a warm, damp summer. The reconstruction of the monasteries represents to most Tibetans an act of self-assertion against the Chinese occupation. This fusion of religion and politics means that centres of unrest arise within the monasteries, which in turn brings official repression in its train.

Abbot Gendüb's monastery, which is very remote, is situated south of Litang, and was founded in the fifteenth century. Gendüb, who was born in 1924, entered the monastery as a young novice; in 1956, the Chinese army took it by storm and razed it to the ground. Gendüb was put in a re-education camp, was made to marry and, at the outbreak of the Cultural Revolution in 1966, found himself in a forced labour brigade. After over 10 years of labour, he was released, the sole survivor of his monastic community. In the 1980s, Gendüb obtained permission to rebuild his monastery and now presides over five old and eight young fully ordained monks, 140 novices, and a dozen laymen. The abbot described the life of the monastery to me.

'With the help of Buddha, I was able to rebuild the monastery. But I fear that I shall not live long enough to pass on all my knowledge. We lack the money to invite famous teachers. But I teach my novices not only Buddhist texts, but also Tibetan grammar and, although it is prohibited, Chinese, simple mathematics, geography and the history of Tibet. I also pass on my modest knowledge of English to the older novices. Each novice must also perform manual labour, either in the kitchen, the carpentry workshop, or the smithy. Between the age of 16 and full ordination, each novice has one day a week free. I insist on the mixture of religious and secular teaching because between the ages of 18 and 20 all the novices must decide whether to take the oath for full ordination or to return to the lay condition. How is a young man to survive if he leaves the monastery having learned nothing but reciting Buddhist sutras? He can then only return to his family, if they will indeed accept him back. Those who speak no Chinese can only get unqualified work.'

I was surprised; Gendüb was the first abbot I had met who had made sure his charges were educated in both religious and secular matters. He continued to explain that he wants only fully motivated monks for his monastery. He was concerned that otherwise the institution would degenerate into nothing more than a tourist attraction. The sheer number of monks in Tibet means that in many towns there is a lack of qualified young Tibetans, encouraging the influx of better-trained Chinese. The abbot then referred to Jigme Puntsok as a shining example of the future of Tibet.

Jigme Puntsok, who was born in 1933, is president of the large monastic university of Larung Gar near Serthar in southern Amdo, which he founded in 1985. My first sight of the university was breathtaking. It emerges from the end of a gorge, its 2,000 small log cabins resembling a colourful carpet spread out on the grass. At that time, almost 10,000 nuns and monks were studying there; the students had come from all five Tibetan Buddhist religious schools, as well as both Bön traditions. This monastic university is unique in many ways. Its nuns are given equal opportunities and the academy is open to all Tibetan schools, and to all nations (1,000 Han Chinese also study here). The only prerequisite is the willingness to lead a monastic life. The six-year curriculum comprises all aspects of Tibetan culture, including Buddhist philosophy and hermeneutics, Tantra, Dzogchen (an advanced kind of meditation), astrology, medicine, history, painting, grammar and writing. After successfully completing their degrees, nuns and monks return to their home monasteries in order to transfer their knowledge. It is Jigme Puntsok's goal to form a new spiritual elite within Tibet who will pass their knowledge on to the next generation. His efforts are vital for the revival of Tibetan culture: two generations of teachers are missing as a result of the Cultural Revolution.

In the summer of 2001 the Chinese authorities dealt this promising project a heavy blow. They limited the enrolments to a maximum of 1,500 Tibetans. Han Chinese students had to leave the university immediately, as did most of the nuns. The Chinese then demolished the majority of the humble dwellings there. Larung Gar was undoubtedly a thorn in the sides of the Chinese. The university gave the whole monastic system a fresh, profound impetus, pushing at the official line, which tolerates monastic institutions provided they act solely as religious bodies and tourist attractions. The number of Han Chinese students wanting to study there must have been threatening as well.

Few people can escape being captivated by Tibet and its people. Nowhere have I experienced the sky so close to the earth and the air so pure and clear. Since Tibet is shielded on all quarters by high, almost invincible mountains, it was protected from foreign influences and developed a unique culture. It is only in the last few centuries that modern weapons managed to conquer Tibet's natural defences and it now faces challenges not only from the Chinese occupation but from an influx of tourism.

But I remain confident. Most Tibetans I met were strong, physically and mentally. Their blood is infused with an untameable pride and love of their country, culture and, above all, religion. The nomads, who scratch a living from nature and are continuously threatened by nature, have developed an attitude of unique respect towards their environment. I can only hope that the swathe of immigrants arriving from China will not water down Tibet's unique character and that it will survive for centuries to come.

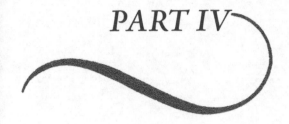

# PART IV

# Secrets of the
# Taklamakan Desert

# A Second Mecca

Although China cautiously opened up under the leadership of Deng Xiaoping, who came to full power in 1980, the Taklamakan Desert remained closed for many years to foreign visitors. A year after I first visited China in 1984, I travelled to Kashgar, in the far west of the remote province of Xinjiang. I planned to explore the famous ruined cities of Niya and Loulan, which lie on the southern and central Silk Road, but Khotan, from where the journey should begin – and anywhere beyond it – was still completely off limits.

Niya and Loulan were once two of the most important and prosperous Silk Road oasis cities. Yet for centuries they lay forgotten and buried beneath the shifting desert sands. Niya, the Pompeii of the East, is believed to have once been the ancient kingdom of Jin Jüe but at some point in the fifth century AD it disappeared without trace. It was rediscovered in 1901, by Aurel Stein. The remains of Loulan are situated on the banks of the now dried-up lake of Lop Nur. It, too, was an ancient kingdom and a strategic point along the Silk Road and was also enveloped by the sands of the Taklamakan. It remained hidden until Sven Hedin discovered it in 1900.

At the peak of their prosperity, Niya and Loulan were under China's political sphere of influence. Culturally, however, they were oriented to the west – to India and Sogdia, in present-day Uzbekistan. The different routes of the Silk Road, which crossed the Tarim Basin to the north and south, injected yet more cultural diversity.[1] As well as being the centre of communication and trade between East and West, Xinjiang's strategic location ensured a turbulent era. The region first came under Chinese control at the end of the second century BC, when Emperor Wudi expelled the Xiongnu from Gansu and the Tarim Basin. This first period of Chinese sovereignty came to an end following the fall of the Western Jin dynasty (AD 263–316) and only at the beginning of the

Tang Dynasty (618–907) was China able to reconquer the Tarim Basin. It was not at peace for long, as in 659 a new power made its appearance in Central Asia: Tibet, its armies spreading like a whirlwind, occupying the Tarim Basin from 670 to 692.

After a further period of Chinese domination, an Arab–Turkish army defeated the Chinese in 751 at the river Talas in the south of Kazakhstan, after which the rebellion of An Lushan broke out in central China, raging from 755–63, resulting in the withdrawal of Chinese troops from the western regions. Tibet began again to fill the power vacuum left by the Chinese and by 791 had conquered the whole territory south of the Tian Shan, the 'Heavenly Mountains'.[2] Sixty years later, they were in turn driven out by the Uigurs, who still predominantly occupy the region today. It was not until 1758 that China was able to reconquer the land, which has since been known as Xinjiang ('New Territory').

In between the wars and rebellions, trade flourished. Silk, lacquer, paper and animal hides filtered from east to west and, in the opposite direction, gold, glass, incense and ivory. Cultures, philosophies and religions were also borne on the caravans that ceaselessly trod the Silk Road. Between the two poles of the Silk Road was Iran, which, with interruptions, was at war with Rome and Byzantium for seven centuries. As a result, transcontinental trade was carried on via middlemen. In Central Asia these middlemen were Sogdians, who represented a panoply of religions: Zoroastrianism, Buddhism, Hinduism and Nestorian Christianity. Like bees, the Sogdian traders disseminated these religions in the areas where they were active and had their trading posts. Adding to the cultural mix were missionaries, who penetrated along the trade routes through Central Asia to China, either to attend to the members of their religions who were living there, or to actively spread their religions among the native populations. The oasis towns of the Tarim Basin became melting-pots, yet much of the archaeological evidence of this still lies undiscovered, beneath the sand.

Ten years after my first visit to China, the gates to the Taklamakan were finally opened to me, and late one autumn afternoon I arrived in Urumqi, the capital of Xinjiang. My travelling companion was Jean-Daniel Carrard, an enthusiastic alpinist and delta-wing pilot, who was the first to fly from Mount McKinley (6,194 metres), the highest mountain in North America.

From Urumqi we drove to Khotan, gateway to the Southern Silk Road and our entry point into the Taklamakan. Over 1,000 years ago, Khotan was the centre of a prosperous Buddhist kingdom on the Southern Silk Road. It once exported great quantities of silk, harvested from its many mulberry orchards, as well as jade and pottery. Today its main economy is agriculture. From Khotan we planned to drive to Minfeng, which lies on the southern edge of the Tarim Basin, and from there to Niya.

We were seated in a huge Unimog lorry which, together with its driver Li, we had hired from a Chinese oil company for the next six weeks. There were three other Chinese accompanying us. Wang, our interpreter and the organiser of the expedition, was an experienced desert traveller. The turbulence of the Cultural Revolution had left its mark on him and given him nerves of steel. When he was 13 years old, the school he attended was closed and he was detailed for work in a factory, where he was put through various 're-education' programmes over the following six years. When he was finally released he went back to school and then on to university to study English and Business Management. Wang Li was our cook and next to him sat Sheng Chen Chou, deputy director of the Historical Museum in Urumqi. The Cultural Relics Bureau had sent him with us to watch us and make sure that we did not carry out any forbidden excavations. He was enthusiastic about the expedition, because even he would not have been able to visit Niya or Loulan without a special permit. We, too, were lucky to have him with us for he knew a great deal about the past civilisations of the Tarim Basin and turned out to be an excellent cook, who could also expertly slaughter and gut a sheep. A few years after our expedition he was promoted to the post of director of the Cultural Relics Bureau of Xinjiang, which provided me with a friend at the top of this important authority.

As we drove we discussed the name of the Taklamakan Desert which, with an area of 338,000 square kilometres, is the second largest pure sand desert in the world after the Rub' al-Khali in Arabia. Wang explained that Taklamakan is an Uigur word meaning roughly 'Once you enter, you will never come out again'. The famous Buddhist monk Xuanzang, who in 629 began a 15-year pilgrimage from China to India, had described the Southern Silk Road in discouraging terms as well:

> [On leaving Niya,] The traveller enters an immeasurable desert of shifting sands. This desert extends endlessly in all directions, and no one can find his way in it. Travellers have no other clues for their orientation than the human bones and animal remains left behind by the caravans that were there before them.[3]

The Taklamakan's reputation as one of the world's harshest deserts is not undeserved. There are few other places in the world where the difference between the amount of rainfall and the evaporation of that rainfall is so extreme. In the eastern portion of the desert the average precipitation is less than 10 millimetres a year while the evaporation potential amounts to 2,900 millimetres. There is even the phenomenon of the so-called 'devil's rain', when the few raindrops that fall evaporate before reaching the ground. In summer, the temperature on the ground can reach 80°C and in winter it rarely rises above freezing.

There is, however, another interpretation of Taklamakan – 'Vineyard' – which, although incongruous today, was probably an accurate description of the oasis towns that once thrived here. Two thousand years ago the climate was vastly different. Like pearls on a necklace, fertile oasis towns were lined up along the Silk Road and it was not until the ninth century when life in them began to be extinguished – a consequence of the climatic desiccation of Central Asia and the collapse of China and Tibet. Through elaborate irrigation systems the towns had managed to sustain human life and protect it from the searing heat and constantly encroaching sand. Today, where heavily laden trade caravans once passed, only the silence of an ocean of sand rules. It is thanks to this dry climate, though, that the ruins of Niya and Loulan and the treasures they contain are preserved.

'This desert also has a Chinese name,' added Sheng, 'Liu Sha, meaning "Wandering Sands".' As a result of the constantly blowing north-eastern winds, some of the sand dunes can migrate southwards as much as 50 metres in a year. The road on which we were driving was 60 kilometres further south than it was 1,600 years ago.

In the evening we reached Minfeng, where it seemed time had stood still since 1970. In the main square stood a three-metre-high stone stele, celebrating the achievements of the Cultural Revolution in both Chinese and Cyrillic characters. The stele matches the larger-than-life-size stone statue of the 'Great Steersman' Mao Zedong in Kashgar. Up to the late 1970s, such statues were ubiquitous in China, but they had since been torn down from their plinths – except in Xinjiang. Perhaps the townspeople foresaw that their statue could mutate into a tourist attraction.

At any rate few, if any, tourists had ever found their way to Minfeng until we arrived. As soon as Jean-Daniel and I got out of the truck, we attracted a large crowd. Hundreds of people turned out to stare at the two long-nosed 'foreign devils'. On two occasions, we caused the traffic to come to a standstill, as carts drawn by donkeys or oxen, cycles, and even some cars, stopped in their tracks to inspect us. A few especially bold youths came over and pulled at the hair on our arms, to make sure it was real and not, as in Chinese opera, glued on. An old woman was walking past carrying a large bowl full of soup; seeing us, she gave a cry and clapped her hands together in front of her face in horror, as if she had come face to face with the devil. The bowl fell to the ground and shattered. Feeling guilty, we hurried to our spartan lodgings, followed by a long trail of curious people.

After a few days' stocking up with supplies in Minfeng, we set out for Niya. Two sheep bleating in panic and a couple of chickens were loaded into the back of the Unimog – our meat supply for the journey – and we set off at full speed along a sandy track, following the shallow river Niya northwards. Two millennia ago, it actually reached Niya, but today it seeps into the ground 70 kilometres south of the ruins. The leaves of the tamarisks that line the river were shining golden in the sunshine. Now and again a fox crossed our path, and a group of camels stampeded at the approach of our snarling truck. After a five-hour drive, we overtook an asthmatic tractor, in the open trailer of which more than 40 people were crammed together like cattle. We stopped to ask them about Niya.

I greeted their leader, an imam in a turban, with 'As-salaam aleikum!' ('Peace be with you')

'Wa aleikum as-salaam,' he answered, somewhat taken aback at hearing a foreigner speaking Arabic. I was lucky – Imam Hassan's Arabic was probably not much better than mine as he had taught himself. 'We are on our way', he said, 'to the Mazar, the mausoleum of Ja'far al-Sadiq.'

Ja'far al-Sadiq (not to be confused with the Sixth Imam of Shi'a Islam who has the same name) was a seventeenth-century Muslim saint and mystic, a descendant of the Prophet, who spread Islam in eastern Turkestan and is widely venerated throughout the region. The imam told me that they would much rather be going on a pilgrimage to Mecca but that, because the number of pilgrims each year is limited and the cost of travel is so great, they treat Sadiq's mausoleum as a 'second Mecca'. 'To us, three pilgrimages to the Mazar of Ja'far al-Sadiq are equivalent to the journey to Mecca,' he explained.

The imam then gave me a sceptical look, and asked: 'Are you a Muslim? You have a terrible accent, but you speak classical Arabic, the language of our

Prophet.' I was forced to disappoint him, but he was right about one thing: I had indeed learned classical Arabic, in Switzerland, from an educated Egyptian. But Hassan comforted me: 'Never mind, perhaps you will still find your way to Islam. But it is a thousand times better to be a Christian than a Communist.'

Towards evening, we reached the settlement of Kabakasgan, which consisted of about a score of clay cottages, and visited the nearby Mazar of Ja'far al-Sadiq. Our route took us past numerous graves, each consisting of a small mound of clay with a rectangular wooden fence around it. Next to each of them, wooden poles up to three metres in height were stuck in the sand, to which colourful pieces of cloth were tied. There were also other larger graves that were subterranean, their burial chambers built of tree trunks. Through a wooden gate decorated with many flags, horses' tails and animal skins, we passed Sadiq's grave, which consisted of a simple wooden structure. It was completely covered by a forest of red, yellow, white and green flags with prayers from the Koran written on them. I felt myself transported to Tibet. Inside the mausoleum, an equally colourful sight greeted the eye: dozens, if not hundreds, of coloured wimples, and at the centre the sarcophagus, covered with a dark red cloth. On this were printed views of Mecca, the Muslim creed, and the names of Muhammad and his son-in-law Ali.

Legend and fact have entwined around Ja'far al-Sadiq. The faithful of the region believe in a story that, around 730, about a century after the death of the Prophet, a descendant of the Prophet, also called Ja'far al-Sadiq, came to eastern Turkestan to convert unbelievers. At the spot where the mausoleum is, Sadiq and his companions were attacked by troops of the Buddhist kingdom of Khotan. To save them from the massacre by the infidels that threatened them, Allah created a sandstorm in the night, which concealed them. The next morning, the officers of the army of Khotan thought that Sadiq had escaped under cover of darkness. They accused one another of a lack of vigilance, and in their quarrel killed each other. Then came a second sandstorm that buried their bodies.

Another tradition tells of a dream that a rich trader had in the eighteenth century, in which he was told to erect a mausoleum in this spot in honour of the earlier, mythical Sadiq. Indeed, the architecture and construction of the mausoleum does suggest it was built in the eighteenth century. This is a typical case of a mythical figure being projected onto a historical figure, fusing the two. In so doing, the mythical Sadiq has been given a factual, historic root and the historical Sadiq has been given a more mystical and divine status. Since the mythical Sadiq defeated his enemies by summoning a sandstorm, a place near an ancient desert ruin covered by sand was a fitting place to erect a mausoleum for the historical Sadiq.

# *T*he *Guardian of Niya*

We spent that night in the two-roomed house of Baikerly, the guardian of the ruins of Niya, 40 kilometres away. For the past 20 years, Baikerly has armed himself with an ancient rifle and ridden once a month to Niya to check that looters haven't disturbed the ruins. His task is not without danger – he has been shot at twice – and the rewards are slim – he receives an annual stipend of 100 renminbi (roughly US$12). By comparison, a fat sheep costs 160 renminbi. While his wife was preparing fresh spaghetti, Baikerly proudly told us a little bit about his life. The family provides for themselves, raising sheep and goats, cultivating a small amount of millet and breeding hunting falcons that they sell in the bazaar of Minfeng for good money. Guarding the ruins of Niya is a matter of honour to Baikerly; he doesn't do it for the money. His grandfather, Sadak, worked for Aurel Stein in Niya and in the ruined town of Endere. He used to tell how Stein made an important find in Endere thanks to him. It had to do with a wooden tablet inscribed in Kharoshthi.[4]

Indeed, Baikerly's grandfather had made an essential contribution to the reconstruction of the history of Endere. In 1901, Aurel Stein carried out his first excavation of Niya and returned in the autumn of 1906. At the conclusion of this second excavation, he planned to return to the ruined town of Endere, 150 kilometres south-east of Niya, which he had also visited in 1901. He reported:

> Sadak, a young cultivator from the Mazar working with my party, had on hearing of my intended move to Endere told me of an 'akhta' [an inscribed wooden document] he had come upon a year or two before while prospecting for treasure close to the old fort of Endere. When he brought it I was surprised to find a tablet of a rectangular Kharoshthi document. The writing clearly proved

that it belonged to the same early period as the wooden documents of the Niya site, i.e. the 3rd century.[5]

Stein was puzzled by this find, as he was convinced that Endere had been founded only in the seventh century. He based this dating on the travel report of the Buddhist pilgrim, Xuanzang, who around the year AD 643 or 644 described the place as barren. Could Endere, perhaps, be older? Stein hurried to Endere with Sadak, arriving there on 8 November 1906.

I hurried to the spot where Sadak declared that he had found the Kharoshthi tablet, which he had brought to me at Imam Jafar Sadiq, now marked [as a ruin] E VI. Setting the men at once to work we had most of the ruin E VI cleared by nightfall. From the floor was recovered a Kharoshthi document, showing nine lines of clear Kharoshthi writing.[6]

Now Stein realised that Endere had already existed in the first centuries AD. This first town on the site fell into ruins in the late sixth century, and was rebuilt only about 10 years after Xuanzang travelled through this area around the year AD 655.

That evening, I could not have guessed that I would four years later make one of my most important discoveries in Endere, precisely near this ruin.

The following day, we drove north into the desert. Thanks to Baikerly, who functioned as a guide, we were able to circumvent the dunes and avoid the soft hollows in which our six-ton vehicle would otherwise have got bogged down. Twenty kilometres before Niya, we drove through a grove of poplars that had been dead for over 1,500 years, their gnarled boughs raised defiantly to the sky. They were silent witnesses to the fact that, instead of the large barren expanse of desert, a forest had flourished here over 1,000 years ago. Further along, we caught sight of a wooden bridge that was about 2,000 years old, under which no water had flowed for a long time. It was lost in the sands, looking as helpless as a beetle lying on its back, unable to right itself. At walking pace, we drove on past tamarisk hills and ruins, until we set up camp between two large ruins, not far from the large Buddhist stupa.

The ruins of Niya are scattered widely throughout the oasis, which covers about 50 square kilometres, and the remains of about 150 dwellings have been found here. The majority were on small, terrace-like platforms of clay or loess, which suggested that the terrain had formerly been marshy, although today there are neither reeds nor live tamarisks – the water has long since dried up.

Sheng explained that the architecture was typical of all ancient oasis settlements: 'First, supporting rings were carved in tree trunks of as large a size as possible, which were then dug into the ground horizontally. Next, pillars of poplar or tamarisk wood were driven into the rings, and between them walls of woven reeds or tamarisk branches were erected and painted over with clay. Did you notice? Baikerly's house was built according to the same method.'

Baikerly nodded, explaining that this was the best way of adapting to the desert and its climate. A few months before, a commissar had come from Minfeng and tried to persuade him to replace his roof of poplar wood and clay with one made of corrugated iron. Baikerly refused. In summer, the temperature in the house would have become unbearable.

We spent the following days exploring the ruins on foot. Without any digging, we found in the sand bronze coins and needles, earrings, semi-precious stones from necklaces, cloth fragments of wool and silk, felt shoes and caps, several human skeletons and a vast quantity of fragments of red pottery ornamented with line patterns. We handed over all the small valuable finds to Sheng and buried the larger, less valuable, objects back in the sand. It was often hard to stop ourselves from properly excavating. On one occasion, we discovered a wide wooden lid covering a completely intact and probably quite large clay amphora buried in the sand. Jean-Daniel and I were bursting with curiosity. What was inside it? But Sheng laid down the law, forbidding any digging. Reluctantly, we closed 'our' amphora again, and covered it up with sand.

On our last day, we made an extraordinary find: two intact wooden coffins. Was this Niya's cemetery? There was no mention of it in Stein's report of his excavations – was it possible that we were the first to discover it? Our hearts beat faster: it was likely that mummies still remained, undisturbed, inside the coffins. The richest and most important archaeological finds are often made in cemeteries, because of the burial objects they contain. But once again Sheng did not allow us to even touch the coffin lids. A year after our visit, a Sino-Japanese team found 'our cemetery' and excavated a double grave containing the mummies of a ruler of the kingdom of Jin Jüe and his wife, both wrapped in silk brocade.[7]

After three days of monotonous driving eastwards, we reached the district capital town of Ruoqiang, which consisted mainly of ugly concrete buildings in the Soviet style of the 1960s. This abrupt encounter with 'civilisation' was a shock to our systems. Since Kabakasgan, we had been living in the open and camping in tents. Now we were confronted with the ugly face of modern society. In a dilapidated barracks now serving as a hotel, we were squeezed into bare, unheated rooms with all the charm of a mortuary. Instead of taking a freshly prepared evening meal beside a cosy campfire, as in Niya, we made our way to the canteen, where we found over 100 drunken policemen, who were taking part in an annual district conference. The air of the dining hall was pregnant with smoke and cheap alcohol fumes; the policemen were shouting, yelling, belching and spitting on the floor, which was strewn with empty bottles. A Chinese version of rock music was blaring from the loudspeakers. At one table, an officer, wearing sunglasses and evidently having great difficulty in standing upright, was making a speech that no one was listening to. It ended with an invitation – instantly complied with – to drain a glassful of their local gut-rot in one draught. At first, we were unnoticed, but soon a few heavily made-up prostitutes approached. Despite the cold, they were scantily clad, smelt of the cheapest perfume and each was uglier than the next. They clearly thought they could expect more from us than from the policemen. Abandoning the policemen's laps, they staggered towards us, eyes rolling expectantly, whereupon Jean-Daniel, Wang, Sheng and I quickly escaped.

The following day, we drove into the surrounding pebble desert to visit the ruins of Old Miran. When the town was abandoned at the end of the ninth century, there was no protective sand to cover the buildings, so they were exposed to the full fury of the winds. For this reason, no traces of wooden structures are found there, only very thick clay buildings that survived the wind. Nevertheless, Aurel Stein, who engaged in archaeological work there in the winter of 1906–7 and in 1914, was able to find rich treasure in Miran. In the huge Tibetan fortress, in a pile of rubbish that still smelled bad, he found over 200 Tibetan documents written on wood and paper – the lack of any Chinese documents showed that Tibet, at that time, had full control of this part of the Silk Road. Rubbish heaps over 1,000 years old often retain their smell – the sand in which they are buried acts as a preservative. In view of this, Stein developed a very special method of dating:

> I have had occasion to acquire a rather extensive experience in clearing ancient rubbish heaps, and know how to diagnose them. But for intensity of sheer dirt and age-persisting smelliness I shall always put the rich 'castings' of Tibetan warriors in the front rank. The recollection of these Miran fort perfumes was fresh enough a year afterwards to guide me rightly in the chronological determination of another site.[8]

The rectangular fortress was built by the Tibetans in around AD 760 to control three strategically important trade routes: the Southern Silk Road from Dunhuang to Khotan and Kashgar, a direct route to Lhasa over the Chiman Tagh Mountains and another road to Lhasa through the Tsaidam Desert. Thanks to Miran and other forts in the Tarim Basin, around Turfan, and in the present-day province of Gansu, Tibet was able to interrupt China's trade connections with Sogdia, thus robbing the Middle Kingdom of an important source of income. At the time, Tibet, which was twice its present size, waged war on China for almost two centuries.[9] Despite its small population, Tibet was able, thanks to general conscription, to put large armies in the field. In the front lines, Tibetans used non-Tibetan cavalry as cannon fodder, followed by Tibetan archers on horseback. Heavy infantry formed the nucleus. The soldiers wore long coats of mail and iron helmets, and were equipped with long lances and swords, as well as bows and arrows. Behind the soldiers stood the artillery, consisting of dozens of catapults. Although we only spent a day in Miran, we found several fine iron rings from such coats of mail in the fortress.

As in Endere, the Tibetan occupation of the eighth and ninth centuries had been preceded by a first settlement in the third–fifth centuries AD. West of the fortress, Stein discovered some splendid Buddhist wall paintings dating from the second half of the third century. They showed a surprising influence from northern India and the eastern Mediterranean. While digging, Stein remembered,

> a delicately-painted dado of beautiful winged angels began to show on the wall, I felt completely taken by surprise. How could I have expected, by the desolate shores of Lop Nor, in the very heart of innermost Asia, to come upon such classical representations of Cherubim! And what were these graceful heads, recalling cherished scenes of Christian imagery, doing here on the walls of what beyond all doubt was a Buddhist sanctuary?[10]

An equally surprising find was the signature of a painter: 'This fresco is [the work] of Tita' (a genitive form of the name Titus).[11] Buddhist Miran at that time was culturally oriented to India and Asia Minor, not to China.

I asked Sheng whether all the murals were still there. He replied that a few of the murals were still in place, but buried under a layer of rubble three metres thick. It turned out that most of them had either been removed by Stein in 1907 and 1914 and taken to New Delhi, or else destroyed by Zuicho Tachibana, a Japanese spy posing as an archaeologist. Sadly, the paintings in

Delhi's National Museum have not been on show for many years. 'If India does not appreciate them, they should be given back to China,' said Sheng, visibly annoyed.

Before setting out on our expedition, I had hoped that I would meet a contemporary of Hedin's or Stein's. I had had no luck until that day, when I met Villayati, an Uigur archaeologist who was to accompany us to Loulan. He told me of a very old man named Kumran Banyas who lived in New Miran. He was born, he said, in the nineteenth century, near Karakoshun, the former Lake Lop Nor, and had experienced the 're-migration' of this lake to the north into its old bed, and the drying up of Lake Karakoshun, as described by Hedin. I pricked up my ears at this; it was possible that he had known Hedin and Stein

On our arrival in New Miran, Villayati took us to Kumran's house. As we walked into the internal courtyard of the pretty little farmhouse, screened from the wind and the outside world by some tall poplars, Kumran Banyas shuffled towards us. Wearing a white Uigur cap, his lively face was distinguished by a white goatee, high cheekbones and large, deep-set brown eyes. He looked questioningly at the group of strangers and appeared at first not to be pleased at our visit. But then he recognised his friend Villayati, and agreed to talk to the two foreigners. We were shown into a small, bare room that served Kumran both as bedroom and living room. He invited us to take a seat on his bed, a traditional Chinese *kang* – a large clay bench with several horizontal channels running through it in which glowing embers are placed in winter, warming the surface evenly. The *kang* was covered with a colourful blanket decorated with bright Tibetan patterns. Kumran sat opposite us on a stool next to the wood stove. A simple light bulb hung from the ceiling, casting a pale glow through the room. Our conversation was slow and passed through various filters, since Kumran spoke in an ancient Tangut dialect that had practically died out. Villayati translated this into Uigur and Wang translated from Uigur into English.

Kumran was 108 years old. Born in 1886 in a small village on Lake Karakoshun, he lived almost exclusively on fish and barley. In the summer, he would paddle out onto the lake in a dug-out canoe and catch the fish with wooden harpoons. The fish would be laid out on the shore to dry or buried in the hot sand. A few weeks later, they were dug up again and chopped into fishmeal. In winter, catching fish was more difficult, because the surface of the lake was frozen for months on end. They had to bore holes in the thick ice at regular intervals and stretch out woven reed nets between the holes. Then the whole village would gather and trample on the ice, shouting loudly to drive the fish towards the nets. As the water of Lake Karakoshun was fresh, it was also their drinking water – there was no need to dig any wells. Kumran's family kept a few chickens and sheep on the farm and sometimes went hunting for hares or gazelles with falcons or eagles. Fruit was unknown to them, however. With a grin, Kumran told us of the time when he first saw a large melon in a field: 'I quickly shot an arrow at this unknown creature, to stop it running away'. The most exciting event for him was hunting not fruit but wild boar through the reed thickets along the lake-shore; it was a dangerous activity: for every five boar killed, one hunter or beater got injured.

This seemingly idyllic childhood didn't last for long. Even when he was young, the Tarim and Lachin-Darya rivers – the Uigur word 'Darya' means 'River' – which came from the Altun Shan mountains in the south, bore less and less water, so that Karakoshun became shallower and a ring of small brackish marshes formed around it. The lake's retreat was unstoppable and soon Kumran and the other villagers had to embark on a long trek to get to its retreating shore. The village gradually lost the basis of its existence and the people began to move away. When Kumran was about 30, an epidemic of plague broke out in the village and Kumran, one of the last remaining members, was forced to finally leave and move to Miran.

Amazingly, Kumran could well remember Sven Hedin. He told us: 'I was about 12 years old when Etzin [as the Uigurs called Hedin] came from Russia to Lake Karakoshun, accompanied by two Russian soldiers. I met him at the south-west end of the lake, where I was living, east of the village of Abdal.'

Had Kumran also known the British explorer Aurel Stein? He thought briefly, then asked whether I meant the 'thief of the paintings from Miran'. 'Yes, I did work for Stein once, about 10 years before Lake Karakoshun disappeared.' Kumran was probably referring to Stein's second visit in 1914. With agitation in his voice, he compared the two explorers: 'Etzin was interested in surveying the country, drawing maps, and taking photographs, whereas Stein attempted to find as many objects as he could, and take them away with him. He promised every excavation worker a reward if he found anything. He also took the paintings from the temple in Miran. I helped to wrap statues, coins, written wooden tablets and paintings in cotton and pack them in large padded boxes, which were then taken by camel to Kashgar.'

It was evident that Stein did not enjoy Kumran's approval.

I felt grateful towards this ancient fisherman, for his tale had given me much and his reminiscences of Hedin had helped me to forge a link to my own youthful dreams of the 'wandering lake'. We stood up to leave and Kumran accompanied us through the courtyard to the gate. He kept hold of my hand for a long time and wished me good luck and success for my journey to Loulan. If I should come back to Miran, he added, I must visit him again.

# *T*he Wandering Lake

It was dawn when we left New Miran and headed along an old, rarely used track eastwards in the direction of Dunhuang. Jean-Daniel and I were excited, for we were, at the time, the first Europeans to travel to Loulan since Aurel Stein made excavations there in 1906 and 1914. The area around Loulan and the lake of Lop Nor had been a prohibited military zone since the 1960s, as China's nuclear testing grounds are situated about 145 kilometres north-west of Loulan. Between 1964 and 1980, 21 plutonium and hydrogen bombs were detonated here above ground; from 1975 on, a further 20 underground tests followed, the last one of these was six weeks before our expedition. Exploring the area around Lop Nor up to then had been permitted only in exceptional cases and then only to Chinese archaeologists; on a few occasions Japanese scientists were permitted.

Lop Nor was first mentioned at the time of the Warring States (475–221 BC) and the Western Han (202 BC–AD 9). In the West the Greek geographer, Marinos of Tyre, was the first to speak of Lop Nor towards the first century AD and of the Tarim, which he called Öchardes and Bautisus. His information had come from a merchant named Maes Titianus, who was active in the China trade. Around two millennia later, in 1876, Nikolai Przhevalsky followed the course of the Tarim south-eastwards, starting from Korla, until he came upon the freshwater Lake Karakoshun, which he identified as the mysterious Lop Nor.

His claim was refuted by the geographer Ferdinand von Richthofen (who coined the expression 'Silk Road'), because Przhevalsky's supposed Lop Nor was located one degree further south than Chinese sources indicated and because Chinese sources mentioned a salt lake, whereas Przhevalsky described a freshwater lake. Von Richthofen concluded that Przhevalsky must have discovered a different, newly formed lake, and that the original Lop Nor must be located further north. To this, Przhevalsky raised the objection that there were no more lakes north of Karakoshun.

The young Sven Hedin, who studied under von Richthofen from 1889 to 1892, was eager to test his teacher's theory. In 1896, he followed the Tarim and the Konche Darya as far as the western shore of Lake Karakoshun. The closeness of the lake shore to the rivers as well as conversations with locals led Hedin to assume that Karakoshun could not have been more than 170 years old. Even at this time, Hedin noted the considerable shrinking of the lake. On returning to the Tarim Basin in 1899, he undertook a journey by raft of about 900 kilometres on the Tarim. He noticed that the Kum Darya had also totally dried up. Kum Darya means 'Sand River', and is also known as Kuruk Darya, 'Dry River'. Hedin suggested that the historical course of the Tarim was located here and that the true Lop Nor had been an extension of it. In early 1900, Hedin followed the Kum Darya eastwards and eventually found traces of the ancient Lop Nor. In March of that year, Hedin made his greatest discovery, although it was due, largely, to the mistake of his Uigur guide, Ördek. One evening, it turned out that Ördek had left his spade at the site of the ruins. He returned to fetch it, but got lost in a sandstorm. After wandering blindly in the dark for hours, he found the ruins of Loulan. He reported to Hedin that he had seen several houses in ruins, and 'richly carved planks of wood'. Hedin's water supply was beginning to run out, and the hot summer was approaching, so he resolved to return the following year to 'Ördek's town', which Stein later called 'L.B.' In March 1901, 10 kilometres east of 'Ördek's town', Hedin found the actual garrison town of Loulan, which in 1906 Stein labelled on his map as 'L.A.'.

Hedin realised that the elusive Lop Nor was a 'wandering lake':

> Anyone who has followed the course of the river [Tarim] as far as its dissolution and annihilation understands that its final point, Lop Nor, must be a wandering lake, a lake that periodically migrates from north to south and from south to north, just like the brass weight on the end of an oscillating pendulum, the pendulum in this case being the Tarim.[12]

With the Tarim's change of course shortly before the year 330, Lop Nor lost its water supply and disappeared. Lop Nor had 'wandered' over the centuries from Loulan to the location of Lake Karakoshun.

Having found some marshes of recent origin north-east of Lake Karakoshun, Hedin asserted: 'I am convinced that in some years we shall find the lake back in the place where, according to Chinese reports, it used to be and where, as Richthofen acutely proved in theory, it must in fact have been located.'[13]

Hedin saw his prophecy come true. When he was in Turfan in February 1928, his former guide Tokta Akhun reported to him that the Tarim had for some years been flowing again through its old bed of the Kuruk Darya and that Lop Nor had returned into a depression north-east of Loulan. Hedin at once sent his colleague, Erik Norin, to investigate; Norin confirmed Tokta Akhun's descriptions, and also found a number of small, shallow freshwater lakes in the delta of the new Tarim. Six years later, Hedin set off for the last time on a river journey, allowing himself to drift down the Konche and then the Kuruk Darya, until he reached the new Lop Nor. On the way, he passed the place where the Konche Darya had taken its new course eastwards in 1921 and where the authorities had tried in vain to force the river to return into its old bed by building a dam. This Lop Nor, which came into being in 1921, dried up again due to irrigation, in 1972–73. Since 2004 a new Lop Nor has formed about 20 kilometres north-east of its position in 1921–73.

At first, the track crossed a desolate stony desert – nothing but grey rocks as far as the eye could see. After five hours we left the road and turned north into the bed of the weakly flowing Lachin Darya. At last, towards evening, a narrow ravine opened out and before us spread the bed of what had been Lake Karakoshun. It was here that our new friend Kumran Banyas had lived over 70 years earlier and here that Przhevalsky and Hedin had explored the lake in small boats. Today, there was nothing but an endless desert of shimmering white salt deposits, which indicated danger. Salt comes to the surface of the lake floor when it is washed up by water from below; this means that beneath the stony but thin crust of the lake floor there lies a treacherous marsh.

After a night camped at the shore of the lake, we crept out of our sleeping-bags with the first rays of the sun and, our spirits high, were soon ready to leave. To the north, the salty surface of the lake floor stretched into the distance, while to the east small sand dunes could be made out. Since Loulan was north-east of our campsite, the question as to the best travel route arose. Villayati was convinced that we should drive north over the salt plain and later turn east. The alternative route through the sandy desert and the *yardang* – the chalky deposits several metres in height on the floor of Lop Nor – would, he claimed, have been at least twice as far. This idea seemed too risky to me, for our heavy Unimog might break through the thin salty crust. I preferred the longer route, but Villayati's pride was piqued and he spoke up loudly in favour of the shorter way across the salty plain. To save his 'face', the members of the Chinese team took his side. In the end, against my inner reservations, I allowed myself to be persuaded and we set off in a northerly direction.

We had travelled less than a kilometre when suddenly the left front wheel of our truck broke through the thin salty crust, throwing us against the windscreen. The heavy vehicle was completely stuck. We got out and placed the wooden planks we had with us for such situations under the wheels. The camping table, together with all of our wooden boxes, also had to be sacrificed. The situation was serious – water had already begun to collect around the rear wheels – but in our haste, we made the mistake of leaving the heavy barrels containing water and diesel fuel on the back of the lorry, instead of unloading them to make it as light as possible. Li was able to drive the truck about three metres backwards before the wooden planks broke and the truck began to sink still further into the bog, its engine smoking ominously.

We set to work in silence. First, we unloaded all the baggage, then the 600 litres of diesel and the 500 litres of water. Wang attempted to dig the wheels free, but this proved hopeless – the deeper he dug away the mud, the more water filled the hollow. We grabbed anything we could do without from our camp – camping chairs, blankets, scraps of wood – and wedged them beneath the wheels. Li, with hesitant steps, walked to the driver's cabin and pulled himself through the door, which was now at a worryingly crooked angle. We all knew that this was the last chance to free the truck from the marsh. When Li started the engine, I felt like averting my eyes. The truck reminded me of a scared camel fighting desperately to escape a lingering death. Cautiously, Li accelerated. Nothing happened, except that the camping chairs were crushed and the blankets flung through the air. Li sat down miserably on one of the diesel barrels and fixed the helpless truck with a depressed stare.

We made our assessment of the situation. It was clear that we would not get the truck out without help and the Dunhuang track was over 70 kilometres away. Moreover, Villayati told us, two lorries a week at most drove along it. We had no satellite telephone. Our only alternative was a hike of about 100 kilometres through the desert to the nearest settlement. After years of intensive preparation and so near to Loulan, our dream had suddenly vanished into an unreachable distance.

As we sat wretchedly in the gathering dusk, Villayati suddenly remembered something important. On the eve of our departure from Ruoqiang, he had heard that a Chinese team with a four-wheel-drive truck was travelling along the same stretch of road as we were, to the site of the old Lop Nor, to carry out a meteorological survey. According to Villayati, the truck was due to pass through the narrow gorge of the Lachin Darya that night. We would have to try to intercept it there. This was an unexpected ray of hope, particularly since expeditions only find themselves in that area a couple of times a year. The energetic Wang, to whom the success of the expedition was a question of honour, resolved immediately to set off on foot, which meant a dangerous night walk of five hours through the desert. But this was our only hope. Wang felt responsible for the day's mishap and refused to be accompanied by Jean-Daniel or me. He detailed Villayati to go with him instead. While the two of them filled their rucksacks with water and some food, Jean-Daniel entered our geographical coordinates into his GPS, which he then gave to Wang to enable him to find his way back to us again.

The next morning, Jean-Daniel and I climbed a high hill and desperately scanned the horizon. There was no sign of our two colleagues. After several tense hours I suddenly spied a growing cloud of dust, which could only have been made by a truck. Soon I could make out two dots that appeared to be moving in our direction from the gorge of the Lachin Darya. Two trucks had come to our rescue! As fast as we could, we ran back to the Unimog, and arrived at the same time as the trucks reached the edge of the dangerous salty plain. Wang, dead-tired but beaming, came up to me and told me how they had walked without stopping until three in the morning, when they finally came upon the camp of the Chinese expedition and guided them to us the following morning.

The drivers of the Chinese team were expertly examining the ground and beginning to unload their own heavy baggage, to reduce the risk of breaking through the crust themselves. Then they drove at a snail's pace to the Unimog, stopping at a distance from the site of the accident. Steel wires on the winches of both trucks were then let out to their maximum length and fixed to the Unimog. Now came the moment of truth: would the two relatively light Chinese trucks succeed in pulling the heavy Unimog out of the mud?

Li had already started the motor. The front wheels of the two Chinese trucks began to dig threateningly deep into the ground and the wire cables stretched to the limit. We waited at a prudent distance – and suddenly, our Unimog gave a great bound backwards, and was once more on terra firma. Our saviours left quickly and we waved our thanks to them from beside the rescued truck.

For the next four days, we drove in the direction of Loulan at walking pace, finding our way with the aid of an old map made by Hedin and checking our position with the GPS. Like Ariadne's thread, we carefully entered the points measured along the route to help us find our way back. We drove through sand dunes and *yardangs* up to a metre high, which from a distance resembled the backs of large sharks. Wind erosion had dug long and deep furrows between the *yardangs* and the terrain was so broken up that we were repeatedly forced to explore on foot before proceeding. In one day we covered only 18 kilometres. It became so dry and arid that all life had vanished. The last animal we found, some distance from the shore of the dried-up Karakoshun, was a dead bird. But we could see that there had once been life in the Lop Desert from the large numbers of shells covering the ground – the only evidence to show that the entire desert was once a lake.

As we slowly made our way to Loulan, my mind wandered 2,000 years back in time, to when the Sogdian merchants of the Silk Road plied this same route. To avoid the heat of the day, and to spare the camels, of which there were over 100, the caravans would not travel by day, like us, but at night. Since there were no wells along this section of the road, they carried blocks of ice for water. For every eight camels, there was one camel-driver, who was responsible for his yoked-together animals. Each camel was laden with silk, precious lacquered goods and a new, expensive commodity, paper.

The first real paper suitable for writing was invented at the beginning of the second century AD. It was made from hemp fibre, textile waste or the remnants of fishing-nets. But archaeological finds reveal rough, felt-like papers used for packaging as early as the second century BC. Lighter and simpler to use than wooden tablets or bamboo strips and cheaper than woven silk, this new material became highly desirable.

Starting in Dunhuang, the caravans would often stop for several days in Loulan, to allow their weary camels to regain their strength and sell some of their goods to the administration of the city or to Chinese soldiers stationed there. Many might have visited Loulan's temple to ask Buddha to protect them from the ferocious bandits that plagued their onward route, despite the fact that most caravans were also protected by hired mercenaries armed with lances and crossbows, another Chinese invention.

The mercenaries, like the camel-drivers, would accompany a merchant caravan to Kashgar, nearly 2,000 kilometres from Dunhuang, where the caravan would then regroup and take on supplies. From Kashgar it would push on to the town of Afrasiab – today's Samarkand – in the heart of Sogdia, where any remaining goods would be sold to Persian merchants. This was the end of the line for Sogdian caravans – it was forbidden to travel further into Iran. From the Persians, the Sogdian trader would buy glass objects, gold ornaments and asbestos, which was prized then as a material for candlewicks and even clothing. In late summer the caravan would set off again on its long trek back to Dunhuang. The rhythm of a merchant's life was determined by the seasons. Caravans were only able to travel in autumn and winter; in spring the dreaded sandstorms raged and in summer the heat was too great, even at night.

We soon found it impossible to continue driving through the maze of *yardangs*, which had grown steadily higher and more dense, and so we decided to cover the remaining 25 kilometres to Loulan on foot. Before dawn, the moon lighting our way, we set off, heavily laden. In addition to our photographic equipment, each of us carried water, dried meat, noodle soup and a sleeping-bag – provisions sufficient for four days. We left our tents and the rest of our baggage in the Unimog.

It was an exhausting trek, as the *yardangs* run west to east, whereas we were moving from south to north. We were forced to cross them in their hundreds. After about five hours of trudging, we came upon some Stone Age arrowheads and, soon after that, what used to be an orchard – the first traces of the settlement of Loulan. More than 20 long rows of dried-up apricot trees, probably dating from the fourth century AD, stood before us. There were still some apricot stones lying on the ground. Immediately beyond the orchard, there was a large piece of land dotted with black and red potsherds, some of which had fine geometrical patterns. Some time after midday, Villayati suddenly cried: 'Loulan, Loulan!' In the distance the silhouette of the stupa of Loulan was clearly visible. We were lucky that the stupa could be seen from so far away and that the terrain was flat, since we discovered that Loulan's position was entered differently on Stein's two maps – a discrepancy of nearly 12 kilometres.[14]

Our first exploration of Loulan showed that little had changed there since Stein's visit 80 years earlier. Everything looked just as it had in Stein's old, yellowing photos, of which I had brought a few copies. Goethe's saying came into my mind: 'The earth is the shroud of the world.' Everything organic is transitory and dissolves into small particles that cover the earth. It is the archaeologist who finally dissects this earthen shroud. There were shards of red and grey pottery lying near most of the ruined houses and lightly brushing away sand and rubble, revealed almost perfectly preserved scraps of silk, linen and wool, pieces of felt and leather. We found a number of copper coins with rectangular holes in the middle, although most of them were broken. There were few small coins in use at the time and so amounts of lesser value were created simply by breaking coins.

The small town of Loulan was densely populated, as is evidenced by the poplar pillars that are scattered all around. It is dominated by two buildings, a 12-metre-high tower of clay bricks that Stein interpreted as a stupa and Hedin as a watchtower, and a 12 metre-long brick building, which was most likely the base of the Chinese military commander. It was here that Hedin made one of his most important archaeological finds. In a rubbish-heap, he discovered hundreds of Chinese documents written on wood, paper and silk. It is these documents, along with items found by Stein in his later excavations, that have enabled the history of Loulan to be reconstructed.

The earliest mention of Loulan, in a letter from Motun, ruler of Xiongnu, to the Chinese emperor Wen-Ti, dates from 176 BC. In it, Motun exalts the victory of his general over the Yüeh-chih and the conquest of Loulan, together with 28 other states. However, the citizens of Loulan misused its strategic location on the Central Silk Road to plunder Chinese trading caravans, which led to a Chinese reprisal under General Cao Po-nu in 108 BC. When Loulan once again turned to the Xiongnu, China sent a second punitive expedition in 77 BC, installing a Chinese commander. The final flourishing of Loulan began when General So Man assumed office around the year AD 260. The unknown author of the so-called 'Classic of the Waters' reported: 'So Man took over the office of the general; at the head of 1,000 soldiers he came to Loulan, in order to set up an agricultural colony there. He built a white house.'[15] This 'white house' is no doubt identical with the large clay-brick building in Loulan, which was once whitewashed with chalk.

The small garrison town appears to have been soon forgotten, for the last dated document, of AD 330, was still written in the name of the last Western Jin emperor, whose rule had ended in 316. So by 330 Loulan must already have been isolated from the central government for 14 years. Around this time, Loulan was abandoned, most likely due to the drying-up of the Kuruk Darya and of Lop Nor. The military garrison was then moved about 55 kilometres southwards, to Haitou, called by Stein 'L.K.'

*   *   *

That evening, after hours exploring every inch of Loulan, we sat around a small campfire on the edge of the ruins. On the horizon glowed an intense red sunset, which turned gradually to violet. Everyone in the team was in high spirits – in spite of all the obstacles, we had reached Loulan. In the features of the indefatigable Wang, in particular, satisfaction but also relief could be read. Sheng, too, radiated contentment, for now he was a member of the very exclusive circle of Chinese archaeologists who had visited both Niya and Loulan.

I was happy at having fulfilled the dream of my youth; the 27-year wait had been worth it. But I was also melancholy, for the following days meant bidding farewell to the desert and its treasures and to our Chinese colleagues, who had become friends.

# $S$keletons in the Sand

It was October 1998 and we were gathered near the ruins of the remote fortress of Mazar Tagh, which had once lain on a caravan route between the Northern and Southern Silk Roads, for an expedition into the heart of the Taklamakan Desert. Our group included a photographer, Urs Möckli, who was to prove an excellent navigator; a second navigator, Ernst Rüegg, who in his spare time goes in search of water veins with his divining-rod as a service to architects; and a Norwegian cameraman, Jon Jerstad, who was documenting the expedition on film for a German TV channel. On the Chinese side was Wu, our interpreter, who had also organised the expedition. Last but not least were a Chinese cook, three Uigur camel-drivers and 15 well-fed camels.

Our goal was the vanished oasis town of Dandan Oilik, which had never relaxed its hold on me since I had devoured Sven Hedin's book *Through Asia* over 30 years before. Hedin had discovered the ruins of the town on 24 January 1896, thanks to the help of two Uigur hunters. Stein later set off into the Taklamakan Desert on the trail of Hedin, mapped Dandan Oilik and excavated several Buddhist shrines. Finds of ancient Chinese documents made it clear that the town had been sacked by Tibetan troops by AD 768 and was finally abandoned in 790.

The last people to reach Dandan Oilik before us had done so in 1928: the German Emil Trinkler and the Swiss Walter Bosshard. They recorded their departure from Dandan in the following words: 'On 25 March the camel-bells sounded for the last time in this ancient settlement. Desert peace reigned again over the logs and debris. Who will be the next European to come here?'[16] Chinese archaeologists believed it impossible to find the town, since it was covered by sand dunes, and so it would be quite an accomplishment if we managed to rediscover it.

Our camels were laden with over 1.7 tons of material, including 750 litres of water, which was for human consumption only. The animals would have to make do with the salty water that we hoped to find in the desert, as the water table is only a few yards deep. Our food supplies were supplemented with two sheep and a few hens. We had wrapped the water canisters in white cloth to reflect the sunlight and protect them from the heat of the sun and, before we set off, checked each carefully to ensure they were all full. In April 1895, about 180 kilometres west of Mazar Tagh, Sven Hedin had ordered the leader of his caravan to load enough water for a 10-day trek through the desert. However, Hedin never checked to make sure his instructions had been carried out – an omission that proved fatal. The leader of the caravan thought he would be able to find water in the desert and only filled their containers with water for four days. When Hedin discovered this two days into their journey, he made his second mistake: instead of turning back, he allowed himself to be persuaded by the assurances of the caravan leader and continued as planned. Two of the five men on the expedition and all but one of the camels paid for this with their lives, dying of thirst. Hedin and two camel-drivers narrowly escaped the same fate.

Our camels lumbered grumpily into motion. We would walk for the duration of the journey and only loaded each camel with 120 kilos of baggage as the terrain – huge, soft sand dunes – would have exhausted them otherwise. I was fascinated by the camels which, with their disproportionately long necks, reminded me of dinosaurs. They seemed to have come to life from the famous Gothic tapestries of the Apocalypse of St John at Angers, which I had seen as a boy and which had made a powerful impression on me.

We crossed the dried-up bed of the Khotan Darya, which at that point carries water only every few years. Mazar Tagh slowly vanished beyond the horizon behind us. Our trek into the unknown had begun. We were physically in very good shape and our mood was optimistic, though we had no idea whether we would find Dandan Oilik. We started where most would have stopped.

By the evening of the first leg of the journey, the camel-drivers had become uneasy. We had so far left them in ignorance about the goal of our expedition, concerned that if they had known they might not have come at all. So now with their camels – their sole possessions – they were to follow four Europeans to a city in ruins, of which they had no knowledge. When we broke this news to them their leader, Ibrahim, was horrified. He became angry and furiously hissed at me: 'You Europeans only spoke of the "normal" desert trek from

Mazar Tagh to the hamlet of Tunguz Basti so we left our spades by the well on that route. How can we dig for water for our camels without spades? We have never heard of these ruins and you do not know where they are. Tomorrow we shall turn back!'

I tried to calm Ibrahim down by telling him that we had two spades and that Ernst could find water with his divining rod. I assured him that if any camel died we would pay him twice its value and that our GPS would prevent us from getting lost. The Uigurs debated beside the campfire for hours, keeping us on tenterhooks and trying our patience. Wu began to taunt them: 'Are you more afraid in your own familiar desert than the long-nosed Europeans, to whom it is strange? Are you men or mice?!'

This had the desired effect. Their pride piqued, they agreed to continue, on condition that they could turn back as soon as the water supplies sank below 300 litres.

The next morning I reduced the water ration from five to four litres per person per day. I didn't want our stay in Dandan Oilik to be cut short by a lack of water if the search took longer than planned. We were hoping to reach the ruins in six to seven days but thirst would be our constant companion. Our mouths and throats already felt sticky and rough. I began to entertain fantasies of a glass of cool, sparkling beer.

The only things we had to help us in the search for Dandan Oilik were the maps of Sven Hedin and Aurel Stein, who had carried out excavations there in the winter of 1900–1. I knew from experience how inaccurate such old maps are, where deviations of five kilometres or more are the rule. I was also concerned that, in a sea of undulating sand dunes, we might easily fail to see the ruins and pass them by if they happened to be beyond the high crest of a dune. We entered Stein's cartographic data as a guide into the GPS and hoped that it would take us near enough to Dandan Oilik so that we would be able to see it from a distance.

All of us except the camel-drivers advanced separately, each on the crest of a different hill. We could, however, not afford to lose sight of one another. Since the desert swallowed up all sounds, calling or shouting for someone who had become lost would be futile. As long as the weather stayed clear, anyone who did get lost would have the chance of finding and following the tracks of the camels; but the dreaded sandstorms, which can blow up without warning, obliterate even the largest hoof prints in minutes and reduce visibility to a few yards.

The structure of our days was strictly regimented. We rose at 6.30 a.m. in bitter cold, struck the tents and enjoyed a breakfast of unleavened bread, fried eggs, tinned meat, an apple and coffee. Each of us was given a litre of water for his water bottle for the day. Loading the animals took an hour and was carried out in darkness. By the time the sun rose at 8.30, the caravan was ready to leave. Whereas earlier on we had endeavoured to warm our bodies with hot coffee, now the sun gave us warmth, caressing our cold skins with its warm rays.

The distance to be covered each day was 20 kilometres as the crow flies but we avoided the highest dunes, so that we were actually walking up to 35 kilometres a day. The first three hours were usually quite pleasant, but after that the sun began to burn mercilessly. Its rays, which were gently warming a few hours before, were now piercingly hot. There was no escaping them for a moment, no shade anywhere. In such an oven, you feel like tearing all your clothes off, but the threat of dehydration and the burning sun prevent you from doing so. During the unbearable midday heat, where temperatures reached 50 degrees, the caravan rested for a full hour (still in the blazing sun), and we refreshed ourselves with juicy melons. The Taklamakan has become so hostile to life that no permanent existence is possible there for either humans or animals. We threw our melon peels in the sand – and even an hour later, not so much as an ant had appeared to feed on them. Not even scorpions can survive. In the coming weeks, we did not encounter a single human being. As Urs aptly remarked: 'Compared to the Taklamakan the Sahara is overpopulated.'

We camped each day at 6.30 in the evening. In spite of our exhaustion and a desire to collapse where we stood, we had to unload the camels and put up the tents quickly, before night fell. Even when that was finished, there were other things that needed attention: puncturing the blood-filled blisters on our feet, cleaning the sand off the cameras, lighting the fire. The cook would also be busy; a sheep bleating in panic would be grabbed, its head turned towards Mecca, and with a muttered prayer, its throat slit.

At night the sky full of twinkling stars was an indescribable sight. The absence of artificial light showed the Milky Way with amazing clarity and shooting stars enlivened the scene. Apart from the quiet noises of the camp, the surrounding desert was utterly silent. The peace and distant sea of light above me aroused such a feeling of security that I preferred to sleep in the open air outside the tent. The desert night raises intangible questions and inspires a deep sense of humility. Man may be the pinnacle of creation on earth but in relation to the endless galaxies a desert sky contains, we are nothing but stardust.

Although gigantic processes like stellar explosions and the movements of comets happen in the cosmos, observed from a distance it gives the impression of perfect order. Maybe such considerations led to both the birth of religious notions and the beginnings of scientific law. It is perhaps no coincidence that the great monotheistic religions were born in desert-like regions.

For my body, walking up the steep dunes was torment. I took three steps forward and slid back two. But to the spirit, the desert bestows an unimaginable sense of freedom. Everyday problems lose their importance and an immeasurably wide horizon opens up. Anything not essential to life becomes superfluous. The desert makes it clear to me to what an extent human life in cities, with its duties, rules and prohibitions, forces us into a Procrustean bed.[17] All the things we are supposed to do, are obliged to do, or are not allowed to do impose on us a straitjacket of norms. If, like the victims of Procrustes, we are too tall, we are cut down; if too short, we are stretched to uniform size. The compulsions of the current norms pervert us into false, reduced versions of ourselves, into bonsai people. But isn't it necessary to swim upstream if we want to reach the source?

This was pertinently expressed by a Christian hermit in Egypt in the fourth century: 'The time is coming when humanity will turn mad; and when they see someone who is not, they will abuse him, saying: "You must be crazy because you are not like us!"'[18] The experience of liberation in the desert leaves its mark on the spirit: many desert travellers report leaving the desert as different people from who they were when they entered it. Wilfred Thesiger, one of the greatest desert explorers of the twentieth century, confessed:

> No man can live [in the desert] and emerge unchanged. He will carry, however faint, the imprint of the desert, the brand which marks the nomad; and he will have within him the yearning to return, either weak or insistent, according to his nature. For this cruel landscape can cast a spell which no temperate climate can match.[19]

The desert is cruel. It exposes our pretensions and denials and forces us to confront who we really are and what we can do. It is wrong to think there is nothing in the desert, for in it we find ourselves.

When trekking in the desert, there is no avoiding yourself or the other members of the expedition. Strengths and weaknesses become mercilessly apparent. Disputes concerning the length of the exhausting stages of the journey or the time of departure are inevitable. Yet the space in the desert is so vast that conflicts literally dissipate in the sand, and the warmth-giving campfire rapidly restores a mood of reconciliation.

After a march of four days, the progress of our caravan slowed down because the camels were thirsty. A laden camel covering long distances in difficult terrain needs water every four to five days. The animals had now become irritable, for they could hear the water splashing in the canisters they were carrying. When we unloaded the canisters in the evening, they dashed their heads against them furiously. When the cook was about to open a canister, the frantic animals besieged him. The camel-drivers were also uneasy and insisted that we break off the expedition and sacrifice the water reserves for their animals. We absolutely had to find water, but where were we to dig? The camel-drivers had no idea. In this critical situation, Ernst proved himself as a water-diviner. He searched for a long, tense hour with his plastic divining-rod, conjuring the water in Swiss: 'Water, water, where are you? The camels are thirsty. Give me a sign, quickly!'

He worked himself into a trance and cursed the concealed ground water, until we began to fear for his sanity. Then, in a small hollow, he at last signalled that he had found water and the sceptical camel-drivers began to dig. At a depth of three metres, the walls of the sandy hole took on a dark colour. The animals, which just before had been bellowing wildly, formed a circle around the damp hole and stared down into it with hopeful eyes. The drivers continued to dig by the bleak light of the moon. Finally, at four metres, one of them dipped a bucket into the hole and it slowly filled with very brackish water. It looked barely drinkable, even for camels, but they downed it with relish. The drivers continued to work in relays until dawn, so that each camel finally got 25 litres of water.

The next day we made a macabre discovery. Three human skeletons, their bones bleached white by the sun, lay before us, presumably exposed by a sandstorm. From a distance we had seen gleaming white objects, which turned out to be their smoothly polished skulls. Red potsherds lay beside them. Who were these people? Inhabitants of Dandan? Lost travellers? Treasure-seekers? Although it was tempting to stop and start searching the area more closely we decided to continue.

We left the three skeletons, but our minds remained with them. We were torn between feelings of excitement at the prospect of nearing Dandan Oilik and dull fear. We did not speak of our personal anxieties, but only of the fear of not finding what we sought. My own mortality in this unforgiving desert had been brought home to me, but I forced myself through it.

If our calculations were correct, we would reach Dandan Oilik the following day. I was tired and was lagging more than a kilometre behind Ernst and Urs, who were leading the caravan that day. Suddenly they stopped, stood still, and in the distance I could make out that they were gesticulating wildly. Had they discovered something? Hope gave my weary legs new energy and I hurried to join them. Silently but with a meaningful look, Urs handed me the binoculars. I could see some slim wooden pillars sticking up out of the sand. After walking for a few more hours, the ruins of a city were spread out before us. We had rediscovered the vanished city of Dandan Oilik! Like Sven Hedin a century before me, I was simply overwhelmed.

> Who could have imagined that in the interior of the dread Desert of Gobi . . . actual cities slumbered under the sand, cities wind-driven for thousands of years, the ruined survivors of a once-flourishing civilization? And yet there stood I amid the wreckage and devastation of an ancient people, within whose dwellings none had ever entered save the sand-storm . . . there stood I like the prince in the enchanted wood, having awakened to new life the city which had slumbered for a thousand years, or at any rate rescued the memory of its existence from oblivion.[20]

# $D$iscoveries in Dandan Oilik

On leaving Dandan Oilik on 25 March 1928, Trinkler and Bosshard had buried, near a ruined temple, an empty tin can in which they had placed their visiting cards with the wry message: 'To the poor fellow who trusts that he will find something here.'[21] They were mistaken; our team was to make some incredibly rich discoveries.

Inside the ruins of the city, we initially oriented ourselves with the help of Stein's plan. Although this was almost a century old, little had changed. We found 13 of the 15 ruins recorded by Stein, as well as three additional ones. A low sand dune divided the city into a northern and southern half, while a ditch, presumably a former river bed, separated the western part from the eastern.

As with other ancient settlements in the Taklamakan, it was striking how few ruins remained. Most buildings were simple clay structures, which had long since decomposed. Only the more elaborate houses, shrines and monasteries had wooden supports and rough walls made with mortar. Half-timbered buildings of this kind were more suited to withstand the eroding power of the wind than were simple houses of clay. At least 10 of the 16 ruins identified by us were Buddhist shrines of one or two storeys, which were once painted inside and out. Inside a small internal room there would have been, more than a millennium ago, a large statue of Buddha on a plinth. In view of the numerous temples in Dandan Oilik, I am convinced that it was primarily a place of pilgrimage and only secondarily an urban settlement. The city was not on any main travelling route, but on a road connecting those that ran along the Keriya Darya and the Khotan Darya.

As to the date of Dandan Oilik's foundation, we are groping in the dark. Dated literary and numismatic finds have been traced to the seventh and eighth centuries AD, but some of the works of art discovered were created

**31** Bönpo pilgrims on the sixty-kilometre pilgrimage route around Mount Bön Ri, Tibet

**32** Young Bönpo monks in the monastery of Nangshig, Aba, eastern Tibet

**33** The Bön monastery Pa Lha Puk, founded in the eleventh century AD, central Tibet

**34** Representation of Sati Ersang, one of the oldest Bön murals in Tibet, Pa Lha Puk monastery

**35** Inside a *gyodar*, a stupa-shaped arrangement of hundreds of prayer flags, Amdo, eastern Tibet

**36** The Bönpo physician monk of Nangshig monastery, with Therese Weber and the author

37  Dancers with pierced
cheeks at the Lu Rol
ritual, Tewo, eastern Tibet

38  A richly ornamented
Khampa woman at the
Horse Festival of Litang,
eastern Tibet

**39** A Khampa wearing the pelt of a snow leopard, Litang, eastern Tibet

**40** The Horse Festival of Litang

**41** A proud Tibetan Golok nomad, eastern Tibet

**42** Appliqué *thangka* of Samtenling monastery, displayed at the New Year's Festival in Aba, eastern Tibet

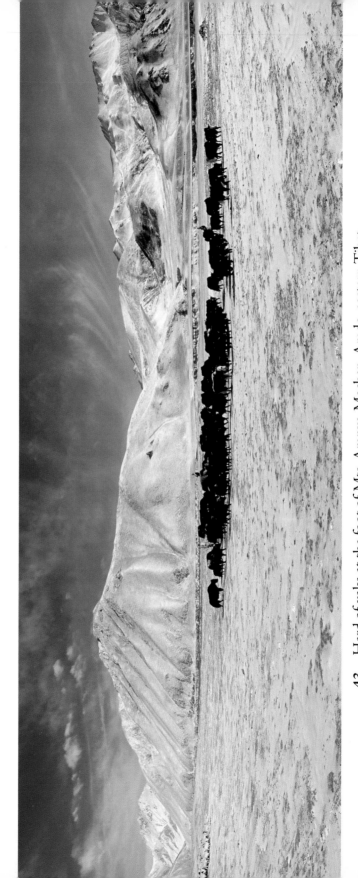

43   Herd of yaks at the foot of Mts. Amnye-Machen, Amdo, eastern Tibet

**44** Golok Tibetans throwing *lungta* papers into a sacrificial fire at Nangshig monastery, eastern Tibet

**45** The Taklamakan Desert, north-western China – 'Once you enter it, you never come out'

**46** Imam Sheikh Abd al-Bakr in front of the mausoleum of Imam Ja'far al-Sadiq, Kabakasgan, Taklamakan

**47** Traditional silk making in Khotan, Taklamakan

48   A ruin in Niya, Taklamakan, first–fourth century AD

49   Kumran Banyas, aged 108, talks of his meetings with Sven Hedin and Aurel Stein, Miran, Taklamakan

**50**  Ruins in Loulan – former archives, the seat of government and, on the right, the stupa, third–fourth century AD, Lop Nor Desert

**51**  Uigur camel-breeder, southern Taklamakan

52  The author's caravan on the way to Dandan Oilik, Taklamakan

53  The newly discovered Buddhist shrine D 13 at Dandan Oilik

**54** Eighth-century murals of gods and goddesses in Dandan Oilik, f.l.t.r.
Weshparkar, Hariti, Zurvan

**55** Paper amulet in the Khotanese language and Brahmi script, eighth century
AD, Dandan Oilik

56 Star orbits at night over the stupa of Endere, Taklamakan

57 A young falconer, Taklamakan

**58** The Bronze Age necropolis of Xiaohe, c. 1800 BC, Lop Nor Desert

**59** Crossing an unexplored part of the Lop Nor Desert

**60**  Ruin L.M. ii with four
pillar bases, first–fourth century
AD, Lop Nor Desert

**61**  Bronze coins discovered in
ruin L.M. ii, Lop Nor Desert

**62**  Beacon tower, second
century BC –fourth century AD,
L.R. i, Lop Nor Desert

earlier, between the fifth and the eighth centuries. What is certain is that Dandan Oilik was a prosperous city up to the middle of the eighth century AD, although it began to decline from 756 onwards, when Tibet invaded the Tarim Basim for the second time. At the same time, the rebellion of An Lushan was threatening the ruling Chinese Tang Dynasty. To quell the revolt, most Chinese troops were recalled from the Tarim Basin to central China. In a letter dated 768 AD, addressed to the King of Khotan, the Chinese military commander complains about pillaging gangs of robbers – probably Tibetans – and asks for the suspension of forced labour. The wealthy inhabitants had apparently already left their city and found refuge in the vicinity of Khotan. Only the monks, the lower strata of society and some military personnel had remained behind.

The latest date found among the Chinese documents of Dandan is 790; one year later, Kucha, the headquarters of the Chinese military administration that had remained in the Tarim Basin, capitulated to the Tibetans, thereby putting an end to almost a thousand years of Chinese presence in this part of Turkestan. Encroaching sands, political unrest and waning population figures soon engendered catastrophic consequences. The last inhabitants left the oasis and the rich and fertile settlement soon became swallowed by the desert.

Such disasters were often worked into myths, in which the event was reinterpreted as divine punishment. Such a myth, which reminds us of Sodom and Gomorrah, fits the decline of Dandan perfectly, and is told by the famous wandering monk, Xuanzang. A Buddhist saint was refused drinking water by the citizens of Ho lao lo chia, he cursed the city and while the inhabitants mocked him, 'sand began to rain from the skies and continued for seven days and nights until the whole of the buildings were buried.'

In all of the ruins at Dandan Oilik, we found innumerable red, grey and black ceramic shards; in some places they lay so densely that they took on the appearance of an oriental carpet. We found millstones more than a metre in diameter, combs made of wood, horn and bone, a pointed Phrygian cap made of felt, three leather-soled shoes woven of thick woollen yarn, an intact ceramic jug, two wooden gateway arch beams and numerous fragments of bronze coins. As in Mazar Tagh and Niya, we also found slag in a kiln, a by-product of iron-smelting.

Since Aurel Stein had often made his most illuminating finds – written documents – in ancient garbage-heaps, we directed our attention to one, more than a millennium old, which was close to the ruins of small houses. There we found a well-preserved coin from the Kaiyuan period (AD 713–41) of Emperor Xuanzong; small pieces of material woven of silk and inscribed; and then something rare: a crumpled-up paper document, covered on both sides with delicate writing. I later had this document deciphered by a professor at Harvard University, who told me that the language is Middle Khotanese, the script italic Brahmi. The text is written as a dialogue between the Buddha and seven snake spirits, called nagas, which reveals that the document is an amulet against sickness. While the role of nagas as tutelary spirits is known from documents in other languages, this is the first and only example in the entire Khotanese literature. The fact that the names of the seven snake spirits are listed is also unique.[22]

Following this exciting find, we searched for a site that was mentioned by both Hedin and Stein. The former wrote: 'By pure chance the men's spade unearthed a number of gypsum figures in relief, each from four to eight inches high and flat on the back, showing that they had served as wall decorations. They represented images of Buddha, some sitting, some standing.'[23] And indeed, thanks to Stein's map, only a few centimetres under the sand we discovered dozens of such stucco figures dating from the sixth to the eighth century AD. I felt a curious affinity with my predecessors Hedin and Stein, who had gazed on the same figures a century earlier.

'Shall we take a few?' asked one of my colleagues. It was tempting, but we had agreed to leave any objects that we found at the site and fill in all our excavations before we left. We would give their exact GPS coordinates to archaeologists in Urumqi so that they would be able find them again later.

We began excavating a small temple in the former monastery of Hukuo but it was almost completely buried by a sand dune. We succeeded in finding the paintings of small seated Buddhas described by Stein on the inside of the southern wall, but the sand above continually slid down and in again.

Excavating Hukuo monastery was a hopeless task, unless we were to remove all the sand so we turned our attention to another group of ruins. In a temple there, Stein had discovered the unique clay statue of the Buddhist tutelary god Lokapala Vaishravana standing on a dwarf, lying on the ground, undamaged except for its head. Vaishravana was the Buddhist adaptation of the Hindu deity Kubera, the god of wealth. Vaishravana was worshipped as the cosmic guardian in the north, and as the protector of traders and also of the kingdom of Khotan to which Dandan Oilik belonged. Such adaptations of deities from other religions marked the assimilative power of Buddhism, which sees 'foreign' gods as culturally conditioned, differing visualisations of identical truths and concepts. The sturdily built dwarf represented malicious forces that can be temporally subjugated, but never definitely defeated. This combination of the protective deity standing on a demonic figure that can at any time try to shake him off is quite ambivalent.

Just beside Vaishravana, Stein found a painting of a lightly clad woman, to whose left thigh a cupid is clinging, bathing in a pool between lotus blossoms. Beside the pool, a horseman was visible. Aurel Stein connected the curious scene with a legend told by the pilgrim monk Xuanzang, according to which the widow of a river god, thirsting for love, dried out the Khotan River, which was essential to the survival of the oasis city. When the King of Khotan besought her to allow the water of the river to flow again, she insisted: 'Not before you give me a man!' For this, a minister sacrificed himself, riding into the river, whereupon the goddess drew him down into her subterranean palace.

From Stein's ground plan, we worked out where to dig. After four hours, we met with bitter disappointment. We had been digging in the right place, but the large figure was destroyed and the dwarf's head was missing. Of the painted naked goddess, only traces of the belly were visible. Evidently, the temple had been reopened following Stein's discovery.

Shortly before sunset, I was sitting deep in thought beside a few short wooden stakes sticking out of the sand, not far from the vandalised shrine. Absent-mindedly, I swept the sand away with my hand between two stakes and felt a harder object beneath. I continued to remove sand, until I suddenly unearthed a clay wall covered in traces of white paint. I remembered that murals were always painted on whitewashed walls. Some careful work with a brush indeed turned out to reveal murals. I was even more excited, since this ruin was missing from Aurel Stein's map but the diminishing light forced me to stop and I returned reluctantly to the camp.

On my return, I found out how rapidly situations and moods can change. Urs and Wu came to meet me with worried looks on their faces. 'The camels have gone crazy with thirst; they attack the cook as soon as he opens a water canister.'

The camel-drivers had returned, ill-tempered, from a long search for water without success. They were now crouching on the ground and the camels, their front legs tied tightly together to prevent them from running away, were bellowing furiously.

Ibrahim stood up and came over to me, his eyes lowered. 'Tomorrow we will give the camels half of the water reserve, then set off at once for the Keriya River, which is three days' march away. You Europeans can do what you like.'

I could not bear to leave Dandan Oilik without further excavating the highly promising murals I had found earlier, but we could not let the camels leave. We racked our brains, worked out alternative plans, only to reject them again at once. It suddenly occurred to me that 98 years earlier, Stein had reported having watered the camels somewhere north of the city. I frantically scoured Stein's map and found, in a hollow two kilometres north of our camp, the entry 'well'. Ernst's skills were once again called for. The Uigurs, who by now had supreme confidence in his powers, jumped up, undid the animals' bonds and shortly before midnight set off together with Ernst and Urs. Three hours later, Ernst and Urs returned, happy. For the second time, Ernst had saved the expedition from turning back. Not far from the place marked by Stein, he had found plenty of good water for the desperate camels.

In the morning, our team once again united, we continued to excavate what turned out to be a temple. We numbered it D 13. Among its murals we found not only the feet of three large standing Buddhas and the symbolic representation of the 1,000 Buddhas sitting in meditation, sketched with stencils and then painted in colour, but also rare motifs, such as images of worshippers bearing in their hands open lotus blossoms or buds. These are symbols of the purity of the spirit in a world of sin, which also expresses the wish of Buddhist believers to be reborn in Buddha Amitabha's paradise Sukhavati. We uncovered a white divinity seated on a red camel, a row of riders dressed in white, seated on piebald horses, and two striking groups of three deities each. I immediately realised the unusual importance of this discovery: these motifs had never before been found on the Southern Silk Road as murals, but only on wooden votive tablets.

On later analysis of the figures I became convinced that they represented Sogdian deities adopted from Buddhism. The orientation of my search towards the Sogdian pantheon was also based on Aurel Stein's discovery of documents in Chinese and Kharoshthi, which not only mentioned Sogdian traders in Dandan, but also indicated that in the last decades of the eighth century AD one of the political leaders of Dandan was a Sogdian. He had the title of sabao, which was usually given in the Chinese Empire to the head of a local community of Sogdian traders who organised his community's civic and religious life and applied the law when necessary.

While the Sogdian language, culture and religion were of Iranian nature, the Sogdian religion did not strictly follow the organised state religion of Zoroastrianism as was the case in Sassanian Iran. Sogdian Zoroastrianism included several pre-Zoroastrian, more ancient Iranian deities and favoured an obvious worship of images that orthodox Zoroastrianism frowned upon. The Sogdians represented many of their deities using visual forms adopted from Buddhism and Hindu deities. The cultural realm of the Sogdians, who were organised as independent city-states on the territory of present Uzbekistan and western Kyrgyzstan, was twice confronted with strong cultural influence from the Indian subcontinent: first during the Kidarite era (fifth century AD) and second during the Hephtalite period (early sixth century AD).

I believe that the white deity riding on a red camel represents the Sogdian god of victory, Washagn (called Veretragna in Iran). In the centre of both triads of deities sits a female deity holding one or two babies in her arms. She is Hariti, who in Buddhist mythology was originally a child-devouring ogress and then was converted by Buddha into a child-protecting goddess. Her cult expanded from India to Central Asia, China and Japan. Within a Sogdian context, Hariti was probably associated with the goddess of fertility, Anahita.

A three-headed deity on the left of the first triad possibly represents the Sogdian wind god, Weshparkar, in the shape of the Hindu god, Shiva. Weshparkar was a Sogdian adaptation of the ancient Aryan god Vayu who, like Shiva, appeared as creator and destroyer of life. In line with Hindu tradition, Weshparkar/Maheshvara is shown in the mural with his mount, Nandi, a black bull. On the right side of this triad, another three-headed deity who holds the sun and the moon in his hands could represent Zurvan, the Sogdian god of time and fate, who also appears in the form of the Hindu god, Brahma.

In the second triad, the left male deity is again three-headed; he holds arrows and a bow as well as a cockerel. Close to his left knee stands a peacock. This bird indicates that the god is the Sogdian god of victory Washagn, but this time in the form of the Indian war god Kartikeya. On the right side finally sits a boar-headed medicine deity called a 'Graha'.

The discovery of this temple was of the utmost importance. No murals had so far been discovered in the Taklamakan that so clearly showed this fusion of Sogdian, Buddhist and Hindu elements. The paintings from the eighth century AD reveal that the spread of Indian influence percolated through Sogdia before reaching the Tarim Basin. Although I was sure that further excavations would unearth many more finds, we had to leave Dandan Oilik as our supplies were dwindling. We covered our discoveries with sand and, under a darkening sky full of the promise of a sandstorm to further erase our presence, we readied ourselves to leave. It was as if we were preparing a new burial for the discovered temple.

# Black Hurricane

We mounted our 'ships of the desert' before sunrise and rode as quickly as possible eastwards across 90-metre-high dunes to the river Keriya Darya, which we reached on the evening of the following day. It lay before us, wide and sluggish, like an overfed snake. Ibrahim led the caravan across a ford. I wanted to photograph the camels reflected in the water from the river but soon got stuck up to my knees in clinging mud. With every attempt to free myself from its embrace, I dug myself in deeper. Urs struggled out to me, took my photo equipment, money and passport and carried them to the shore. While Ernst and the three camel-drivers looked on and Jon recorded the spectacle on film, Urs returned and ended up getting stuck too. A few Uigurs had gathered on the bank and were casting uneasy glances in our direction. I shouted to Wu to make a long rope with the cords used to tie the baggage onto the camels, throw me one end and tie the other to a camel, so it could pull me out. But Ibrahim shook his head; he thought this would take too long, by which time I would have drowned.

I had sunk up to my waist in muddy water and could barely move. Images of a film from 1927, in which one of Sven Hedin's camels got stuck in a ford and drowned in the mud, flashed before me. Finally, four of the Uigurs came to the rescue. They freed Urs and then hurried to me and circled round, taking care not to stop in one place. While the locals pulled me by the arms, Urs dug my legs out, first the right, then the left. Exhausted, he then staggered back to shore. The Uigurs pulled until they had finally freed me and dragged me to the shore, where they dropped me like a sack of flour. Thanks to them I was spared the irony of drowning in the desert.

Two days later we set out from our camp at the oasis of Tunguz Basti on a seven-hour camel ride to the antique fortress of Karadong, which lies on an ancient route that once linked the Northern and Southern Silk Roads. Both the camels and the three drivers continually wandered from the track, the camels because they loved to eat fresh tamarisk leaves, and the drivers because they were looking for the *dayong* root, an aphrodisiac much sought-after in China (a root could be sold in Yütian for 30 to 35 renminbi).

We reached Karadong in the late afternoon and climbed a small sandhill. Putting up the tents could wait. From here, we could see the ruins of the 2,000-year-old fortress spread before us in the soft evening light. As we were photographing the scene we noticed that the camels were huddled unusually close together and alternately bellowing loudly and sticking their muzzles in the sand. Ibrahim called to Wu excitedly: 'A hot wind is coming!'

Sure enough, the horizon had begun to take on a poisonous-looking yellow-green tinge and the sky darkened dramatically. We hurriedly packed up our cameras and ran to the camels, who were now kneeling on the ground and laying their long necks on each other. Before we could unload them, the storm hit us like a punch of heat and sand, throwing us to the ground. It was impossible to stand upright. We crawled to the camels and huddled close to their huge bulks, trying to shield ourselves from the worst of it.

It was a *kara buran*, a black hurricane. In an instant, day had turned to night and it became bitterly cold. Wu crawled to the blankets that were used as camel saddles and distributed them among us; in seconds he was completely covered in sand, almost unrecognisable. Four hours later and the storm was still raging ferociously. We had no choice but to lie where we were, huddled in the sand, our stomachs empty and our throats parched. Sand covered us thickly like a shroud. I could well understand how people thought the untameable force of the *kara buran* was alive, the work of demonic spirits. Travellers who lost contact with their caravans in such sandstorms had little hope for survival. These black hurricanes obliterate tracks in minutes and remodel the landscape. New sand dunes form, a tamarisk tree that was a vital landmark is hidden; a buried skeleton suddenly shows itself to the living.

In the early hours of the morning, the sandstorm blew itself out and gradually subsided. At the first rays of dawn we rose and set about getting rid of the sand. It was everywhere: in the baggage, in our hair, eyes, noses and mouths; even our teeth grated with it. But now the air was clear, as after a cleansing thunderstorm and soon we set off to explore Karadong. By far the largest ruin was a fortress or a fortified caravanserai of the time of the Later Han Dynasty (AD 24–220). On the clay walls of the fortress there would once have stood numerous wooden structures plastered with clay. As in Dandan Oilik, I was confronted here with traces of vandalism: one of the great cross-beams of the eastern gate had been burned. Inside the fortress were the ruins of a large two-storey dwelling-house.

Hedin reached Karadong in 1896, the first foreigner to do so, according to local accounts. On his return, he described several Buddhist wall paintings, but they seemed to have disappeared when Aurel Stein explored Karadong nearly a decade later. The mystery of where the paintings had gone was solved 100 years later when the Uigur archaeologist, Idriss Abduressul, came upon two small temple ruins that had been exhumed from the desert by a recent sandstorm. Here Idriss found the paintings that Hedin had discovered. They date from the third century AD and, like those of Miran, are among the oldest extant Buddhist murals in the world. To the north of these two little temples huge sand dunes have prevented any more excavations.

The expedition was drawing to an end and a feeling of anticlimax had settled over the group. There was little motivation to visit Endere, the last place we had planned to explore. Each of us was thinking out a plan of his own. Urs wished to take more photographs in Khotan, Jon wanted to record traditional Uigur music in Yutian, and Ernst to stroll through a bazaar. At Tunguz Basti, we spent the night in the house of one of our camel-drivers, who was also the chief of the oasis. On the expedition, he had been a modest man, under the command of Ibrahim, but at home he was transformed. Neighbours from all around flocked to the house and greeted him respectfully. He received them at the far end of a long room, where he sat elevated on the *kang*, while the guests squatted on the floor in two long rows. The scene was almost ceremonial – subjects paying homage to their ruler.

In the evening, however, the real 'rulers' drove up in three brand-new Toyota Land Cruisers. It was a 10-man delegation from the provincial capital Urumqi, ostensibly come to investigate the living conditions of the villagers. The chief had no choice but to entertain them at his expense, with a freshly slaughtered sheep and great quantities of cheap spirits. The following morning, all the members of the delegation were presented with skins, wool, *dayong* and strong drink. Ibrahim told me angrily that another group would follow in a few months' time – a real plague of locusts. Soon after, we said goodbye to the camel-drivers and to the camels that had served us so well, and we set off in two jeeps that had arrived punctually the day before. We drove along a sandy track beside the meandering Keriya Darya and after a few hours drew up at a road toll. A soldier demanded 500 renminbi instead of the expected 200. It transpired that the officials, who had passed through before us, had told him that the two last vehicles in the convoy – that is, ours – would pay the toll for the whole group. We had no choice.

A few days later, we were confident that we would reach the village of Hortang, 240 kilometres east of Yütian, by midday, for the road, which was as straight as an arrow, had recently been resurfaced. From Hortang, a desert track led to the hamlet Andier, where we were to swap our jeeps for camels. However, our two drivers had resolved on a go-slow strike, and crept at 40 kilometres per hour along the road, although it was in excellent condition and devoid of traffic. After only a few hours, we turned into an open-air garage in the small town of Yawatong to repair 'damage' to the motors of both vehicles. The drivers promptly disappeared for two hours, leaving the jeeps with a mechanic who had no idea what he was supposed to be repairing. With some embarrassment, Wu explained the reason for this annoying turn of events. A month or so before, we had had to leave one of our two vehicles behind on the way to the fortress of Mazar Tagh, because the gearbox was damaged. Two days earlier, I had discovered that it was still defective and loudly voiced my dissatisfaction. At this, the drivers felt they had lost face, and were now taking their revenge. We did not reach Andier until long past midnight. The drivers grinned gloatingly, for they would be able to sleep late the following morning, whilst we had to set off early with the new camel caravan towards Endere.

As with Dandan Oilik and Karadong, Endere was first visited by Sven Hedin in 1900 and subsequently briefly excavated by Stein in 1901 and 1906. Based on coins found next to the main stupa in the western area (Buddhism flourished here, too), it was probably settled around the third century AD. But towards the end of the sixth century AD, the city was abandoned. When Xuangzang returned from India to central China via the Southern Silk Road in 643 or 644, he found the stretch between Minfeng and Cherchen depopulated. His mention of a long-since-abandoned desert town called Tuhuoluo most likely relates to Endere. After the Tang rulers regained control over the Southern Silk Road towards the end of the seventh century, they re-established an administrative centre in Endere. A Chinese scraffito from AD 719 supports this, writing of the death of a Chinese commander-in-chief in a battle between China and the 'great Tibetans'. By the end of the eighth century, however, the

Tibetans had expelled the Chinese from Endere. When the Endere River changed its course in the ninth century, the settlement was abandoned for the second and final time.

We began our explorations of Endere in the oldest part of the settlement, which dates from the first century and is dominated by a stupa and the nearby ruins of a high wall. We found areas the size of football fields covered with red and black potsherds, where pottery kilns had once stood, as well as fragments of copper coins.

On the way to the fortress, about a kilometre to the east, we passed two further stupas standing alone in the desert, bearing witness to the omnipresence of Buddha. In the centre of the fortress, which was built around 630 there is a forest of slender poplar pillars in the sand; these are the ruins of the buried main Buddhist temple, which had been founded during the first period of settlement of Endere. Here Stein had discovered not only several dozen documents written on paper, which served as amulets or were presented by the faithful as small votive tablets, but also three virtually life-size figures of red- and white-painted clay. We were saddened to find fragments of red and white clay in the sand, betraying the fact that looters had dug up the temple again not long ago, and destroyed the fragile statues. Close to the temple lies a small shrine where Stein found some particularly rich Buddhist murals dating from the seventh–eighth centuries AD. He had not removed them, but when we reached the shrine we discovered a gaping hole and bare walls disfigured by traces of chisels. Salim, the son of the local watchman, told us how his father had caught two intruders at this place just a few weeks before, but they had driven him away with rifle shots. They were not vandals, but professional treasure-looters who work on commission selling to private collectors and thus helping to ensure that these priceless artefacts disappear forever. The authorities evidently lack the funds, and presumably also the interest, to protect these archaeological treasures more effectively.

To the west of the fortress, I came upon a finely turned wooden pillar, which was probably one of the supporting pillars of the military commander's brick residence. Salim was convinced that treasure-looters had dragged it to this spot and left it there. Kasim, the archaeologist who was travelling with us, resolved to have the pillar taken to the archaeological museum in Khotan. Together with the camel-drivers, he tied a rope around it, and 55-year-old Ali, the head of the camel-drivers, heaved it onto his back and set off for our camp, two kilometres away, with this burden.

On a wall in one of the rooms in the commander's residence, Aurel Stein had discovered an important Tibetan inscription, which I now wanted to find. The task was not easy as most of the pillars, signifying where buildings would once have stood, stuck barely five centimetres out of the sand. After carefully figuring out the most likely spot, Ernst began to dig and after a few minutes, the wall began to emerge. On the wall were two sets of writing: one short, vertical inscription in Chinese and a horizontal Tibetan inscription three lines long. Both inscriptions relate to the history of the fort. The Chinese one mentions the imperial ambassador Xin Lizhan and the Tibetan one reads as follows: 'At Pyagpag in the province of Upper Jom Lom this army was outwitted, and a tiger's meal was obtained. Eat until you are fat.' Stein interpreted this text as the recording of a Chinese defeat around AD 790 with many enemies killed. After photographing the inscriptions, we covered them up completely with sand again. I wondered at the pendulum swings of history. Twelve hundred years ago, Tibet was fighting China on a huge front and drove the proud Tang Dynasty off the Silk Road. How different from today, where the Chinese dragon has swallowed the Tibetan snow-leopard and Tibet has become Chinese territory.

Three days later, we were hit by another sandstorm. It was one of the luckiest things that could have happened. The following morning, we were exploring the ruins to the south of the fortress. We came to Stein's ruin 'E VI', where in 1906 the British explorer had found important wooden documents in Kharoshthi characters.[24] Beside the remnants of the weathered stupa lay the 'gift' of the previous day's sandstorm. On the ground, I found two greyish steatite stones with writing on them. I soon realised that the two stones were part of the same inscription. The writing looked Indian, and I was fairly certain that it was Kharoshthi.[25]

My heart beat faster, as I realised this could be the first Kharoshthi inscription on stone from the Shan Shan Empire – a sensational find. I was unable to read the Kharoshthi script (which died out in the fifth century) but I guessed that as it was written in Kharoshthi it was related to the administrative workings of the settlement, rather than religious matters, which were usually written in Brahmi. When I returned from the trip a Kharoshthi specialist confirmed that my discovery was highly interesting. The language of the text is Prakrit, also called Central Asian Gandhari and its script is Kharoshthi. Although such documents written on wood or leather had already been found, this was the first inscription on stone from the Shan Shan kingdom.

The text is a proclamation listing the titles of a king of Shan Shan who prides himself on being a 'crusher of his enemies'. Although the king's name and the date are lost, the ruler referred to is most probably King Amgoka (who ruled in the third century), but his predecessors, Pepiya and Tajaka, cannot be totally ruled out. Since the list contains titles usually applied to Kushana rulers, we can infer that Shan Shan was at that time a kind of semi-independent vassal of the Kushana Empire of northern India. This fact suggests that the inscription pre-dates the seventeenth year of Amgoka's reign around AD 263, when the king had to yield to Chinese overlordship. After this date, Amgoka and his successors discontinued the use of almost all Indian titles. Another interesting clue is provided by the word 'hinargami', which was most probably the ancient and hitherto-unknown name of Endere. The most important finding stemming from this inscription concerns the introduction of Mahayana Buddhism into Shan Shan, for it also includes the title 'mahayana-samprastida': the one 'who has set forth on the Great Vehicle', namely Mahayana Buddhism.[26] This is the earliest official proclamation of this title in Shan Shan, and it demonstrates that Mahayana Buddhism benefited from royal support already during the first half of Amgoka's reign, several decades earlier than previously assumed.[27]

# A Blank Space on the Map

My third Taklamakan expedition of 2003 had failed to locate the ancient city of Calmadana (Qiemo), abandoned in the seventh or eighth century AD and not discovered since, but my appetite for exploring uncharted places had not dwindled. Four years later I found myself at the start of winter with two colleagues from my former expedition to Dandan Oilik, Ernst and Urs, plus a Swiss cameraman called Ueli Nüesch and a six-strong Chinese support crew at the western edge of the dreaded Lop Nor Desert.

This expedition was to be a particularly challenging one. Because of the harsh environment, brutal weather and the fact that the northern part is closed off by the army, Lop Nor is the least-explored part of the Taklamakan. We planned to cross a part of it that was completely unmapped and had never been explored, during the bitter months of winter. Our goal was to reach several ancient sites that dated from the second century BC and the fourth century AD and to pave the way for future archaeological investigations.

The first of these sites was to be two neighbouring fortresses, named 'L.K.' and 'L.L.' by Aurel Stein, who had briefly investigated them in February 1914, as well as two ancient settlements, L.M. and L.R.[28] A Uigur hunter called Tokhta Akhun first discovered L.K. in 1910 and later led Stein there. I was especially keen to rediscover the L.R. settlement, as it had been visited only once by Stein's worker, Afraz Gul, in 1915. Stein himself had never been there and no photographs or sketch plans of its ruins exist. The only other expedition able to reach L.K. and L.L. was a Chinese survey team in 1988, but it failed to find either settlement. Stein and the Chinese team had approached the site from the south-east, where travel was relatively 'easy' over low dunes, gravel and salt-encrusted ground. I decided to start in the west and advance over a tight system of high dunes.

Both fortresses stand on the site of an ancient caravan trail that once linked the Middle and Southern Silk Roads. It would have taken camel caravans three days to cover the 55 kilometres from Loulan in the north to L.K. and an additional six days from there to Miran in the south. A letter written in AD 328 by Minister Li Bo and found near the Konche Darya suggests that L.K. was at that time the seat of the governor of the Western Regions – as today's Xinjiang was then called – underscoring the strategic importance of the fortress.

The Chinese name of L.K., 'Haitou', is revealing. It translates literally as 'head' (*tou*) of a 'lake' (*hai*), suggesting that Haitou stood at the south-western shore of Lake Lop Nor, at whose northern end Loulan was situated. The lake would have been fed by waters from the Konche Darya, whose tributaries watered the whole area between L.K. and L.R. Numerous ancient riverbeds visible on a satellite picture give the incorrect impression that this north-western part of the desert had been a swamp two to three millennia ago. But I knew from other parts of the Taklamakan that these rivers never carried water at the same time, since they tend to meander and often change their course. The area we were headed for was, two millennia ago, neither a desert nor a marsh, but most likely a steppe dotted with a few fertile oases. These settlements were abandoned at the end of the fourth century AD when the lake had disappeared and the neighbouring regional dynasties in western China of the Former Liang (320–376) and Later Liang (386–403) collapsed, which damaged trade on the Middle and Southern Silk Roads.

For this expedition, I decided not to use camels but special desert vehicles that I rented from an oil company in Korla. The trucks were four-wheeled monsters weighing seven tons each; their immense tyres over a metre high. Given the size of the tyres and the power of the eight-litre engines, they are among the best desert vehicles in the world. In spite of the practicalities of using camels on desert expeditions, this journey was different. It was unlikely that we would find water in the high dunes; even if we found a waterhole, it would be frozen. To carry ice for drinking water for both humans and camels would also be useless as we would have no way of thawing it. Much valuable time would also have been lost on the short winter days in loading and unloading the camels.

The start of the journey gave us a foretaste of what the desert had in store for us. Ernst, Urs, Ueli and I had left Korla before dawn and gone ahead of the trucks, which were being driven in on semitrailers, to reconnoitre a place where they could enter the desert. We had to cross the deep bed of the river Tarim and pass through a thick forest of dead trees; it was essential that the trucks did not get entangled in this maze or slit open their tyres on the razor-sharp tree trunks. On the afternoon that we set out, a sandstorm was raging, obliterating the sun. A fog had also descended, reducing visibility to less than 20 metres. An icy wind howled as we began searching the terrain on foot.

Urs and I muffled up, covered our faces with scarves – a chink open for the eyes – and marched against the wind. Even with this protection, the desert welcomed us with an icy jet of fine sand that immediately entered eyes, mouth and nose. We searched for an entry into the ravine of the riverbed, crossed it and entered the forest. Urs stayed at its edge and I ventured inside after having marked his position on the GPS. After a few moments, I had lost sight of him and advanced into the sandstorm. But luck was with me. Following a small gully, I found a safe way out of the labyrinth of dead trees into the open desert that was dotted with high tamarisk mounds. I hurried back to Urs. We reached the road just in time to meet the semitrailers emerging out of the sandstorm. Within minutes the desert trucks had been offloaded and we began guiding them towards the ravine. Night had fallen and they advanced cautiously with their headlights on; in the fog thick with sand they looked like fire-breathing dragons. We had entered, as Ueli noted, the 'vault of Lop Nor'. The expedition had begun.

As with my two previous expeditions, we guided the Chinese support crew. This time, however, we had no maps to guide us since this part of the desert had never been explored. For navigation we only had a satellite picture that showed the high dune systems and, about 80 kilometres east of our entry point, some ancient riverbeds.[29] Although the drivers had never worked with foreigners, they were from the start extremely cooperative, trusting that we valued our lives as much as they did theirs. The bitter cold made driving in this difficult terrain a tough and very tiring experience, but at the end of the expedition they told us that they had enjoyed helping us to search for ways through the dune labyrinths.

On the second day the high dunes appeared. They were no ordinary dunes but complex systems that spread out like a gigantic net over huge areas. Some of them were virtually perpendicular walls blocking our path; others looked like immense stepped pyramids, and could only be surmounted in stages. Our advance was further handicapped by the fact that the wind mostly blew from the north-east, which meant that we had to climb the dunes on the soft lee side. On several weary days, we covered less than six kilometres as the crow flies. The engines would roar and pound, the trucks groaning under the effort and transferring their painful juddering to our already-bruised bodies.

A few days into the expedition we encountered areas covered with the remains of ancient freshwater snails, reminding us that this utterly dry sand desert had, many thousands of years ago, been a lake. Pieces of petrified horsetails – one of the oldest plants on earth – were further clues that life did once flourish here millennia ago. We also discovered man-made relics. One was the remains of an unknown dwelling standing on top of a small hill. From the textile we found inside, I judged it to be about 500 to 700 years old, built at a time when the desert had not yet reached the Tarim River.

It had taken us 10 incredibly hard days to cover 113 kilometres as the crow flies but at last we reached the L.K. fortress. While walking the last few kilometres we found several ancient relics, including two ceremonial stone axes made from green jade, a worked piece of yellow, almost transparent selenite (similar in appearance to jade), several worked flints, three stone spindles and some coarse pottery. In Lop Nor the ancient Chinese always built their fortresses and settlements on sites that had been occupied since prehistoric times, with easy access to water.

Although abandoned for 16 centuries and badly battered by the wind, the fortress still looked impressive in its solitude. Shaped like an irregular oblong, its massive walls, built of alternating thick layers of clay and poplar trunks and strong branches laid crosswise, were in some sections still standing. The walls would have been covered in clay originally, supporting a parapet. As at Karadong, a wide gateway on the north-east side gave entry to the fort. It was closed by two strong wooden doors, one of which was still lying intact on the ground. Although L.K. was much more solidly constructed than Loulan, its strong walls were badly breached by the raging wind, which in this desert is the worst enemy of anything man-made.

The ferocious power of the wind, which blows from the Gobi, is much worse than in the other parts of the Taklamakan lying to the west of Lop Nor. It erodes all structures and even the earth itself. In most parts of the Taklamakan one sometimes walks upon earth that has been untouched for millennia but in Lop Nor it has been mostly swept away and replaced by yardangs or sand. The wind is devastating, not because of the fierce sandstorms, but because it blows, uninterrupted, from the same direction. As one of our drivers remarked, 'The wind in Lop Nor neither rests nor sleeps.' It is like a gigantic grinding machine, the sand its abrasive paper.

The interior of the fortress was a scene of utter destruction. Countless heavy wooden beams and posts littered the ground in its centre. Stein had seen dozens of these posts still standing, but I found only very few of them upright, the rest lying around in wild heaps. Stein had removed several of the posts during his brief excavation and since his visit a century ago the wind had widened the breaches in the walls and wreaked further havoc. Still, I managed to identify all the rooms mentioned by Stein and discovered an additional one next to the gate that once belonged to a narrow, two-storeyed building. Although we excavated it to the ground, we only chanced upon minor finds such as fragments of coins, a clay spindle, some rough blue glass beads, two strings made out of camel hair and some grey and red pottery shards. Like Stein, we didn't find any inscribed documents.

With time, the nights became colder and colder, the thermometer reaching -30°C. If the sky remained cloudy, temperatures would hardly rise during the day and the strong wind produced a chill factor of an additional -10 to -15°C. Every movement required a special effort. Hands and faces became swollen. Our tears froze on our cheeks and miniature icicles formed at the corners of the eyes as well as on our noses and moustaches. The daily morning march, before sunrise, from the camp to the ruins was signalled by a cacophony of unattractive noises. We gasped, sneezed, spat, groaned, farted and belched – like our trucks, whose spluttering engines had to run in neutral gear for half an hour before they were ready to move. We remained a sniffing caravan of miserable and frozen individuals until the sun rose on the horizon and energised us.

On one such morning I decided to walk to the second fortress, L.L., whose outline one could guess from the walls of L.K. It was much smaller than L.K., with a dune running from its west side into the desert. The interior of the fort offered an even more desolate picture than L.K. Nothing remained, apart from a few huge posts lying on the ground. Everything else had been swept away by the winds into the desert. Our digging resulted only in some blue and amber beads, a millstone, a small shield-shaped bronze plate, and an intact *wuzhu* coin. The name 'wuzhu' means 'five grains' and referred to the original weight of the coin, which was 3.5 grams. The *wuzhu* had the traditional shape of Chinese coins – round with a square hole in the middle – which carries a cosmological meaning since the circle symbolises heaven and the square earth. The *wuzhu* was introduced in the second century BC and was kept in circulation for more than 700 years.

Every afternoon during our excavations at L.L. the wind increased and started a minor sandstorm. Against the fading sun, the running sand looked like hundreds of golden snakes fleeing away. Soon, ground and sky merged at the horizon and the landscape would lose all its shape.

In spite of Stein's and our efforts, the two fortresses remained shrouded in mystery. No one really knows exactly when they were constructed or when they were abandoned. What is more intriguing is the question of why two fortresses were built in this utterly barren landscape and standing only five kilometres apart. They would have been costly to build and maintain. Was one a military fortress and the other one a caravanserai? Or were they built at different times? At L.K. I had noticed that a layer of poplar trunks inside the outer walls was blackened by fire. Perhaps the fort had burned down and been later rebuilt? This is not unlikely when we consider the fact that China twice lost control of the Lop Nor and the neighbouring areas between c. AD 15–75 and AD 140–260, when nomadic hordes from the north attacked and plundered the region.

After a week of excavating, we had to leave both forts, and our questions remained unanswered. Finding our next targets, L.M. and L.R., was to be an even bigger challenge. The settlements were about four kilometres apart, but neither was on the satellite picture; Stein's inaccurate map was of no help either. We divided the vast search area into three sectors. Urs took the western, Ernst the northern and I the north-western. I had drawn the lucky straw, for within only a few minutes of search I found a decorated bronze pot broken into more than 40 pieces. Such a sophisticated object didn't point to a semi-nomadic prehistoric settlement, but to one dating from the Han (202 BC–AD 220), Wei (AD 220–65) or Western Jin (AD 263–316) dynasties.

After a few hours I came across the remains of an ancient orchard, its trees aligned in long rows. From previous experiences, I knew that such orchards were usually only a couple of kilometres away from settlements so I climbed the high dunes nearby and began to search the landscape with my binoculars. Soon I caught in one single sweep of the binoculars not one but two ruins. Looking against the sunset I clearly saw in two places, about one kilometre apart, several regularly arranged wooden beams jutting out of the sand. These were two of the five ruins of L.M. last visited by Aurel Stein 93 years ago.

The first ruin stood south of an ancient riverbed with four other houses located north of it. Two thousand years ago this river would have been the source of life for the settlement. The first ruin consisted of a large room measuring 8 x 10 metres, and at least two lateral rooms. On the floor lay dozens of thick poplar posts. A few of them, including some elegantly carved architraves, lay in the spots where they had once formed the walls, and nearby were some bases with sockets for the pillars that supported the roof. Scattered on the ground we found some blue and amber glass beads, a large wooden ladle, textile fragments made from linen, hemp, silk and felt, a piece of woollen tapestry with geometric patterns in red, blue, orange and yellow and two pieces of fine, yellow glass with a line decoration shaped like a large 'Z'. They most probably came from a vessel where the glass had been blown into a mould – a Roman technique invented in the last century BC. Such a fine vessel must have been imported from the Roman Empire and so the two fragments were important evidence of the ancient trade between East and West. The small glass beads were most probably made locally.[30]

Less than one kilometre to the north-west of the first ruin (L.M. i) stood the smaller ruin (L.M. ii) on top of a five-metre-high, wind-eroded ridge. In the main room of this structure lay four large oblong poplar bases with sockets, marking the place where the massive beams had once supported the roof. Here I discovered another important find. When I stepped inside the room, dozens of small bronze coins littering the floor caught my eye. Some were piled on top of each other and had corroded together. They looked as if they had been dropped accidentally only yesterday. I had found the 'Bank of L.M.'!

Such coins would have come from China proper and were also locally produced in the semi-independent kingdom of Kucha. In contrast to the West, where coins used to be struck, Chinese coins were cast in moulds. I soon noticed that the hoard consisted of two types: a few 'Kucha *wuzhu*' coins, but mostly Kucha small coins without inscriptions. Since the latter were of very low value, they were linked together with a string running through the central hole. These strings usually numbered 100 or 1,000 coins, the latter weighing almost three kilograms. On the floor of this same room I found a long tubular, greenish-blue glass bead and another aquamarine glass bead consisting of five flattened spheroids clinging together, as well as a fine copper vessel affixed to a hollow bronze rod, maybe a part of an oil lamp.

Two questions immediately arose: how was it possible that Stein didn't notice the coins, since he claimed to have cleared this room completely? Perhaps he had stopped before reaching the ground. Then, why did so much money remain scattered inside the room? Did its inhabitants flee in haste before an advancing enemy – the singed walls of L.K. and L.L. came to mind – or was it left there by someone staying in the house after its owners had abandoned it?

Excavations in the three other ruins, L.M. iii, iv and v, gave no clues as to when and why the settlement was abandoned but I discovered in the third ruin a wonderful green jade axe. Since it was so well kept I assumed that it wasn't meant for daily use and that it instead served a ceremonial purpose in the Han-Jin dynasty, and hence didn't stem from prehistoric times.

The settlement of L.R. was even more difficult to find. It had only been found by Afraz Gul in 1915 and since then nobody had laid eyes on it. Because of the constantly shifting sand dunes, there was a risk that the site had been buried. But again, luck was on our side. Having once more divided the search area into three sectors, the discovery this time fell to Urs. From a high dune the view through his binoculars offered the sight of two groups of standing posts and of a mound resembling a stupa. We had rediscovered L.R., 92 years after the first and last person had seen the ruins.

These ancient settlements would have consisted of many more buildings than the ruins that remained, whose walls were strengthened by poplar beams and posts. In addition to the three ruins, several places dotted with shards and bronze fragments indicated that more simple clay buildings had once stood here but had been destroyed by the wind. L.M. and L.R. would once have been lively settlements.

As with all five dwellings of L.M., the axis of the long side of the houses L.R. ii and L.R. iii was oriented to the north-east so that the winds blowing from the Gobi would only hit the short side, causing less damage. While at the smaller ruin, L.R. ii, we only found one huge poplar pillar still stuck in the socket of its base, at the larger ruin, L.R. iii, we found next to dozens of poplar posts and beams all four of the wooden pillars that had supported the roof. We also found one large base with socket as well as two wooden capitals with scroll-shaped brackets at each end cut in one piece, looking similar to Ionic volutes. This house would have consisted of five to six living rooms and at least three stables for goats and sheep and for storing millet and other cereals (we found thousands of cereal grains under the sand). The four pillars encouraged us to excavate the main room and search for the remaining three bases. The first pillar base was badly weathered, having been exposed to the sun and wind, but the other three were in pristine condition, preserved by the dry sand, and had kept their original brown-reddish colour. The bases were incorporated into the floor, which consisted of a layer of wood covered by rubbish mixed with straw, for insulation purposes, and finally a thin coat of clay. In a refuse heap close to the door, whose wooden threshold we excavated as well, we found eight bronze tacks, which would have been used to fix leather onto the wooden frame of a saddle.

At the southern side of the house we found dozens of freshwater snail shells encrusted in the ground of a long, narrow depression. Obviously the inhabitants had had access to running water. But, as in every oasis, man must fight the advance of the desert by planting tight rows of trees and bushes, as we had seen at L.M., and by maintaining irrigation systems. If such measures were neglected, the desert would have recaptured what man had created from it. Such settlements would have then fallen into oblivion and disappeared, until a lucky archaeologist had the fortune to uncover their history again. We were careful to measure all the ruins, draw detailed plans and list all our finds.

The L.R. i ruin had a major surprise in store for us. It turned out to be neither a dwelling, as Stein had assumed based on Afraz Gul's description, nor a stupa, as it appeared from the distance. It consisted of two sections lying on the top of separate small mesas, 3.5 and 5.5 metres high. On the lower one we found fine poplar posts and branches; on the higher one were two piles of unusually thick and long beams, some of which had fallen to the ground. The top of the mesa was crowned by a tight layer of poplar branches and covered by rough blocks of clay, recalling the construction method used at both fortresses. The intricacy of its design, aimed clearly at strengthening the building, suggested that it hadn't been an ordinary house. I carefully inspected the beams. Two beams 4.5 metres long had 11 holes, once serving as an architrave and as a lower cross-beam for the wall-supporting pillars lying next to them. I discovered on the western side of the mesa two short beams measuring only 85 centimetres, at both ends of which 25 centimetre-long wooden pegs were stuck. There was no doubt that these were two window frames.

It dawned on me that this was the ruin of an ancient beacon tower – the first one ever found inside Lop Nor. Like those standing west of Dunhuang and along the Konche Darya near Yingpän, this tower would have consisted of a five-metre-high concrete mesa with a room on top, built out of strong wooden beams and thick layers of mud. The only entrance would have been here, reached either by a ladder that could be lifted, or by a rope. The two window frames formed the embrasures for archers. It made sense that the remains of these two embrasures lay on the western upper slope of the mesa, since it was from the north-west that any likely enemy, such as the Xiongnu, would approach. The discovery of this beacon tower throws new light on the debate surrounding the huge tower at Loulan, which Stein and Chinese archaeologists believed was a Buddhist stupa, but Hedin assumed was a beacon tower.

Looking closely at the GPS data I quickly noticed that the L.M. settlement and both fortresses stood in a line south-east of the L.R settlement. These four sites thus form a 14-kilometre, virtually straight line stretching from L.K. in the south-east to L.R. in the north-west. The beacon tower at L.R. and both fortresses would have had direct contact with each other via smoke signals in the day and fire signals at night. The two agricultural settlements must have supplied the two fortresses or fortified caravanserais with the required foodstuffs and other goods necessary to be self-reliant.

Yet, still more mysteries remained. Had Buddhism reached this region prior to its abandonment? Neither Stein nor I could find any indication of a connection to Buddhism – no temples, figures or documents. Another enigma was the location of cemeteries in these settlements. As with some other sites in the Taklamakan we didn't find any evidence of tombs and still wonder at how the dead were buried in the heart of Lop Nor in those days.

On the last day of our stay I set out on an exploratory walk to the north-west. After having crossed a small riverbed I found at a distance of just over a kilometre from L.R. iii, a place scattered with dozens of very coarse black, grey and red pottery shards and a worked flint. All of these fragments were prehistoric and indicated a small Neolithic settlement. Encouraged by this I continued to march. I crossed a wide riverbed totally filled with sand and for every kilometre I advanced beyond it the landscape became more dreary and desolate. Not even a dead tree or a tamarisk cone broke up the monotony – just sand, yardangs and the steep embankments of more sand-filled riverbeds. An environment more hostile to life was hard to imagine, but I still wondered if this mysterious desert held yet more secrets in its depths – more settlements, more signs that people once lived in its harshness.

For now, however, they would have to remain undiscovered. Our water and food supplies had run dangerously low and we had no choice but to begin our long trek to the northern edge of the desert.

# Epilogue

People often ask me why I go to such effort, forsaking a life of comfort and safety just to explore 'dead' cultures. Sometimes I ask myself the same question. Everybody longs for experiences beyond those of our regulated, everyday lives. My own desires and aspirations are satisfied through travel and the discoveries that I make on the nomad's trail. A Chinese friend inspired by Confucius once told me, 'instead of worrying about life after death, it is much more rewarding to cultivate life before death'.

The richness of Asia, its cultures and its peoples, has taught me to live in the here and now. But, just as the traditional towns and villages of Tibet, Mongolia and China are being bulldozed for uniform concrete blocks to rise in their place, so the unique and diverse cultural heritage of these countries is being ruthlessly standardised; ancient religions and customs degraded to folklore. By exploring these threatened cultures and recording their past and present riches, I am attempting to make a modest contribution to the preservation of their heritage. A broader understanding of the past helps to understand the present better.

Zen Buddhism stresses that Buddha exists nowhere other than in the present, within ourselves. There is no Bodhisattva Guanyin whom we can implore, no future Buddha Maitreya to initiate a perfect age, nor a Buddha Amitabha who can promise us rebirth in paradise. Every symphony remains incomplete; every paradise is provisional; behind every horizon there waits another. I will continue and never arrive. The quest will never end.

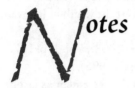# Notes

## Introduction

1  T.E. Lawrence, *Seven Pillars of Wisdom* (1926), p. 23.
2  Wilfred Thesiger, *The Life of my Choice* (2000), p. 115.

## Part I

1  On the Church of the East, see: Christoph Baumer, *The Church of the East* (2006).
2  J.L. Dutreuil de Rhins and F. Grenard, *Mission scientifique dans la Haute Asie* (1890–95), Vol. 3, p. 134f.
3  A.H. Francke, *Antiquities of Indian Tibet* (1992), Vol. I, pp. 58ff. Emil Trinkler, *The Storm-Swept Roof of Asia* (1931), p. 37. Helmut de Terra, *Durch Urwelten am Indus* (1940), p. 80f.
4  My additional explorations in other former or present centres of the Church of the East, for instance in Yemen, central China or Kerala (southern India) are not mentioned here, since these places are located outside Inner Asia.
5  William Moorcroft and George Trebeck, 'Travels in India' (1989), Vol. I, p. 429f.
6  Christoph Baumer, *The Church of the East* (2006), p. 195f.
7  S.B. Sutton, *In China's Border Provinces* (1974), p. 164.
8  Gertrude L. Bell, *Amurath to Amurath* (1911), p. 311f.
9  Benjamin Domara bears the title of 'cor-bishop' and is the deputy of the bishop.
10  See www.anca.org. The European Parliament condemned this act of state vandalism on 16 February 2006 with an overwhelming majority.

11 Justin Perkins, *A Residence of Eight Years in Persia among the Nestorian Christians* (1843), p. 380.

12 Asahel Grant, *The Nestorians; or the Lost Tribes* (1841), p. 178f.

13 John 1:29.

14 Immediately before flight from Egypt, Moses had the blood of sacrificial lambs smeared on the doorposts of the Israelites' houses, to avert the wrath of Jehovah from their inhabitants (Exodus 12).

15 'Ata-Malik Juvaini, *The History of the World-Conqueror* (1958), Vol. 1, p. 167.

16 Tirkesh Hojaniyazov and Chary Yazlyev, 'Ancient Merv' (1996), p. 2.

17 The theme of the heavenly ladder is also found in the Old Testament as Jacob's ladder (Genesis 28:1–22).

18 The most important subterranean mosques are: Shakpak Ata, Sultan Ata, Karaman Ata, Shopan Ata and Beket Ata. In addition to these the separate necropolises of Koshkar-Ata, Kalin-Ata, Hanga Baba, Ushtam, Kenty-Baba and Karagasti Aulie exist.

19 The second impetus to this myth was provided by the Buddhist Khan Yelü Dashi of the Kara Khitai Empire, who inflicted a crushing defeat on the two powerful Muslim rulers Rukn ad-Din and Sanjar in present eastern Uzbekistan in 1137 and 1141.

## Part II

1 In Mahayana Buddhism, Bodhisattvas are enlightened beings who, out of compassion, renounce their own entry into nirvana until all living creatures have been saved.

2 Henry Yule, *The Book of Ser Marco Polo* (1926), Vol. I, pp. 246.

3 The Persian historian and Grand Vizier Rashid al-Din (1247–1318) describes the necropolis briefly. See Rashid al-Din, *The Successors of Genghis Khan* (1971), pp. 31, 228, 311f.

4 This anecdote can be found in Erich Haenisch (ed.), *Die geheime Geschichte der Mongolen (The Secret History of the Mongols)* (1948), p. 3, where is it not attributed to Genghis Khan but to a mythical female ancestor. The anecdote is, however, considerably older: it is found in pre-Christian Scythian, Sogdian and Iranian traditions, and among Aesop's fables. See: 'Ata-Malik Juvaini, *The History of the World-Conqueror* (1958), Vol. I, p. 41; Boris Marshak, *Legends, Tales and Fables in the Art of the Sogdians* (2002), p. 89f; and Renate Rolle, *Die Welt der Skythen* (1980), p. 145.

5 Skiing has been known in northern Eurasia for thousands of years, for skis of ash wood 4,500 years old were found there. See Michel Egloff and Yuri Piotrovsky et al., *Trésors des steppes* (2006), p. 27.

6  Quoted in Vladimir Kubarev, *New Turkish Sculptures of Mongolia and the Altai* (2000), p. 6.
7  Sergei Kliachtornyi, 'Une "Ile de Pâques" dans les montagnes de Mongolie', *Les Scythes. Dossiers d'archéologie* (June 1994), p. 52f. There is presumably a remote connection between these Europoid stone figures and the Scythian stone images north of the Black Sea.
8  Wilhelm von Rubruk, *Reisen zum Grosskhan der Mongolen* (1984), p. 59.
9  Herodotus, *The Histories* (1954), p. 260.
10  In Hans-Georg Hüttel, 'Karakorum, eine historische Skizze' (2005), p. 134.
11  Ibid. This piece of advice is also attributed to Lu Jia (d. 157 BC), who served as counsellor to Emperor Gaozu, founder of the Han Dynasty. Ssu-Ma Ch'ien, *Shih chi* (1971), p. 277f.
12  William of Rubruk: *Reisen zum Grosskhan der Mongolen* (1984), p. 206.
13  Ibid., p. 175, author's translation.
14  Ibid., p. 163f, author's translation.
15  See p. 172.
16  Christopher Atwood, *Encyclopedia of Mongolia and the Mongolian Empire* (2004), p. 428.

## Part III

1  See p. 123f.
2  For photographs of Tholing and Tsaparang from the time before the Cultural Revolution, see Li Gotami Govinda, *Tibet in Pictures* (1979), Vol. II, pp. 148–83.
3  C. Wessels, *Early Jesuit Travellers in Central Asia* (1924), p. 66.
4  Jürgen Aschoff, *Tsaparang – Königsstadt in Westtibet* (1989), p. 59.
5  Ibid., pp. 59, 84.
6  Bruno Baumann, *Kailash* (2002), p. 222f.
7  On Bön, see Christoph Baumer, *Tibet's Ancient Religion, Bön* (2002).
8  Ippolito Desideri, *An Account of Tibet* (1932), p. 83f.
9  The Drigungpa are a sub-group of the monastic order of the Kagyüpa. The other important Buddhist orders of Tibet still existing today are the Nyingmapa, the Sakyapa and the Gelugpa, as well as the Jonangpa in eastern Tibet. See Christoph Baumer, *Tibet's Ancient Religion, Bön* (2002), pp. 125–34, 175f.
10  Mani stones are stones engraved with Buddhist mantras, that is, short religious prayers. The name comes from the mantra of the Bodhisattva of compassion, Chenresi: 'Om Mani Padme Hum'.
11  Ekai Kawaguchi, *Three Years in Tibet* (1979), p. 173f.
12  Sven Hedin, *Transhimalaja* (1909), Vol. II, p. 166.

13  Ibid., p. 170. I observed a similar custom in the Fomu Cave at Mount Wutai Shan, China's holiest Buddhist pilgrimage destination.
14  F.M. Bailey, 'Through Bhutan and Southern Tibet' (1924), p. 295.
15  Christoph Baumer: *Tibet's Ancient Religion, Bön* (2002), p. 74f; Hugh Richardson, *A Corpus of Early Tibetan Inscriptions* (1985), pp. 64–71.
16  Namkhai Norbu, *Journey among the Tibetan Nomads* (1997), p. 70.

## Part IV

1  On the cultural history of the Southern Silk Road in Xinjiang, see: Christoph Baumer, *Southern Silk Road* (2003).
2  Tibet was also for a time in control of the region around Beshbalik (Beiting), which is located north of the Tian Shan and borders on today's Mongolia.
3  René Grousset, *Die Reise nach Westen* (1986), p. 231, author's translation.
4  Kharoshthi is a northern Indian script that was used to write languages of central India called Prakrit. Kharoshthi is derived from the Aramaic script, and was used as an administration script from the fourth century BC until the fourth–fifth centuries AD. In the Tarim Basin, wood was used to write on up to the early fourth century AD, as paper was expensive and could not be rewritten on, whereas with wood a text no longer needed could be planed off.
5  Marc Aurel Stein, *Ruins of Desert Cathay* (1912), Vol. I, p. 300f.
6  Marc Aurel Stein, *Serindia* (1921), p. 276.
7  Feng Zhao and Zhiyoung Yu, *Legacy of the Desert King* (2000).
8  Marc Aurel Stein, *Ruins of Desert Cathay* (1912), Vol. I, p. 442.
9  The Sino-Tibetan wars lasted, with interruptions, from AD 641 to AD 821. See Christoph Baumer and Therese Weber, *Eastern Tibet* (2005), pp. 32f, 40f, 65f.
10  Marc Aurel Stein, *Ruins of Desert Cathay* (1912), Vol. I, p. 457.
11  Marc Aurel Stein, *Serindia* (1921), p. 276.
12  Sven Hedin, *Im Herzen von Asien* (1903), Vol. I, p. 107, author's translation.
13  Ibid., Vol. II, p. 84, author's translation.
14  The older, better map comes from Stein's work *Serindia*, and the later one from *Innermost Asia*. See Marc Aurel Stein and Major K. Mason, *Memoir on Maps of Chinese Turkistan and Kansu* (1923), pp. 79f, 83, 85, 87, 90, 95, 112f, 142.
15  Quoted in Christoph Baumer, *Southern Silk Road* (2003), p. 135.
16  Walter Bosshard, *Hazards of Asia's Highlands and Deserts* (undated), p. 91.
17  Procrustes was a bandit in Greek legend. He would tie his victims to the 'bed of Procrustes' and maim or stretch them until they were an exact fit.
18  Yushi Nomura & Henri Nouwen, *Weisheit aus der Wüste* (2002), p. 31.
19  Wilfred Thesiger, *Arabian Sands* (1960), p. XIII.

20  Sven Hedin, *Through Asia* (1899) p. 787.

21  Emil Trinkler, *The Storm-Swept Roof of Asia* (1931), p. 197.

22  The paper amulet is now in the Archaeological Institute of Xinjiang at Urumqi.

23  Hedin, *Through Asia* (1899) p. 783

24  See above, p. 147.

25  The inscription was handed over to the archaeological museum in Khotan.

26  The whole translation reads: 'In the year ... of the lord, the great king, the king [of kings ...], crusher of his enemies, who is his own army, whose ... who is worshipped ... who has set forth on the Great Vehicle [Mahayana], who is fixed in the true dharma, of great majesty ... The names of the supervisors [are] Okaripa, Sirsha, Kutre. This ??? at Hinarga.' See Richard Salomon, 'A Stone Inscription in Central Asian Gandhari from Endere' (1999), p. 4.

27  Hinayana and Mahayana are two forms of Buddhism. In the older, Hinayana, the 'small vehicle', each person strives to attain his own nirvana. In Mahayana, the 'large vehicle', by contrast, enlightened persons renounce entry into nirvana, in order, as merciful Bodhisattvas, to help others also to attain nirvana. Mahayana Buddhism emerged in the first century AD.

28  Stein labelled all ruins he visited in Lop Nor with two letters: The first 'L' stands for 'Loulan' and the second Stein allocated in the chronological order of his visits.

29  Stein's maps were unfortunately useless for us since he had never travelled through this part of the desert, and his maps from *Innermost Asia* are flawed by major triangulation mistakes affecting longitudinal indications. On Stein's maps dealing with Lop Nor, all sites, including Loulan, L.K. or Yingpän, are shown 12 to 24 kilometres too far to the west.

30  All finds discovered were left in situ and re-covered with sand.

# Bibliography

Aschoff, Jürgen, *Tsaparang – Königsstadt in Westtibet* (MC Verlag, Munich, 1989)

Atwood, Christopher, *Encyclopedia of Mongolia and the Mongolian Empire* (Facts on File, New York, 2004)

Azarpay, Guitty, *Sogdian Painting. The Pictorial Epic in Oriental Art* (University of California Press, Berkeley, 1981)

Bailey, F.M., 'Through Bhutan and Southern Tibet', *Geographical Journal*, No. 4, 1924.

Baipakov, Karl, *The Site Kuirytobe – Town Keder* (Archaeological Institute of Almaty, 2005)

Baipakov, Karl and Nasyrov, Rakip, *Along the Great Silk Road* (Kramos, Almaty, 1991)

Baumann, Bruno, *Kailash* (Piper, Munich, 2002)

Baumer, Christoph, *Tibet's Ancient Religion, Bön* (Orchid Press, Bangkok, 2002)

Baumer, Christoph, *Southern Silk Road. In the Footsteps of Sir Aurel Stein and Sven Hedin* (Orchid Press, Bangkok, 2003)

Baumer, Christoph, *The Church of the East. An Illustrated History of Assyrian Christianity* (I.B.Tauris, London, 2006)

Baumer, Christoph, 'New Discoveries in the Taklamakan Desert, Xinjiang. Finds from Dandan Oilik and Endere', in Russell-Smith, Lilla (ed.), *From Nisa to Niya. New Discoveries and Studies in Central and Inner Asian Art in Archaeology* (Saffron, London, 2008)

Baumer, Christoph and Weber, Therese, *Eastern Tibet. Bridging Tibet and China* (Orchid Press, Bangkok, 2005)

Belinizki, A.M., *Mittelasien. Kunst der Sogden* (VEB Seemann, Leipzig, 1980)

Bell, Gertrude L., *Amurath to Amurath* (William Heinemann, London, 1911)

Berchem, Max van, *Amida. Matériaux pour l'épigraphie et l'histoire Musulmanes du Diyar-Bekr* (Carl Winters Universitätsbuchhandlung, Heidelberg, 1910)

Bergman, Folke, 'Archaeological Researches in Sinkiang', in Hedin, Sven, *Reports from the Scientific Expedition 1927–35. Publication 7* (Bökförlags Aktiebolaget Thule, Stockholm, 1939)

Bodhidharma, *The Zen Teachings of Bodhidharma*, translated by Red Pine (North Point Press, New York, 1989)

Bollinger, Rudolf, *Revolution zur Einheit. Jemens Kampf um die Unabhängigkeit* (Hoffmann & Campe, Hamburg, 1984)

Bosshard, Walter, *Hazards of Asia's Highlands and Deserts* (Figurehead, London, undated, after 1930)

Brentjes, Vasilievsky, *Schamanenkrone und Weltenbaum* (Seemann, Leipzig, 1989)

Carpini, Johannes von Plano, *Kunde von den Mongolen* (Thorbecke, Sigmaringen, 1997)

Chan, V., *Tibet Handbook* (Moon, Chico, 1994)

Chang, Claudia (ed.), *Of Gold and Grass: Nomads of Kazakhstan* (Foundation for International Arts & Education, Bethesda, 2006)

Chuvin, Pierre (ed.), *Les arts de l'Asie Centrale* (Citadelles et Mazenod, Paris, 1999)

Compareti, Matteo, 'Gli apporti indiani nell'arte della Sogdiana e il ramo marittimo della via della seta' (doctoral thesis, University of Naples, Naples, 2003)

Desideri, Ippolito, *An Account of Tibet*, edited by Filippo de Filippi (Routledge, London, 1932)

Di Cosmo, Nicola, *Ancient China and its Enemies* (Cambridge University Press, Cambridge, 2002)

Dutreuil de Rhins, J.L. and Grenard, F., *Mission scientifique dans la Haute Asie 1890–1895* (Ernest Leroux, Paris, 1898)

Egloff, Michel and Piotrovsky, Yuri et al., *Trésors des steppes* (Laténium, Hauterive, 2006)

Feng Zhao and Zhiyoung Yu, *Legacy of the Desert King. Textiles and Treasures Excavated at Niya on the Silk Road* (China National Silk Museum, Hangzhou, 2000)

Francfort, H.-P. et al., 'Les pétroglyphes de Tamgaly', *Bulletin of the Asia Institute*, Vol. 9 (1995)

Francfort, H.-P. et al., '"Le kourgane de Berel" dans l'Altaï kazakhstanais', in Gillel, Martine (ed.), *Arts Asiatiques*, vol. 55 (Ecole française d'Extrême-Orient, Paris, 2000)

Francke, A.H., *Antiquities of Indian Tibet*. Reprint from the 1914 edition (Asian Educational Services, New Delhi, 1992)

Govinda, Li Gotami, *Tibet in Pictures* (Dharma Publishing, Berkeley, 1979)

Grant, Asahel, *The Nestorians; or the Lost Tribes* (John Murray, London, 1841)

Grousset, René, *Die Reise nach Westen oder wie Hsüan Tsang den Buddhismus nach China holte* (Diederichs, Cologne, 1986)

Gruschke, Andreas, *The Cultural Monuments of Tibet's Outer Provinces* (White Lotus Press, Bangkok, 2001–7)

He Dexiu, 'A Brief Report of the Mummies from the Zaghunluq Site in Chärchän County', in Maier, Victor H. (ed.), *The Bronze Age and Early Iron Age Peoples of Eastern Central Asia* (Institute for the Study of Man, Washington, DC, 1998)

Hedin, Sven, *Through Asia* (Harper, New York and London, 1899)

Hedin, Sven, *Central Asia and Tibet* (Hurst & Blackett, London, 1903)

Hedin, Sven, *Scientific Results of a Journey in Central Asia, 1899–1902* (Lithographic Institute of the General Staff of the Swedish Army, Stockholm, 1904–7)

Hedin, Sven, *Transhimalaja* (Brockhaus, Leipzig 1909–12) [Published in English as *Trans-Himalaya* (Macmillan, London, 1909–13)]

Hedin, Sven, *Southern Tibet, 1906–8* (Lithographic Institute of the General Staff of the Swedish Army, Stockholm, 1916–22)

Hedin, Sven, *General Prschewalsky in Innerasien* (Brockhaus, Leipzig, 1925)

Hedin, Sven, *Mein Leben als Entdecker* (Brockhaus, Leipzig, 1928) [Published in English as *My Life as an Explorer* (Cassell, London, 1926)]

Hedin, Sven, *Auf großer Fahrt* (Brockhaus, Leipzig, 1929) [Published in English as *Across the Gobi Desert* (Routledge, London, 1931)]

Hedin, Sven, *Rätsel der Gobi* (Brockhaus, Leipzig, 1931) [Published in English as *Riddles of the Gobi Desert* (Routledge, London, 1933)]

Hedin, Sven, *Die Flucht des großen Pferdes* (Brockhaus, Leipzig, 1935) [Published in English as *Big Horse's Flight* (Macmillan, London, 1936)]

Hedin, Sven, *Die Seidenstrasse* (Brockhaus, Leipzig, 1936) [Published in English as *The Silk Road* (Routledge, London, 1938)]

Hedin, Sven, *Der wandernde See* (Brockhaus, Leipzig, 1937) [Published in English as *The Wandering Lake* (Routledge, London, 1940)]

Hedin, Sven, 'History of the Expedition in Asia 1927–1935. Parts I–IV', in *Reports from the Scientific Expedition to the North-Western Provinces of China. Publications 23–26* (Elanders Boktryckeri Aktienbolag, Göteborg, 1943–45)

Hedin, Sven, 'Central Asia Atlas' and 'Memoir on maps', in *Reports, Publications 47–49*, with contributions by N. Ambolt and E. Norin (The Sven Hedin Foundation, Stockholm, 1967)

Helfritz, Hans, *Chicago der Wüste* (Hobbing, Berlin, 1932)

Helfritz, Hans, *Entdeckungsreisen in Süd-Arabien* (DuMont, Cologne, 1977)

Herodotus, Herodot, *Geschichten und Geschichte* (Artemis, Zürich, 1990) [Published in English as *The Histories* (Penguin, London, 1954)]

Hojaniyazov, Tirkesh and Yazlyev, Chary, 'Ancient Merv', in *Caspian. Official Publication of TIOGE '96* (Anglo-Caspian Services, London, 1996)

Huntington, Ellsworth, *The Pulse of Asia* (Houghton, Boston, 1907)

Hüttel, Hans-Georg, 'Karakorum, eine historische Skizze', in Müller, Claudius and Wenzel, Jacob (eds), *Dschingis Khan und seine Erben* (Hirmer Verlag, Munich, 2005)

Jacobson, Esther, *The Deer Goddess of Ancient Siberia* (Brill, Leiden, 1993)

Juvaini, 'Ata-Malik, *The History of the World-Conqueror*. Translated from the text of Mirza Mohammed Qazvini by J.A. Boyle, 2 vols (Manchester University Press, Manchester, 1958)

Kawaguchi, Ekai, *Three Years in Tibet* (reprinted by Bibliotheca Himalayica, Bangkok, 1979)

Koslow, Pjotr, *Die Mongolei, Amdo und die tote Stadt Chara-choto* (Brockhaus, Leipzig, 1955)

Kubarev, Vladimir, *New Turkish Sculptures of Mongolia and the Altai* (Institute of Archaeology, Novosibirsk, 2000)

Leont'ev, Nikolaj and Kapel'ko, Vladimir, *Steinstelen der Okunev Kultur* (Deutsches Archäologisches Institut, Berlin, 2002)

Lin Meicun, 'The Last Capital of the Shan Shan Kingdom in Loulan', *Yenching Journal of Chinese Studies*, Vol. 3 (1995)

Lüscher, Geneviève, *Die Hydria von Grächwil* (Chronos, Bern, 2002)

Mahé, A. and J.P., *L'Arménie à l'épreuve des siècles* (Gallimard, Paris, 2005)

Maier, Victor H. (ed.), *The Bronze Age and Early Iron Age Peoples of Eastern Central Asia* (Institute for the Study of Man, Washington, DC, 1998)

Mallory, J.P., *In Search of the Indo-Europeans* (Thames & Hudson, London, 1989)

Marshak, Boris, *Legends, Tales and Fables in the Art of the Sogdians* (Bibliotheca Persica, New York, 2002)

Mode, Markus, 'Die Religion der Sogder im Spiegel ihrer Kunst', in Jettmar, Karl and Kattner, Ellen (eds), *Die vorislamischen Religionen Mittelasiens* (Kohlhammer, Stuttgart, 2003)

Moorcroft, William and Trebeck, George, 'Travels in India. Himalayan Provinces of Hindustan and Punjab in Ladakh and Kashmir' in Wilson, Horace Hayman (ed.), *Peshawar, Kabul, Kunduz and Bokhara; from 1819–1825* (reprinted from the 1841 edition by Asian Educational Services, New Delhi, 1989)

Namkhai Norbu, *Journey among the Tibetan Nomads* (Library of Tibetan Works and Archives, Dharamsala, 1997)

Nomura, Yushi and Nouwen, Henri, *Weisheit aus der Wüste* (Herder, Freiburg, 2002)

Okladnikow, A.P., *Der Hirsch mit dem goldenen Geweih* (Brockhaus, Wiesbaden, 1972)

Perkins, Justin, *A Residence of Eight Years in Persia among the Nestorian Christians* (Allen, Morril & Wardwell, Andover, 1843)

Rashid al-Din, *The Successors of Genghis Khan* (Columbia University Press, New York, 1971)

Rhétoré, Jacques, *Les chrétiens aux bêtes* (Le Cerf, Paris, 2005)

Richardson, Hugh, *Tibet and its History* (Shambala, Boulder, 1982)

Richardson, Hugh, *A Corpus of early Tibetan Inscriptions* (Royal Asiatic Society, London, 1985)

Rolle, Renate, *Die Welt der Skythen* (Bucher, Lucerne, 1980)

Rong Xinjiang, 'Buddhist Images or Zoroastrian Deities? The Mixture of Religions on the Silk Road as seen from Khotan', *Chinese Culture Quarterly*, , Vol. 1, No. 2, 2003

Rubruk, Wilhelm von, *Reisen zum Grosskhan der Mongolen* (Thienemann, Stuttgart, 1984)

Rudenko, Sergei, *Frozen Tombs of Siberia. The Pazyryk Burials from Iron Age Horsemen* (Dent & Sons, London, 1970)

Salomon, Richard, 'A Stone Inscription in Central Asian Gandhari from Endere, Xinjiang' *Bulletin of the Asia Institute*, Vol. 13, 1999

Scharlipp, Wolfgang, *Die frühen Türken in Zentralasien* (Wissenschaftliche Buchgesellschaft, Darmstadt, 1992)

Schiltz, Véronique, *Die Skythen und andere Steppenvölker* (Beck, Munich, 1994)

Sinor, Denis (ed.), *The Cambridge History of Earlier Inner Asia* (Cambridge University Press, Cambridge, 1990)

Ssu-Ma Ch'ien, *Shih chi*. Translated by Burton Watson (Columbia University Press, New York, 1971)

Stein, Marc Aurel, *Sand-Buried Ruins of Khotan* (Hurst & Blackett, London, 1904)

Stein, Marc Aurel, *Ancient Khotan* (Clarendon, Oxford, 1907)

Stein, Marc Aurel, *Ruins of Desert Cathay. Personal Narrative of Exploration in Central Asia and Westernmost China* (Macmillan, London, 1912)

Stein, Marc Aurel, *Serindia* (Clarendon, Oxford, 1921)

Stein, Marc Aurel, *Innermost Asia* (Clarendon, Oxford, 1928)

Stein, Marc Aurel, *On Ancient Central Asian Tracks* (Macmillan, London, 1933)

Stein, Marc Aurel and Major K. Mason, *Memoir on Maps of Chinese Turkistan and Kansu* (Trigonometrical Survey Office, Dehra Dun, 1923)

Strzygowski, Josef, 'Die christlichen Denkmäler von Amida', in Berchem, Max van, *Amida* (Carl Winters Universitätsbuchhandlung, Heidelberg, 1910)

Sutton, S.B., *In China's Border Provinces. The Turbulent Career of Joseph Rock, Botanist-Explorer* (Hastings, New York, 1974)

Terra, Helmut de, *Durch Urwelten am Indus* (Brockhaus, Leipzig, 1940)

Thesiger, Wilfred, *Arabian Sands* (Longmans, Green & Co., London, 1960)

Thesiger, Wilfred, *The Life of my Choice* (HarperCollins, London, 2000)

Trinkler, Emil, *The Storm-Swept Roof of Asia* (Seeley, London, 1931)

Vitebsky, Piers, *Reindeer People. Living with Animals and Spirits in Siberia* (HarperCollins, London, 2005)

Weber, Therese, *The Language of Paper* (Orchid Books, Bangkok, 2007)

Wessels, C., *Early Jesuit Travellers in Central Asia, 1603–1721* (Nijhoff, The Hague, 1924)

Ye'or Bat, *Der Niedergang des orientalischen Christentums unter dem Islam* (Resch, Gräfeling, 2002)

Yule, Henry, *The Book of Ser Marco Polo* (Scribner's Sons, New York, 1926)

Ziegler, Gudrun and Hogh, Alexander (eds), *Die Mongolen* (Wissenschaftliche Buchgesellschaft, Stuttgart, 2005)

# Index

## Places